The Influence of National Competition Policy on the International Competitiveness of Nations

Andreas Mitschke

The Influence of National Competition Policy on the International Competitiveness of Nations

A Contribution to the Debate on International Competition Rules

Physica-Verlag
A Springer Company

Author
Dr. Andreas Mitschke
University of Erlangen-Nuremberg
Lange Gasse 20
90403 Nuremberg
Germany
andreas.mitschke@wiso.uni-erlangen.de

ISBN 978-3-7908-2035-5 e-ISBN 978-3-7908-2036-2

DOI: 10.1007/978-3-7908-2036-2

Contributions to Economics ISSN 1431-1933

Library of Congress Control Number: 2008925130

Cover design: WMXDesign GmbH, Heidelberg

Printed on acid-free paper

9 8 7 6 5 4 3 2 1

springer.com

Preface

Does every open economy profit from economic globalization? Why do some countries profit more than others? What role does national economic policy play with regard to a nation's potential to profit from economic globalization? Is there a need for an international harmonization of economic policy in order to protect global competition and to prevent international conflicts or, to the contrary, is national economic policy a crucial and indispensable instrument for fostering the international competitiveness of an economy?

These questions were the starting point for a research project of the Department of Economics at the University of Nuremberg in 2003. The intention was to take a fresh look at the various harmonization claims which have been raised both in economic literature and by politicians. As politicians, in general, simultaneously also strive for enhancing the international competitiveness of their nation, the project aimed at the relation between harmonization claims on the one hand and the competitiveness debate on the other.

The decision to set the focus of this project on the role of competition policy has been triggered against the background of the ongoing debate on international competition rules. In October 2001, the International Competition Network (ICN) has been established in New York. Furthermore, the Doha Ministerial Declaration of November 2001 envisaged WTO negotiations on international competition rules. Consequently, there was a current need to analyze the effects of an international harmonization of antitrust rules on the international competitiveness of nations. The project intended to contribute to close the gap between current research on international competition rules on the one hand and the existing literature on the international competitiveness of nations on the other. It also offers a framework for future research on this issue. Further research with regard to the advantages of *national* competition policy compared to *international* competition rules would be desirable.

This book is a revised version of my doctoral thesis which has been accepted by the Department of Economics, University of Nuremberg, in May 2007. I want to thank all who encouraged me to carry through this project.

My special thanks go to Prof. Dr. h.c. Werner Lachmann, Ph.D. (Nuremberg) and Prof. Dr. Karl Farmer (Graz) who supervised the dissertation.

Nuremberg, January 2008 *Andreas Mitschke*

Table of Contents

List of Abbreviations

ANZCERTA	Australia-New Zealand Closer Economic Relations Trade Agreement
APEC	Asia-Pacific Economic Cooperation
Art.	Article(s)
BGH	Bundesgerichtshof (German Federal Court of Justice)
BGHZ	Entscheidungen des Bundesgerichtshofes in Zivilsachen (Decisions of the German Federal Court of Justice in Civil Matters)
Cf.	confer
Chap./Chaps.	Chapter/s
DIAC	Draft International Antitrust Code
DoJ	(US) Department of Justice
EC	European Community; EC Treaty
ECMR	European Community Merger Regulation
ECN	European Competition Network
Ed(s)	Editor(s)
Edn	Edition
e.g.	exempli gratia (for example)
EPA	European Patent Agreement
EOS	Economies of Scale
EU	European Union
EWG	Europäische Wirtschaftsgemeinschaft (European Economic Community)
FDI	Foreign Direct Investment
FTAA	Free Trade Area of the Americas
FTAIA	Foreign Trade Antitrust Improvements Act
FTC	Federal Trade Commission
GATT	General Agreement on Tariffs and Trade
GDP	Gross Domestic Product
GWB	Gesetz gegen Wettbewerbsbeschränkungen (German Antitrust Act)
HDI	Human Development Index
IAA	International Antitrust Authority
IAEAA	International Antitrust Enforcement Assistance Act

Ibid.	Ibidem (the same)
ICN	International Competition Network
i.e.	id est (that is to say)
IMF	International Monetary Fund
IPC	International Patent Classification
ITO	International Trade Organization
MC	Marginal Costs
MLAT	Mutual Legal Assistance Treaty
MOS	Minimum Optimal Scale
NAFTA	North American Free Trade Agreement
No	Number
OAS	Organization of American States
OECD	Organization of Economic Cooperation and Development
OJ	Official Journal of the European Union
Op. cit.	opere citato (in the work already quoted)
OPEC	Organization of the Petroleum Exporting Countries
PCT	Patent Cooperation Treaty
PQLI	Physical Quality of Life Index
RCA	Revealed Comparative Advantage
R&D	Research and Development
Sec.	Section
SII	Structural Impediments Initiative
SME	Small and Medium-Sized Enterprises
TFP	Total Factor Productivity
TRAMs	Agreement on Trade Related Antitrust Measures
TRIMS	Agreement on Trade-Related Investment Measures
TRIPS	Agreement on Trade-Related Aspects of Intellectual Property Rights
TT-BER	Technology Transfer Block Exemption Regulation
UN	United Nations
UNCTAD	United Nations Conference on Trade and Development
UNIDO	United Nations Industrial Development Organization
UN-RBP	United Nations Set of Multilaterally Agreed Equitable Principles and Rules for the Control of Restrictive Business Practices
US	United States (of America)
VoIP	Voice over Internet Protocol
Vol	Volume
WIPO	World Intellectual Property Rights Organization
WTO	World Trade Organization

1 Introduction

1.1 Connecting Two Current Debates

The world economy is moving toward a single market, since the liberalization and international integration of national markets has become a crucial feature of world trade over the last decades. As a consequence of this economic globalization, both enterprises and national economies must cope with competition from abroad. The intensified international competition between enterprises is generally considered one of the most important positive effects of globalization, whereas national governments often find it difficult to adjust their economic policy to the new international regulatory competition. On the one hand, they have to strengthen the international competitiveness of their national economy.[1] They can do so by means of improved conditions for foreign investors, by supporting domestic enterprises and by creating so called national champions – possibly a danger for competition and free trade. On the other hand, national governments attempt to reduce the international competitive pressure. They are in search of international coordination and harmonization as a last resort[2], officially on the grounds that without creating a so-called *level playing field*, there could be no fair global competition.[3]

Consequently, as regards the internationalization of antitrust, two fields of economic research in competition policy have gained in importance in times of economic globalization. Firstly, globalization has resurrected the debate whether there is a need for international competition rules against private anticompetitive practices and how these rules could be implemented in the best way. This is because competition policy receives a growing importance in the course of further globalization; fair trade policy and the promotion of free trade generally have as a prerequisite the existence of good competition policy. The opening of national markets, the increasing

1 Lachmann (1998) p. 106.
2 Cf. Richter and Furubotn (2003) pp. 524f.
3 Cf. Mitschke (2005) pp. 32ff.

number of mergers and mega-mergers, the internationalization of business activities and the restructuring of global markets can only become a positive factor of international welfare, international competition and international competitiveness when there is a stable basis for sound competition policy. One could say that the success of economic globalization depends on the success of competition policy. Nevertheless, competition policy is still 'one of those fields where cross-jurisdictional activities contrast with lacking supranational governance competences ... competition policy continues to be done by nation-states'[4]. Hence many economists and jurists plead for international competition rules against restrictive business practices. The question about the necessity of an international political regime which governs all international competition restraints, caused by private persons and enterprises, has already been discussed during the negotiations about the liberalization of international trade (Havana-Charter) and the creation of an International Trade Organization (ITO) in the wake of World War II. The gradual elimination of state-induced restraints to trade (e.g. tariffs, import quotas, export subsidies, and anti-dumping), which has been the central aim of the General Agreement on Tariffs and Trade (GATT) ratified in 1948, was supposed to be accompanied by an agreement within the Havana-Charter[5] which leads to an internationally coordinated fight against privately induced restraints to international trade (e.g. cartels, mergers), with a focus on the coordination of procedural law. In contrast to the GATT, the Havana-Charter has not been ratified so that the establishment of international competition rules has never been put in concrete terms and has not been realized up to now. Nonetheless, since the early nineties of the 20th century, when the foundation of the World Trade Organization (WTO) in 1994 improved the administration and protection of international fair trade, several economists have revived the debate about the necessity and forms of international competition policy as a second pillar of fair international competition.

Secondly, the concept of the international competitiveness of nations has become a significant issue for all open economies. Globalization causes fundamental structural changes both within national economies and within international relations so that many countries fear a loss of economic competitiveness and welfare, especially with regard to the welfare

4 Budzinski and Christiansen (2004) p. 1.

5 Chapter V ('Restrictive Business Practices') of the Havana Charter for an International Trade Organization (UN Doc. E/Conf. 2778, 1948) was a multilateral agreement including international competition rules and empowering the ITO to investigate anticompetitive business practices which have a negative effect on international trade (cf. Zanettin (2002) p. 2).

of certain sections of the population which are in danger to become the economic losers of globalization. On the one hand, it is said that national governments have lost their former position to control the national economy because the big international enterprises have emancipated themselves from national politics. Especially international capital has become footloose in search of optimal conditions for new investments. Consequently, national governments could be disciplined by international enterprises and by global markets; the scope for arbitrary and autocratic national politics has become smaller. On the other hand, it has to be stressed that national economic policy has gained a new role. The national politicians have to improve locational conditions for foreign investors and they have to adjust politics so that domestic enterprises become more competitive.[6] This means that national economic policy undergoes both a national and an international test.[7] The government has to meet the interests of *national* voters if it wants to maximize its chances of being re-elected. For instance, according to the median voter model developed by Hotelling[8], the government would have to take a position at the median if it wants to win a majority voting. This is a simple two-party model and it is doubtful whether it can explain the complex processes of democratic elections because political parties use many instruments to influence voters and many voters are neither aware of their personal interests nor are they well informed about political and economic issues. Nevertheless, the median voter model can explain why political economics can lead to bad economic politics. These deficiencies, which characterize democratic elections and majority votings, do not occur equally with regard to the *international* test national governments are undergoing on global markets. Governments have to meet the interests of domestic and foreign investors who know exactly what investment conditions they need and who decide rationally without being influenced by political propaganda. In this way, national governments are increasingly disciplined by mobile input factors. They are forced to practice a good and successful economic policy in order to attract investors and skilled labour force. Consequently, every government has the task to create national (legal) institutions which promote the international competitiveness of the economy. Only a complete international harmonization of economic policy would release national governments from this challenge.

---

6 Rodemer and Dicke (2000) p. 307.

7 Cf. Richter and Furubotn (2003) pp. 29f., 521.

8 Hotelling (1929) pp. 54f.; cf. Downs (1957) pp. 114ff.; Downs (1957a) pp. 135ff.

These two fields of research – the debate about international competition rules and the debate about the international competitiveness of nations – stand in close connection with each other. The discussion of both themes directs the attention to a specific interface of these two issues. The implementation of international competition rules limits or even eliminates national competition policy. The matter in question is to what extent national competition policy has to be regarded as a factor of international competitiveness or to what extent international competition rules could improve the international competitiveness of nations. The importance of national competition policy for the international competitiveness of a nation could be a justification for a keeping up of national competition policy despite the alleged necessity of international competition rules. There could be a trade-off between the aim to improve the international competitiveness of the national economy on the one hand and to establish international competition rules on the other, although both aims could serve to strengthen international competition. Therefore, in contrast to the predominant academic literature which primarily debates about the necessity of international competition rules and about possible and probable legal institutions to implement and enforce them, the following investigation especially analyses the role national competition policy plays for the international competitiveness of nations. The entire investigation will be characterized by a critical attitude towards the current extensive debate on international competition rules, especially with regard to the arguments of the proponents and the consequences of further harmonization. The proponents of international competition rules have put into question the status quo of competition policy; this work will challenge the demand for international competition rules. Therefore, this work will underline the negative effects of international competition rules on the international competitiveness and highlight the positive effects of *national* competition policy on the international competitiveness.

1.2 State of Scientific Research

As regards the debate about international competition rules, economic science and jurisprudence have produced an immense number of publications which primarily are about the status quo of international antitrust and about the question as to whether there is a necessity for international competition rules. While some authors take up an almost neutral position – though rather underlining the limits and deficiencies of the status quo than the limits of an international competition policy regime – several publications have made more or less precise proposals how to design and implement an international competition policy regime (cf. Chap. 2.3). In contrast to this, the number of economists and jurists who reject the claims for international competition rules is relatively small, although their arguments are weighty (cf. Chap. 2.4). Consequently, there is a lack of critical literature that highlights more precisely the disadvantages and potential negative consequences of international competition rules.

Correspondingly, important aspects like the international competitiveness of nations are almost completely neglected in the debate on international competition rules. This is surprising considering the old and well-known debate about the relation between market concentration on the one hand and the international competitiveness and the efficiency of *enterprises* on the other. Economic literature – for example the traditional industrial organization theory and the theory of industrial policy – has dealt with this subject in different ways, both theoretically and empirically, considering the technological, productive, allocative, and dynamic (innovatory) efficiency of company size, market structure, and inter-firm cooperation.[9] This discussion has resulted in two fundamental positions which might, at first sight, appear incompatible or even contradictory.[10] The first position emphasizes the necessity to foster mergers in order to achieve productive efficiency and to become internationally competitive. The Chicago School of Antitrust could be seen as a theoretical basis of this 'efficiency-defense' position, underlining that mergers result in cost-savings that could be passed on to consumers.[11] The second position equates the protection of competition by sound competition policy with the promotion of international competitiveness, economic growth, and innovativeness.[12] For instance, EU publications highlight the role of (European) competition policy because there is, according to the European Commission, 'ample evidence' that vigorous and 'effective competition in the EU internal market makes, through improved productivity and innovation, a decisive con-

[9] The relation between market concentration and the international competitiveness and efficiency of enterprises is described, for instance, in the following works: Berg (1985) pp. 3ff.; Clougherty (2003); Haufler and Nielsen (2005); Isele (2003); Kantzenbach and Kinne (1997) pp. 67-84; Kinne (1997) pp. 9ff., 26ff; Seong (1989); Stennek and Verboven (2001) pp. 3ff.

[10] The so-called Williamson trade-off between technological or productive efficiency on the one hand and allocative efficiency on the other has illustrated this problem.

[11] Cf. Demsetz (1976) pp. 371ff.; Schmidt and Rittaler (1986) pp. 60, 63, 78; Rittaler (1989).

[12] Cf. Dutz and Hayri (1999) pp. 1ff.; Fontenot and Wilhelm (2005) pp. 233-53; European Commission (2004a); Kroes (2006).

tribution to the competitiveness of the European industry'[13]. Similarly, the United Nations Conference on Trade and Development (UNCTAD) has instituted a field of work and issued several publications about the development impact of competition policy and about the role of competition policy for strengthening the international competitiveness of developing countries and their enterprises.[14]

Meanwhile, both positions are in line with conventional wisdom, but they cannot be reconciled completely although the economic globalization and the international integration of national markets have helped to reduce this trade-off between productive efficiency and effective competition. On the other hand, globalization has raised a new question. While the debate on competition policy and international competitiveness hitherto referred to the application of *national* competition law – especially merger law and rules for inter-firm cooperation – to strengthen the productive efficiency, innovativeness and international competitiveness of enterprises, the present debate on *inter*national competition rules brings up the question to what extent the aim to strengthen the international competitiveness of a nation could be impaired by an international harmonization of competition policy. Up to now, the relevant literature on international competitiveness in most cases ignores the impact of competition policy or it does not explicitly distinguish between national and international competition policy, i.e. the advantages of *national* competition policy are not compared with the disadvantages of *inter*national competition rules.[15] Furthermore, the former approaches – i.e. the traditional industrial organization theory, the theory of industrial policy, and the Chicago School of Antitrust Analysis – have reduced the competitiveness debate to a *micro*economic perspective, i.e. the competitiveness of enterprises. The *macro*economic concept of international competitiveness, which also refers to the locational attractiveness of nations, has not been considered yet. Moreover, there are several publica-

[13] European Commission (2004a) p. 20.

[14] UNCTAD (1998, 2004); Lachmann (1999); Brusick et al. (2004); Cernat (2004).

[15] Several publications highlight the role of competition policy as a dimension of economic policy that plays an important role to strengthen the international competitiveness either of domestic firms (cf. Anderson and Khosla (1995) p. 99) or of national industries or nations as a whole (cf. Porter (1990)). Competitiveness considerations have even entered into several competition laws, for example in the Canadian Competition Act (cf. Anderson and Khosla (1995) p. 99) or in the German merger control provisions that allow a ministerial permission to improve the international competitiveness of domestic enterprises. Though, there is no explicit differentiation between a sovereign *national* antitrust policy and internationally harmonized competition rules.

tions about the (workability of an) international competition of competition laws[16], but these examinations either do not analyze the effects of regulatory competition on the international competitiveness of nations[17], or they primarily deal with *protectionist* trade practices that are undoubtedly internationally harmful and governmentally initiated or tolerated trade restrictions.[18] These protectionist trade practices should be part of the area of responsibility of the WTO.[19] In contrast to this, the following investigation focuses on non-protectionist and non-discriminatory national antitrust policies and their effects on the international competitiveness of nations.

To sum up, previous research does not offer a systematic investigation about the advantages of *national* competition policy with regard to the international competitiveness of nations. Though, there are several articles and publications which touch the topic of this investigation. On the one hand, there are publications which underline specific disadvantages of international institutions, especially the political economics of an international antitrust regime[20] and the elimination of the international regulatory competition[21]. On the other hand, there is a field of research that rather highlights the benefits of national competition policy, although this research does not always explicitly differentiate between national and international competition rules and it partly does not refer to the debate on the international competitiveness of nations. Some publications underline the necessity for a specific competition policy for certain countries, but they do not explicitly distinguish between national and international competition rules. For instance, Gal and Anderson/Khosla have analyzed the necessity for a specific competition policy for small market economies.[22] Jorde and Teece have focused on new and particular challenges for anti-

---

16 Cf. Chap. 4.2.5.

17 Cf. Kerber and Budzinski (2003) pp. 411ff.; Kerber and Budzinski (2004) pp. 31ff.; Sinn (1997) pp. 248ff.; Sinn (1999); Sinn (2003) pp. 178ff.

18 Cf. Stearns-Bläsing (2004) pp. 32ff. Besides strategic mergers policies, Stearns-Bläsing especially describes the protectionist use of several market foreclosing practices: export cartels [especially voluntary export restraints], vertical restraints, and R&D cooperation.

19 For instance, voluntary export restraints are generally forbidden by the WTO so that export cartels that serve as a substitute for voluntary export restraints also should be covered by the WTO regime (cf. Stearns-Bläsing (2004) pp. 73, 78).

20 McGinnis (2004); Nagy (2002). Chapter 4.2.3 will deal with this issue.

21 See Chap. 4.2.5.

22 Gal (2003, 2003a); Anderson and Khosla (1995). Chap. 4.3.2.2 will deal with this issue.

trust authorities in industries of rapid technological change.[23] Other authors and international institutions have focused on the role of competition policy for the economic needs of developing countries.[24] Moreover, there are some publications which highlight special functions and aspects of *national* competition policy that are also relevant for the international competitiveness of nations, for example the linkage between antitrust policies and other political interests that are relevant for the international competitiveness of nations.[25]

1.3 Course of Inquiry

The investigation is organized as follows. Chapter 2 gives a survey about the wide discussion as regards the necessity and modalities of international competition rules, starting with a description of the status quo in dealing with private cross-border competition restraints. The different valuation of this status quo is one of the natural starting points for research on international competition rules. Proponents and opponents of international competition rules vary in their analysis of the status quo; furthermore, they have different ideas how to reduce the present deficiencies of international antitrust.

In Chap. 3, the concept of the 'International Competitiveness of Nations' has to be outlined with regard to its development and its theoretical foundation and legitimacy. This concept constitutes the theoretical basis for the work presented here. Chapters 2 and 3 can be considered a preliminary work before dealing with the central question of this investigation.

Chapter 4 delineates and highlights the role of *national* competition policy – compared to international competition rules – for the international competitiveness of nations in order to enrich the discussion on international competition rules. The analysis starts with a description of the general disadvantages of international harmonization and centralization and then, after this preliminary work, the *direct* influence of *national* competition policy on promoting the international competitiveness of the nation will be described. The analysis underlines the positive effects of *national* competition policy to take into account the specific characteristics and interests of the national economy by maintaining a certain degree of flexibility in antitrust. This aspect will be made more precise by an additional

---

23 Jorde and Teece (1990, 1992, 1997).

24 Chapter 4.3.2.3 will deal with this issue.

25 Meessen (2000); McFetridge (1993); Gottwald (1992). Especially Chap. 4.3.2.4 will deal with this issue.

description of the advantages and disadvantages of practicing a rather permissive, protectionist, or strict competition policy on a case-by-case basis under the rule of reason approach.

2 About the Necessity of International Competition Rules

As regards competition policy, globalization has revived the question whether there is a need for international competition rules in order to protect national and global competition, to reduce efficiency and welfare losses as a result of anti-competitive business practices in international trade and to avoid unfair or discriminatory enforcement practices by creating a level playing field. The academic discussion about this subject of international harmonization of procedural and substantive law, centralization and vertical competence allocation is still in progress. There is a majority of economists and jurists who plead for international competition rules.[26] This chapter intends to highlight the crucial aspects of the debate. Chapter 2.1 starts with some introductory remarks on the general harmonization debate, describing the aims, arguments, and instruments of the various harmonization proposals. The subsequent Chap. 2.2 gives an introduction into the status quo of international competition enforcement, focusing on the existing forms of international cooperation. Chapters 2.3 and 2.4 describe the economic arguments both in favour of and against international competition rules and shortly presents the most important currently existing scientific proposals for economic and legal institutions to cope effectively with future international competition restraints. This chapter will not discuss the political probability for an implementation of harmonized antitrust rules. As regards the probable economic consequences – especially the consequences for the international competitiveness of nations – of an internationalized competition policy, this will be the subject of Chap. 4.

---

[26] Cf. Hauser and Schoene (1994) p. 205.

2.1 The General Debate on International Harmonization

The process of economic globalization has called into question the traditional role of national economies and national economic policy making. The rise and development of global markets, international value-added chains, international trade, transnational companies, international mergers and acquisitions, cross-border cartels and unfair strategies, cross-border or even global external effects and many other cross-border activities are a challenge for traditional macroeconomic and political concepts based on sovereign national governance. Globalization has led to a debate about the limits and merits of national policy and sovereignty and about the advantages and disadvantages of alternative modes of international political governance, such as international cooperation, coordination, harmonization, and supranationalization (centralization). These modes can be varied in different ways, they can be based on binding or non-binding agreements, and they also allow for more complex cooperation models like international network governance and multi-level governance. The basic forms of international cooperation can be illustrated by Fig. 2.1, which also shows that international cooperation can be developed stepwise in the course of time.

Supranationalization: Transfer of rights of the state to a supranational institution, which autonomously produces supranational law that has priority over national law.

Centralization: Transfer of certain national competences to an international institution, e.g. the centralized enforcement of an agreement that is based on intergovernmental cooperation.

Harmonization: Bringing national (procedural or substantive) laws in line with each other, for example by implementing international minimum standards or by creating identical laws.

Coordination: Coordinating political action with foreign countries in order to achieve a better solution for a national or international problem. Either ad hoc or by a formal coordination regime.

Cooperation (in the narrow sense): Exchange of information, e.g. general exchange of knowledge or case-specific exchange of information. Notification of political action. Exchange of staff. Technical and financial assistance.

Unilateralism: Preferring one-sided political action without any form of international cooperation, partly even risking international conflicts because of negative cross-border spillovers.

Fig. 2.1: Different Degrees of International Cooperation

As regards the younger historical development of international cooperation efforts, the academic debate before, during and after World War II about an international coordination of economic policy originally concerned the aim to avoid severe global economic crises, i.e. to cope with international macroeconomic imbalances and to stabilize the system of global financial markets. Consequently, the policy coordination debate was focused on fiscal policy, monetary policy, and exchange rate systems, considering both discretionary and formula flexibility.[27] The Bretton Woods international monetary system of fixed exchange rates and its institutions, the International Monetary Fund and the World Bank Group (former International Bank for Reconstruction and Development), were supposed to deal with these subjects on the international level directly after the end of World War II. Furthermore, the protection of international free trade was a crucial issue in the post-war period. This has led to the implementation of the GATT regime in 1948. After the collapse of the Bretton Woods system in 1971, there was only little interest in further international economic cooperation and coordination.[28]

Nonetheless, economic globalization, the increase of global competition, several regional financial crises and further international economic developments in the recent two decades have revived the coordination and harmonization debate. On the one hand, there is a new debate about the international financial architecture.[29] Furthermore, the debate on international cooperation has been widened to include new political issues, focusing on an international harmonization in fields like labour standards, social policy, ecological standards, and antitrust.[30]

Looking at Table 2.1, we see that the proponents of international harmonization in these new fields can use a variety of criteria, aims, and arguments with regard to different fields of policy making. This table does not claim to be complete, but it shows that it is relatively easy to demand an international harmonization in economic policy by means of generally accepted criteria (fairness, efficiency, etc.) and a multitude of arguments, which at least contain a grain of truth. Up to a certain degree, the opponents of harmonization even follow the same aims and apply the same arguments and criteria like the proponents of harmonization, e.g. the promo-

---

27 Cf. Maennig (1992) pp. 15ff.; Wagner (2003) pp. 139ff.

28 Maennig (1992) p. 249.

29 Cf. Eichengreen (1999); cf. Frenkel and Menkhoff (2000); Ho (2000) pp. 939ff.; Jochimsen (2000) pp. 159ff.; cf. Nunnenkamp (2000) pp. 3-11.

30 Some selected publications on the debate about the necessity of social and environmental standards are Adlung et al. (1997); Beaulieu and Gaisford (2002); Berthold and Hilpert (1999); Bhagwati and Hudec (1996); Bhagwati (1995); Busse (2002); Feld (1996); Großmann et al. (2002); Kelly (2003); Rodrik (1996); Suranovic (2002); Flanagan and Gould (2003).

tion of free trade and competition, the avoidance of international conflicts, the aspects of fairness, efficiency, transparency, and subsidiarity, and the enforcement of national law. This phenomenon underlines the problem that many aspects can be viewed from different perspectives. Consequently, the opponents come to different conclusions, either because of different data, different assumptions, different methods, or because of additional criteria, i.e. there are several criteria which mainly could be applied by the opponents of harmonization. For instance, they could highlight the importance of national sovereignty, the responsibility and liability of national politicians, the equality of opportunity of small and underdeveloped countries, and the beneficial role of an international regulatory competition.

Indeed, harmonization claims and the arguments in favour of harmonization could become ubiquitous in times of economic globalization, finally leading to a total international harmonization of national politics if politicians supported these claims. International harmonization and cooperation claims are en vogue in economic science, and this may be a dangerous trend. Therefore, every political field, which could become an object of international harmonization, should be analyzed extensively with respect to both the necessity of an international harmonization and the economic and political consequences of giving up national competences.

This is a difficult task because the criteria, aims and arguments in favour of harmonization often have a moral content, which, in accordance with scientific logic, cannot be falsified. The supporters of international harmonization usually complain about an alleged unfairness in world economy and about social and ecological evils caused by economic globalization. Furthermore, the proponents of harmonization frequently predict severe future problems in case of non-harmonization, which also cannot be falsified easily.

Criteria for harmonization	Political fields of harmonization	Aims and arguments for harmonization		
Fairness and human rights	Social policy; Ecological policy; Antitrust; Tax policy	Creating a level playing field for fair competition	Keeping human rights, e.g. labour standards Avoiding moral arbitrage	Avoiding a race to the bottom, e.g. caused by social and environmental dumping
Efficiency and transparency	Technical standards; Antitrust (merger control)	Reduction of transaction costs Economies of scale	Promoting free trade and competition	Avoiding an inefficient race to the bottom
Constancy and Reliability	Social policy; Ecological policy; Antitrust; Tax policy	Providing for international standards (at least minimum standards) to avoid a race to the bottom	Reducing transaction costs and enhancing international transparency and understanding	Avoiding migration, flight of capital, and moral arbitrage
Enforcement of national law	Competition policy; Patent law; Criminal law; Health policy; Consumer protection policy	Avoiding negative external effects from abroad	Avoiding inefficiencies and limits of unilateral approaches	Avoiding international conflicts resulting from unilateral action (effects doctrine)
Subsidiarity (dealing with global problems)	Antitrust; Environmental policy; Stabilization policy	Protection of global public goods like free competition, a clean environment, a stable world economy	Reduction of negative external effects	Creating a global governance which supports the international understanding
Overcoming national resistance	Social policy; Ecological policy; Antitrust	Bypassing national interest groups	Positive effects of harmonization for national law	International pressure on passive national governments
International division of labour	R&D; Technical test procedures	Economies of scale	Promoting free trade by means of common research and division of labour	Promoting competition by faster diffusion of new technologies

Table 2.1: Aims and Arguments in Favour of International Harmonization

In fact, the economic consequences of both harmonization and non-harmonization are hard to predict, but they could be serious. Although the problems and potential dangers of non-harmonization really exist to a more or less extent, it is doubtful whether they are caused by globalization and non-harmonization because globalization and national economic policy could also become a path to solve these problems because, in the long run, globalization could lead to an international convergence of national welfare and political standards.[31] Consequently, there are no easy answers within the harmonization debate, but there are some principles one should follow in the face of harmonization claims.

Firstly, one should get clear about the question whether the status quo of non-harmonization is really as bad as some proponents of harmonization claim with the intention to put the people and politicians on alert. In many cases, an objective research could come to the result that the status quo generally works well, although there could be some deficiencies and malfunctions, which partly are typical and inevitable for every kind of economic policy and regulation, whether by harmonization or by non-harmonization. Therefore, it is important to seek and analyze less radical alternatives to a far-reaching international harmonization. We will deal with these tasks in Chaps. 2.2, 2.3 and 2.4 with regard to harmonization claims in competition policy.

Secondly, it is possible to uncover contradictory argumentations, to reveal inner tensions and ambivalences within the pro harmonization argumentation. The two opposing groups of economic harmonization, its critics and supporters, hold ambiguous positions because it is a difficult task to weigh the advantages and disadvantages of harmonization and supra-nationalization against each other. Many proponents of international harmonization, for instance, have a fundamental problem with the diminishing power of national governments and the growing influence of multi- and transnational groups of companies and the internationally mobile capital.[32] They want to strengthen the democratically legitimated national parliaments and governments so that national sovereignty does not become a self-deception. On the other hand, some of these economists also demand a political framework governing the economic globalization; they call for an international harmonization of national politics and international standards in order to avoid problems like a harmful race to the bottom. Such harmonization claims have ambivalent effects on the national sovereignty. On

[31] Cf. Mitschke (2005) pp. 31ff.

[32] For more details about the (diminishing) role of national governments in designing the rules of national and global markets in times globalization, see Rodemer and Dicke (2000) pp. 294ff.

the one hand, national governments could regain scope of action in comparison with international enterprises, for example with regard to the protection of labour standards without harming the international competitiveness of the nation. On the other hand, national governments would have to transfer at least a part of their political competencies and rights of disposal to an international institution. This international institution would be characterized by a lack of democratic legitimacy and several additional uncertainties and transaction costs which ensue from relational contracts.[33] It appears that the proponents of international harmonization prefer such a transfer of national sovereignty to an increasing power of the mobile capital. Nevertheless, there remains an inner tension in this position stemming from the clash of two aims, which hardly can be pursued simultaneously: strengthening national sovereignty and democratic processes on the one hand and promoting international solutions and supranational competences on the other.

Thirdly, one should explore the possible negative effects of harmonization with regard to aims like fair and free global competition, increasing global welfare, long-term sustainability, national sovereignty, democratic responsibility and liability of politicians, and with regard to the economic consequences for single nation states, especially for the development of their national welfare and international competitiveness. These negative consequences of international harmonization have to be weighed up against the expected problems in case of non-harmonization. Though, the promised advantages of harmonization are often doubtful because in many cases there is a lack of theoretical and empirical evidence. Moreover, the advantages relate to an uncertain future, depending on a set of assumptions. Furthermore, there are some disadvantages that generally arise in all economic fields in case of harmonization. Harmonization causes the end of international regulatory competition. Countries demanding an international harmonization could be compared with an international oligopoly building a cartel in order to stop the international systems competition and to regain monopolistic power.[34] This cartelization also could be viewed as a collusion of powerful countries at the expense of third parties, for example small and underdeveloped countries and consumers, which rather profit from the state of non-harmonization. In times *before* intensive economic globalization and international harmonization, the national governments were the so-called 'final monopolist', having a wide scope to practice bad economic politics and to harm domestic consumers and tax payers.[35] Glo-

[33] Cf. Richter and Furubotn (2003) pp. 525f.
[34] Cf. Berg (1983) p. 3.
[35] Cf. Kerber (2001) p. 87.

balization and liberalization exposes bad national politics, the international locational competition weakens the monopolistic position of national governments towards their citizens. International harmonization, for instance by erecting an international competition authority, would help build up a new 'final monopolist'.

Concept	No Centralization and Harmonization	Ambivalence between Centralization/Harmonization and No Centralization/No Harmonization	Centralization and Harmonization
Goals of Antitrust Policy	Innovative Antitrust Policies Flexibility and Diversity National Policy Mix Democratic Legitimacy International Competitiveness Industrial Policy	Protection of International Competition against Private Anticompetitive Restraints **Antitrust Policy** Independence from Polit-Economic Influences Avoiding a Race to the Bottom	Simplified and Transparent Antitrust Procedures Reducing Transaction Costs for Merging Enterprises Avoiding Discriminatory and Protectionist Antitrust Enforcement Creating a Level Playing Field Avoiding International Conflicts

Table 2.2: Goals of Harmonization/Centralization versus Goals of Non-Harmonization/Non-Centralization in Antitrust

With regard to harmonization claims in antitrust, table 2.2 shows that both the strategy of harmonization/centralization and the status quo of non-harmonization/non-centralization are characterized by specific advantages, i.e. both strategies and concepts are suitable to achieve specific goals. Furthermore, several goals possibly can be achieved by both strategies. Consequently it is difficult to weigh the advantages against the disadvantages of harmonization and centralization.

2.2 The Status Quo of International Competition Policy

The status quo of international competition policy is characterized by different institutions which generally can be assigned to two opposing strategies. On the one hand, there is the unilateral strategy. International competition policy is still determined by a situation of non-harmonization and international regulatory competition. The two basic legal institutions which characterize this unilateral strategy are the principle of territoriality and the effects doctrine. Both principles could be regarded as not sufficient to solve the problem of international and interjurisdictional conflicts and to guarantee an effective and efficient protection of international competition. Either they do not set the right incentives for governments to enforce national competition law without discriminating foreign enterprises or countries, or there is an inherent potential for inefficiencies and international conflicts.[36]

On the other hand, a cooperative strategy has been developed in order to reduce international conflicts and inefficiencies with regard to the enforcement of national antitrust law on international antitrust cases.[37] Many countries prefer different forms of international cooperation but are rather sceptical about the necessity and efficiency of an international top-down harmonization or even centralization, which would mean a transfer of their sovereign power to an international institution.

2.2.1 Regulatory Competition

Although national and international competition is increasingly characterized by cross-jurisdictional business activities of national and international companies, competition policy still belongs to the central competences of sovereign nation-states. Every sovereign country is able to develop its own

[36] Cf. Lachmann and Mitschke (2006) pp. 560f.

[37] Zanettin (2002) pp. 1f.

competition policy according to its own needs, interests, and convictions. This also includes the willingness and possibility to learn from other countries how to deal with private competition restraints, either by a bottom-up convergence of national competition policy (ex post-harmonization) or by entering into voluntary agreements with other countries, concerning different degrees of cooperation and coordination.

The national independence of competition policy can be justified by its central role within a market economy. Competition policy has a significant influence on market structures, market activities, market outcomes and the general welfare of the people, so that every democratically legitimated government bears a high responsibility for the protection of competition according to the national economic constitution and for its international competitiveness. Nevertheless, national competition policy is part of the international regulatory competition so that governments have to react on international developments. There is a dynamics of mutual learning by trial and error, but finally every country decides on its own how to structure its markets and how to control domestic enterprises. This can be considered a central governmental task in every democratic market economy, so that a transfer of such significant political competencies to an international institution like for example the WTO would have to be based on extremely important arguments like the impossibility of sufficiently fair and efficient international trade in absence of international competition rules.[38]

2.2.2 The Principle of Territoriality

National competition authorities traditionally follow the principle of territoriality as regards the jurisdictional reach of their national competition law.[39] This principle of (formal) territoriality in international law generally determines that no state is allowed to undertake governmental action on foreign territory.[40] This is a fundamental characteristic of every national legal system because international law generally limits the effect of national law to the national territory.[41]

Two aspects have to be distinguished with regard to territoriality. The so-called *subjective* territoriality ('Inländerprinzip') determines that national laws can only be applied with respect to restrictive business prac-

[38] The relation between the international regulatory competition and the international competitiveness of nations will be described more precisely in Chap. 4.2.5.

[39] Cf. Kojima (2001) p. 2; cf. Norton (1979) pp. 576f.

[40] Hobe and Kimminich (2004) pp. 96f.

[41] Cf. Fuchs (2000) p. 356; cf. Immenga (2004) p. 6.

tices which – either in whole or in part – have their origin within the domestic territory. According to the principle of *objective* territoriality ('Inlandsprinzip'), the laws primarily cover restrictive business activities with (intended) substantial effect within the domestic territory, though these anticompetitive practices also could have negative effects outside of the domestic territory.

Consequently, taking both aspects together, enterprises become subject to the competition law of the country which they chose as starting point for their anti-competitive conduct; furthermore, their conduct needs to have a substantial effect on competition within the territory of this country. In most cases, the location of the firm's head office decides on the anti-competitive strategies so that companies are primarily subject to their domestic competition law. Therefore, the principle of territoriality hardly protects competition on foreign markets and does not provide for efficient instruments to fight against restrictive business practices which have their origin in a foreign country. In order to protect international competition effectively by means of the principle of territoriality, all countries would have to implement a modern and effective competition policy and they would have to apply the principle of *subjective* territoriality consequently. In this case, all private competition restraints would be disciplined within their country of origin, independently from their effect on the territory of this country. This would be an important step to protect *international* competition so that every country could do without the prosecution of anti-competitive effects from abroad. The debate about the necessity of international competition rules could be reduced to possible efficiency gains from international merger control and to a strengthening of international cooperation, especially as regards the coordination of parallel investigations and the exchange of information and evidence from abroad.

However, sovereign states are neither selfless enough to implement such an altruistic strategy nor do they have sufficient external incentives to prosecute competition restraints whose negative effects primarily affect foreign markets. To the contrary, governments are likely to protect their internationally active companies so that these companies can make more profit in foreign countries and probably strengthen their international competitiveness, too. Consequently, mere territorial enforcement would fail to protect consumers and producers who are victims of foreign competition restraints.[42] Furthermore, mere territoriality could be an incentive for a so-called race to the bottom in antitrust enforcement resulting from govern-

42 Rosenthal and Nicolaides (1997) pp. 372f.

ments′ aim to attract companies by means of permissive competition policy.[43]

2.2.3 The Effects Doctrine

As a consequence of the unsatisfactory and unreliable implementation and application of the principle of territoriality in many countries, the so-called effects doctrine has become more significant. Historically, the effects doctrine has been the first solution to deal with international anticompetitive business practices on the national level.[44] According to this doctrine, domestic competition law is also applicable to anti-competitive behaviour which has its origin in a foreign country but has a significant anti-competitive effect on domestic markets. In a more extreme approach, pursued by the United States, the effect doctrine also applies to foreign conduct that has a negative effect on the foreign commerce of domestic firms, for example by hampering domestic exporters to enter foreign markets.[45] The national antitrust enforcement and merger regulation covers all enterprises irrespective of their nationality and location. The decisive criterion is – from the point of view of the national competition authority – the anti-competitive impact on domestic markets.

The effects doctrine can be considered a relatively effective and popular tool to protect domestic competition, except for small and developing countries that have no economic and political power to pursue their interests by means of the effects doctrine.[46] Several competition authorities make use of this antitrust instrument, for example the European Commission, the German Federal Cartel Office ('Bundeskartellamt'), the Japan Fair Trade Commission, and the US-Department of Justice.[47] The United States have been the first to adopt the effects doctrine in the 1945 *United States v. Aluminium Co. of America (Alcoa)* case, 'under which the Sherman Act applies even to foreign actors acting abroad when they intend to and do affect US commerce'[48] (so-called 'effects-test'). The Sherman Act generally prohibits restraints of competition that affect commerce between and among the states of the United States and with foreign nations. Though, according to the US Foreign Trade Antitrust Improvements Act of 1982 (FTAIA), which became Sec. 7 of the Sherman Act, there is an ex-

---

43 Worm (2004) p. 141.
44 Zanettin (2002) p. 1.
45 Fullerton and Mazard (2001) p. 409.
46 Cf. Immenga (2004) p. 6.
47 Cf. Rosenthal and Nicolaides (1997) p. 373; cf. Melamed (1998).
48 Fox and Pitofsky (1997) p. 263; cf. Ryngaert (2004) pp. 6f.

ception to apply the effects doctrine. In certain cases, the decisive criterion to apply the effects doctrine on foreign competition restraints is that these restraints have a *direct, substantial, and reasonably foreseeable* effect on trade or commerce. According to Sec. 7, Sec. 1-7 of the Sherman Act (and thus the effects doctrine) shall *not* apply to 'conduct involving trade or commerce (other than import trade or import commerce) with foreign nations *unless* ...

(1) such conduct has a direct, substantial, and reasonably foreseeable effect ...
  (A) on trade and commerce which is not trade or commerce with foreign nations, or on import trade or import commerce with foreign nations; or
  (B) on export trade or export commerce with foreign nations, of a person engaged in such trade or commerce in the United States; and

(2) such effect gives rise to a claim under the provisions of sections 1 to 7 of this title, other than this section' (italic added).

In other words, import trade or import commerce is not covered by the FTAIA so that import trade and import commerce are generally governed by the effects test. Accordingly, the FTAIA primarily refers to restraints on export trade. These restraints only violate the Sherman Act if they have a direct, substantial, and reasonably foreseeable effect on commerce within the United States.[49]

The extraterritorial application of national competition law can cause inefficiencies and international conflicts. Although the effects doctrine is formally accepted by international law, its application can easily harm and undermine the sovereignty of foreign countries. Conflicts especially arise in case that a country applies its competition law to punish a foreign market conduct that is legal or even desired in that foreign country. Foreign countries could feel forced to change their national politics, to open their markets, or to introduce retaliatory measures. Furthermore, there is a realistic danger that the effects doctrine could be misused by powerful economies like the United States and the European Union. They could attack a foreign market conduct although they are not severely affected. Furthermore, they could operate a double standard, fighting against foreign competition restraints which are at the same time allowed in their own markets

[49] Cf. Hovenkamp (2005) p. 768; cf. Tritell (2006) p. 1; cf. Baker and Miller (1997) pp. 83; cf. Robertson and Demetriou (1994) p. 419.

if only foreign countries are negatively affected by these practices (for example in case of export cartels).[50]

In order to reduce the danger of conflicts and the correlating problems of international antitrust enforcement, competition authorities and national governments have developed some further institutions. The so-called balancing approach and the conclusion of bilateral cooperation agreements shall help to avoid international conflicts in antitrust.

2.2.4 Balancing Approach

The application of the effects doctrine by the United States had significant effects on international commerce. This exercise of US power since the Alcoa case in 1945 caused several international conflicts. These conflicts have been a central issue within the academic discussion on international antitrust so that, in order to avoid international conflicts, some US courts have tempered the effects doctrine by implementing an additional interest-balancing test, for the first time in the case of *Timberlane Lumber Co. v. Bank of America* (1976).[51] As a consequence of this test, the extraterritorial application of US antitrust law is limited by a rule of reason, according to which the US courts have to balance the pro-competitive effects of extraterritorial jurisdiction against the negative effects on foreign countries and international relationships.[52] Therefore, the balancing approach can be regarded as a specific form of the effects doctrine.[53] In order to avoid a significant collision with foreign law, the US courts shall – in a first step – analyze the influence of their proceedings and decisions on foreign jurisdictions. Furthermore, the court shall consider the foreign countries′ interest to apply their laws. In concrete terms, ‘the court must consider seven factors: purpose, effect, foreseeability, nationality, location, comparative significance of effects in the United States and elsewhere, and degree of conflict with foreign law and policy. The court is enjoined not to exercise jurisdiction if the ‘interests of, and links to, the United States … [are not] sufficiently strong, vis-à-vis those of other nations, to justify an assertion of extraterritorial authority’’[54].

As regards the legal status of the balancing approach, it has to be pointed out that the rules and guidelines which have been drawn up by the American Law Institute in 1987 (‘Restatement on Foreign Relations Law

[50] Cf. Rosenthal and Nicolaides (1997) pp. 371ff.
[51] Cf. Norton (1979) pp. 588ff.
[52] Cf. Gerber (2000) p. 308.
[53] Basedow (1998) p. 24.
[54] Fox and Pitofsky (1997) p. 264; cf. Immenga (2004) p. 8.

of the United States, Third') and in 1995 by the Department of Justice and the FTC ('Antitrust Enforcement Guidelines for International Operations') are no binding legal norms. Instead, the balancing approach is an administrative regulation demonstrating the current legal practice.[55] In contrast to the effects doctrine which is prescribed by legislation, the interest-balancing test is only supported by the judiciary and executive. Consequently, the balancing approach is a controversial issue because, while the legislative still prescribes the effects doctrine, the courts and the guidelines have introduced this additional criterion of interest-balancing which could exceed and overtax the competences of the courts. Balancing the interests of several countries to apply their laws should not be the task of the judiciary because this gives the courts a wide scope of discretion in the application of the effects doctrine.[56]

In practice, the interest-balancing test is rarely used because this approach is – according to a 1993 decision of the US Supreme Court in *Hartford Fire Insurance Co. v. California*[57] – only relevant in cases of 'true conflicts' between two jurisdictions[58], i.e. in case that domestic laws are contradictory to foreign laws so that it is impossible for companies to comply with both of them. In other words, only if foreign law prescribes a conduct that is forbidden by US law, then the US courts could refrain from applying the effects doctrine.[59] The European Court of Justice holds a similar position, limiting the application of the effects doctrine only in case of contradictions between European and foreign law.

To sum up, the balancing approach can be regarded as a possible unilateral approach to reduce problems and conflicts which arise from unilateralism. The general workability of a balancing approach can not be denied because, compared to the *Act of State Doctrine* which forbids an application of the effects doctrine in case of sovereign acts of foreign countries[60], the balancing approach could be applied similarly. Nonetheless, balancing-tests applied by national courts have not become generally accepted so that bilateral and multilateral cooperation has become increasingly important in international antitrust enforcement.

---

55 Cf. Worm (2004) p. 130; cf. Basedow (1998) pp. 23f.

56 Basedow (1998) pp. 23f.

57 Gill (1994) pp. 109ff.

58 Basedow (1998) p. 25.

59 Ibid. pp. 25, 49.

60 Governments can protect domestic enterprises against foreign antitrust investigations by means of sovereign acts. A prominent example of anti-competitive sovereign acts by foreign countries is the Organization of the Petroleum Exporting Countries, the so-called OPEC cartel.

2.2.5 International Cooperation

The increase in the number of international antitrust cases, the potential for international conflicts – for example because of inconsistent simultaneous proceedings and remedies in the course of so-called mega-mergers – and the deficiencies and inefficiencies of the above mentioned forms of unilateral international competition policy enforcement – for example the limited access to evidence (e.g. documents and witnesses) located in foreign countries, especially in case of international cartels – have made it important for national competition authorities to foster international cooperation in antitrust matters, both through informal and non-binding cooperation and through formal and binding cooperation agreements.[61]

In general, the status quo of international cooperation in antitrust can be described by a dominance of soft cooperation by voluntary dialogue, both bilaterally (often on the basis of official bilateral agreements) and multilaterally, for example in fora like the *International Competition Network (ICN)* and the *Trade and Competition Working Group* of the WTO.[62] The status quo of international antitrust cooperation is far from being characterized by far-reaching forms of coordination. There is 'no coordination of substantive laws, no compromise of domestic control, and no minimum standards'; 'compliance is voluntary' and 'each state is free to refuse cooperation when it wishes and remains guided by its own interests in deciding when to do so'[63]. Exceptions from this status quo of international antitrust only exist in combination with regional trade agreements, especially within the European Community[64] and the Australia-New Zealand Closer Economic Relations Trade Agreement (ANZCERTA)[65].

The purpose of the subsequent chapters is to summarize the fundamental provisions of existing forms of cooperation.[66] Models for future forms of more intensive international cooperation in antitrust will be presented in Chap. 2.3.2.

---

61 Cf. Zanettin (2002) pp. 1f.; cf. Melamed (1999) p. 424.

62 An overview of the existing forms of cooperation can be found in Lloyd and Vautier (1999) pp. 33ff. An overview of the majority of existing cooperation agreements in international antitrust is given in the Inventory of the Competition Policy Agreements, Treaties and other Arrangements Existing in the Western Hemisphere, submitted by the OAS Trade Unit to the FTAA Negotiating Group on Competition Policies, March 22, 2002.

63 Guzman (2004) pp. 369f.

64 Cf. Chap. 2.3.2.2.

65 Cf. Chap. 2.3.2.1.

66 A more detailed description of the existing bilateral, regional, plurilateral, and multilateral agreements can be found in Kennedy (2001) pp. 22ff.

2.2.5.1 *Bilateral Cooperation*

The instrument of bilateral agreements originally has been initiated by a non-binding OECD recommendation about restrictive business practices, adopted in 1967.[67] Since then, many OECD countries have entered into bilateral cooperation which reflects the minimum commitments provided by OECD recommendation.[68] With few exceptions, bilateral cooperation is limited to voluntary information-sharing, both in case of informal cooperation and formal cooperation agreements.[69] Nonetheless, for many competition authorities, the building and maintenance of bilateral relationships with foreign competition authorities has become a crucial and critical element of their own criminal and non-criminal antitrust enforcement program to maintain competitive markets.[70]

2.2.5.1.1 Informal Cooperation

Though informal cooperation is the simplest form of international cooperation, it can serve several purposes. It involves, for instance, (1) the exchange of ideas and positions; (2) the discussion about competition theory; (3) the sharing of knowledge about competition matters in general; and (4) the exchange of non-confidential information, for example so-called agency confidential information, i.e. information that is neither routinely disclosed nor protected by disclosure prohibitions (e.g. views on market definitions, competitive effects, and remedies).[71] This could, over time, promote a common understanding on substantive antitrust principles and an international convergence of best practices.[72] These forms of soft cooperation mostly occur as a dialogue between experts in order to increase the expertise of all participating competition authority[73], but informal cooperation also includes technical assistance in order to help one of the participating competition authority to gain expertise and competence, especially with regard to developing and transforming countries that intend to establish a modern competition policy for the first time. In this case, it is the aim to establish modern national competition rules which correspond to in-

---

67 Cf. Chap. 2.2.5.2.

68 Cf. Lloyd and Vautier (1999) pp. 33ff. An overview of bilateral enforcement cooperation agreements on competition can be found in Holmes et al. (2005) pp. 79ff., and in Kennedy (2001) pp. 22ff.

69 Guzman (2004) p. 369.

70 Tritell and Kraus (2006) p. 2.

71 Ibid. p. 3.

72 Melamed (1999) p. 423.

73 Ibid. p. 425.

ternational standards and to build up resources so that these rules can be enforced. Furthermore, one-sided exchange of information also can aim at helping countries to acquire a 'competition culture'.

2.2.5.1.2 Cooperation Agreements

Bilateral agreements have been signed to establish a reliable and binding framework for cooperation which generally goes far beyond the mere exchange of information and mutual assistance on general matters of competition policy. The more important concern is to provide assistance in case-specific enforcement activities.[74] Certain forms of bilateral cooperation even could be regarded as hard cooperation. In contrast to soft cooperation, hard cooperation aims at a more detailed, mutual, and case-specific enforcement cooperation.[75] According to Zanettin, 'forms of cooperation in which a competition authority is asked, at the request of a foreign agency, to take actions it might not have otherwise taken'[76], have to be assigned to the category of hard cooperation. The principle of *positive comity* is considered to be one of these concepts of hard cooperation. The *exchange of confidential information* is even considered to be a more ambitious form of hard cooperation since 'it usually requires changing existing domestic legislation'[77].

The agreed provisions of a bilateral agreement largely depend on the interests of the two participating countries, but there are several recurrent aspects and basic obligations[78] that can be included into a bilateral agreement and that have to be outlined here because they are – either in whole or in part – the fundamental provisions of existing bilateral agreements, especially those the United States have signed with Canada, the European Union, Australia, and Germany.

Notification. Bilateral agreements generally include the mutual obligation to notify the other government or competition authority of one's own antitrust enforcement activities as soon as possible if these activities affect the

---

74 Ibid. p. 425.

75 Ibid.

76 Zanettin (2002) p. 5.

77 Ibid.

78 Cf. Galloway (2005) pp. 589ff. Galloway has analyzed and compared bilateral agreements to assess whether these agreements reflect specific relationships between the two parties or whether there is a large amount of convergence. He observes a high degree of convergence so that bilateral agreements could be substituted by a multilateral agreement.

other country's important interests.[79] This is in order to avoid international conflicts and to initiate further steps of information sharing and consultation. Therefore, for instance, according to Article II of the agreement between the United States and Canada, each party has to notify its bilateral partner when its antitrust enforcement activities are (1) relevant to the enforcement activities of that country; (2) involve anticompetitive activities, other than mergers or acquisitions, carried out in whole or in part in the territory of the other party, except where the activities occurring in the territory of the other party are insubstantial; (3) involve mergers or acquisitions in which one or more of the parties to the transaction, or a company controlling one or more of the parties to the transaction, is a company incorporated or organized under the laws of the other party or of one of its provinces or states; (4) involve conduct believed to have been required, encouraged or approved by the other party; (5) involve remedies that expressly require or prohibit conduct in the territory of the other party or are otherwise directed at conduct in the territory of the other party; or (6) involve the seeking of information located in the territory of the other party, whether by personal visit by officials of a Party to the territory of the other party or otherwise.[80]

In case of mergers and acquisitions, the notification procedure often has to take into account national confidentiality provisions which intend to prevent disclosure of plans for such a transaction. Hence bilateral agreements often require a notification not later than the time the competition authority starts seeking information or documentary material concerning the proposed transaction, for example not later than the second request for additional information.[81] Though, the merging parties can be asked to notify their merger plans to the other jurisdiction in order to support the international cooperation and coordination of investigations.

Exchange of Information. The general exchange of information can take place both by informal cooperation and by a binding agreement. Bilateral

---

[79] Tritell and Kraus (2006) p. 2.

[80] Article II.2 of the Agreement between the Government of the United States and the Government of Canada Regarding the application of Their Competition and Deceptive Marketing Practice Laws, Washington and Ottawa, August 1995.

[81] Cf. Article II.4 of the Agreement between the Government of the United States and the Government of Canada Regarding the application of Their Competition and Deceptive Marketing Practice Laws, Washington and Ottawa, August 1995. As regards the United States, the second request itself is protected by confidentiality provisions of the Hard-Scott-Rodino Act, so that US competition agencies generally notify earlier (Parisi (1999) p. 21).

agreements often include provisions like for example the obligatory exchange of texts on legal theory, case-law or market studies. Moreover, the parties can agree on a compulsory provision on the exchange of information about any known anticompetitive activities and any innovations introduced into the legal systems in order to improve the application of their respective competition laws. These provisions intend to facilitate the effective application of the national competition laws and to promote a better understanding of each other's legal frameworks. The exchange of information can be promoted by informal and institutional meetings between the representatives of each party's competition authorities.

Consultation. In contrast to mere notification and the general exchange of information, consultation includes a case-specific exchange of information, but does not involve any form of cooperation and coordination. Bilateral consultation among competition authorities is especially important with regard to investigations of restrictive business practices where the enterprises are located in another country, either to resolve unilateral or mutual concerns.[82] For instance, in case of a merger enforcement concerning two foreign enterprises located in the other country, both parties of the bilateral agreement could be allowed to consult the other party in order to share information which the national laws allow to disclose, e.g. as regards each party's analysis of the relevant market, and to 'resolve concerns between the states which arise from enforcement activities'[83].

Besides this form of case-specific consultation, bilateral agreements often give each party the right to request consultations regarding any matter relating to the cooperation agreement. Some bilateral agreements also commit to periodic meetings between the competition authorities about international enforcement issues, for example in order to exchange information on current enforcement efforts and priorities in relation to their competition and deceptive marketing practices laws; to exchange information on economic sectors of common interest; to discuss policy changes that they are considering; and to discuss other matters of mutual interest relating to the application of their competition and deceptive marketing practices laws and the operation of the bilateral agreement. For instance, the US antitrust agencies and the Japan Fair Trade Commission conduct annual consultations since 1976[84]; the officials of the US antitrust agencies and the Canadian competition authorities shall meet at least twice a year.

---

[82] Lloyd and Vautier (1999) p. 36.

[83] Guzman (2004) p. 369.

[84] Melamed (1998).

In sum, consultation can be regarded as a first step to support international antitrust enforcement and to avoid conflicts with other countries with regard to specific antitrust-cases.[85] Nevertheless, mere consultation has many limits. Consultation does not lead to common solutions; each party autonomously decides the case. Furthermore, consultation could become impracticable if many countries are dealing with the same case.

Enforcement Cooperation. By means of a bilateral enforcement cooperation agreement, the two parties generally acknowledge their common interest to cooperate in the enforcement of their competition laws and to promote a better understanding of each other's enforcement policies and activities. In order to achieve these aims, the parties do not have to make any significant changes as regards national law and enforcement activities. The cooperation between both parties is mostly limited to the extent compatible with their respective laws and interests so that the requested party is allowed to take its own interests into account whether to cooperate and to what extent.[86] Consequently, mere cooperation between national competition authorities is not a reliable instrument to protect international competition.[87] Nevertheless, cooperation exceeds the boundaries of mere consultation and involves commitments to assist the other party´s competition authorities, upon request, in locating and securing evidence and witnesses, to share information to the extent legally possible and compatible with each country's interests, to inform each other with respect to anticompetitive activities and enforcement activities involving conduct that may also have an adverse effect on competition within the territory of the other party, and to discuss possible enforcement theories or market definitions, or possible public sources of relevant information. Furthermore, the parties may agree to work together in technical cooperation activities related to competition law enforcement and policy. These activities may include, for instance, the temporary exchange of competition agency personnel for training purposes and the mutual participation of competition agency personnel as lecturers or consultants at training courses on competition law and policy organized by each other´s competition agencies.

Coordination of Investigation and Enforcement Activities with Regard to Related Matters. In contrast to *cooperation* agreements, a *coordination* agreement should be applied in cases of common interest, i.e. when *both* parties have started enforcement activities with regard to a specific matter. In this case, the parties can decide to work closely together and to

85 Lloyd and Vautier (1999) p. 36.
86 Ibid.
87 Koopmann (2000) p. 27.

coordinate, either in whole or in part, and to structure their investigatory and enforcement activities in order to conduct their enforcement activities consistently and not to disrupt the other party's activities with any decision. Therefore, for instance, they share their information and independent analysis when 'significant issues for both sides are involved'[88]. This includes the exchange of information about investigational processes and methods (e.g. methods how to analyze product and geographic markets), publicly available information about the relevant markets, applicable legal principles and precedents, information on remedies (such as divestitures, licensing or behavioural controls), and timetables and deadlines. Coordination also includes the possibility to hold joint meetings with the involved companies, especially in case of a merger or acquisition. Nevertheless, in general, both parties will finally take autonomous decisions, though it is also possible to carry out joint investigations in both territories, to find a common solution, and to assist each other in implementing the proposed remedies.[89] Furthermore, the parties can implement a so-called 'who goes first' procedure, i.e. 'one party may decide to hold back its enforcement activities until the other has reached a decision. If that decision also solves the former party's problem, that party may decide that it no longer needs to take independent action'[90]. In many antitrust cases, which concern both countries, one country is in a better position to investigate and remedy the case because it is affected more directly or the restrictive business practices are primarily conducted in this country. Then it can be useful to let this country take the lead and not to make any own decisions before the other party's investigations are closed.[91]

The decision whether to start coordinated investigations depends on the consideration of several criteria which concern the expected effective results which coordination could produce with regard to enforcement objectives, for example (1) each country's ability to obtain additional and necessary information and to secure effective relief against the anticompetitive business practices; (2) the reduction of costs for the competition authorities and the persons subject to enforcement activities; (3) the potential advantages of coordinated remedies to the competition authorities and to the persons subject to enforcement activities; (4) the observance of applicable deadlines under national legislation. During the process of coordination, each party is free to notify the other party at any time that it intends to limit or terminate coordinated enforcement and to pursue their enforce-

[88] Cf. Lloyd and Vautier (1999) p. 37.
[89] Cf. Melamed (1999) p. 427.
[90] Cf. Lloyd and Vautier (1999) p. 37.
[91] Melamed (1998).

ment activities independently or according to other provisions of the bilateral agreement.

Mutual Legal Assistance Agreements. Mutual Legal Assistance Treaties (MLATs) are a relatively new and intensive form of international antitrust cooperation.[92] The parties assist each other especially in criminal antitrust investigations, i.e. with regard to antitrust crimes like international price-fixing, bid-rigging, market division, and other hardcore cartels. The parties even share confidential evidence that is located in their own country (for example documents and witness testimony) in order to support the other country´s antitrust investigations.[93] Either do they already possess this antitrust evidence or they investigate themselves, for example by means of subpoenas, to collect new evidence for the foreign antitrust authority. Furthermore, besides obtaining evidence, MLATs also can include a close cooperation in parallel investigations.[94] In contrast to the above mentioned forms of cooperation, a prerequisite for this form of far-reaching cooperation is a relatively high similarity of the parties competition laws, especially with regard to the protection of confidential information.

Negative and Positive Comity. A widespread element of bilateral agreements on antitrust cooperation is the negative comity principle (traditional comity). According to this principle, the parties of a bilateral agreement mutually guarantee to notify the other country about antitrust proceedings which may affect important interests of the other country. Furthermore, they limit the extraterritorial application of their antitrust laws by means of a rule of reason, similar to the unilaterally applied interest-balancing test. The parties agree to give careful consideration to the important interests of the other party when applying the own national competition laws according to the effects doctrine, including decisions regarding the initiation of an investigation or proceeding, the scope of an investigation or proceeding and the nature of the remedies or penalties sought in each case. As a part of this, each party abstains from inducing firms to do things that could conflict with the laws and the economic policy of the other country.[95] Both the non-violation of the other country´s laws and sovereignty and the minimization of adverse effects that the own enforcement activities might have on the other's important interests are of special importance. This is in order to avoid international conflicts and to initiate some coordination in

92 Cf. Lloyd and Vautier (1999) pp. 33, 39f.

93 Cf. Worm (2004) p. 159; cf. Melamed (1999) p. 427.

94 Cf. Melamed (1999) p. 427.

95 Meiklejohn (1999) p. 1242.

case of parallel proceedings so that a common solution becomes more likely.

Theoretically, negative comity does not forbid the application of the effects doctrine, but actually negative comity often caused a non-application of the effects-doctrine for reasons of politeness and good relations between the nations. Consequently, negative comity did not always promote the protection of international competition; to the contrary, negative comity often has led to a lack of antitrust enforcement in order to avoid international tensions or conflicts. Furthermore, 'existing agreements do not lay out any details about how this consideration is to be given, do not include any sort of sanction for a failure to take the interests of the other party into account, and say nothing about how the interests of the other state should affect domestic policy decisions.'[96]

As a consequence of these deficiencies of mere negative comity, governments have decided to enter into a second generation of bilateral agreements. The positive comity principle has been developed which can be combined with negative comity. Positive comity has become an important element of bilateral agreements in order to prevent the application of the effects doctrine without giving up the protection of international competition. Instead of applying the own competition laws, a country that is party to an agreement on the application of positive comity may ask the other party to take appropriate measures against an anti-competitive business practice which takes place on the territory of the requested party – generally by firms of the requested country – and affects important interests of the requesting party. This is especially relevant in case of market foreclosure which results from private anticompetitive behaviour and harms the requesting country's exporters.[97] In this case, the requested foreign competition authority is asked to commence investigations against its companies who are suspected of violating important interests of the requesting party

[96] Guzman (2004) pp. 369f.; cf. Meiklejohn (1999) p. 1243.

[97] The 1998 Agreement Between The Government of the United States of America and the European Communities on the Application of Positive Comity Principles in the Enforcement of their Competition Laws includes some presumptions as regards the application of its positive comity provision. In case that the alleged violations especially harm domestic consumers, the domestic competition authorities normally would not defer the enforcement activities to the foreign competition authority, unless the anticompetitive activities 'occur principally in and are directed principally towards the other Party's territory (Article IV 2.(a) of the Agreement Between The Government of the United States of America and the European Communities on the Application of Positive Comity Principles in the Enforcement of their Competition Laws, OJ L 173 of June 18, 1998, Brussels; cf. Fullerton and Mazard (2001) p. 413).

by excluding domestic enterprises from the foreign market. This request is based on a preliminary case analysis by the requesting competition authority. According to Article III of the 1998 bilateral agreement between the United States and the European Union, 'the competition authorities of a Requesting Party may request the competition authorities of a Requested Party to investigate and, if warranted, to remedy anticompetitive activities in accordance with the Requested Party´s competition laws. Such a request may be made regardless of whether the activities also violate the Requesting Party´s competition laws, and regardless of whether the competition authorities of the Requesting Party have commenced or contemplate taking enforcement under their own competition laws.'[98] One aspect of this agreement is of special importance. The crucial feature is that the foreign enterprises violate the competition laws of the requested party so that the requested foreign competition authority can start an investigation against its enterprises. It is not necessary that the competition laws of the requesting party have been violated, too. In this way, international competition policy achieves the aim that anticompetitive business practices are investigated under the competition law in which these practices are – in whole or in part – occurring and probably directly affecting the home market, too. This is a general advantage for the protection of competition because of the following reasons. Firstly, the requested party has a better access to required evidence and frequently it has a genuine interest in starting an investigation in order protect domestic competition and consumers, too.[99] Secondly, a referral of a case on the basis of positive comity can help to start coordinated investigations and to avoid parallel proceedings and conflicts.[100] Thirdly, the requested party generally has better possibilities to remedy the anticompetitive business practices. Fourthly, positive comity does not require the transfer of confidential information. Despite these advantages, 'positive comity is still an under-used tool'[101]; though the small number of positive comity requests also could be a result of its preventive character, i.e. it is likely that countries automatically take into account the other party´s interests in order to avoid a request by the foreign competition authority.

---

98 Article III ('Positive Comity') of the Agreement Between The Government of the United States of America and the European Communities on the Application of Positive Comity Principles in the Enforcement of their Competition Laws, in: Official Journal – L 173 of June 18, 1998, Brussels.

99 Klein (1997).

100 Cf. Budzinski (2002) p. 242.

101 Zanettin (2002) p. 279; cf. Basedow (1998) p. 35.

Nonetheless, positive comity does not solve all problem of international antitrust. First, both parties are not obliged to follow the other party´s matter of concern. On the one hand, the requested party is not obliged to start own investigations and to enforce its competition laws against domestic firms. On the other hand, in case that the requested competition authority had started an own investigation and entered into consultation with the requesting party (for example by setting up so-called joint case teams[102]), the requesting authority is not obliged to accept the requested party´s analysis and the proposed remedies. Instead, if the referring competition authority cannot take sufficient influence on the requested party´s analysis, it still has the sovereignty to start an own antitrust enforcement initiative under its own competition laws if the foreign anticompetitive business practices violate domestic law. Though, this could be difficult because of limits in obtaining necessary (confidential) information and problems in enforcing its results against the foreign companies. Secondly, positive comity necessitates a relatively high degree of similarity between the competition laws of the parties. Otherwise, in case of an underdeveloped competition law of the requested party, positive comity could fail to achieve its purpose.[103] Furthermore, in case that several countries are affected by a competition restraint, similar interests and competition laws are necessary in order to be able to take into account the important interests of all participating countries. In general, bilateral agreements between these countries can be regarded as an incentive and instrument to develop more similar competition laws.

Confidentiality. Bilateral agreements partly include provisions to share *confidential* business information to the extent legally possible and compatible with each country's domestic laws and interests and to maintain the confidentiality of any information that they receive from another authority in confidence. Hence no party of a bilateral antitrust agreement is required to communicate any information – like commercially sensitive information about domestic firms – to the other party if the communication is prohibited by the laws of the party possessing the information or if the disclosure of the information would harm fundamental interests of this party. Nevertheless, cooperation and especially coordination can be promoted by a more permissive practice in sharing confidential information, especially as regards business information. In order to make this possible, confidentiality agreements may require a change of existing domestic legislation, especially in case of comprehensive blocking statutes. Several nations have en-

102 Moeschel (2005a) p. 601.

103 Cf. Wins (2000) p. 88; cf. Meiklejohn (1999) p. 1423.

acted blocking statutes which impede foreign investigatory efforts by banning the transfer of sensitive business information so that its citizens and residents are not allowed to comply with foreign requests or orders to disclose or testify sensitive information.

Although the application of blocking statutes has been reduced, governments are often still unwilling to abandon existing confidentiality rules. On the one hand they are interested to protect confidential information in order to protect the domestic firms′ international competitiveness. Furthermore, they also fear that national competition policy could become less effective if domestic firms are deterred from sharing confidential information to their own domestic competition authority if this information could be communicated to foreign antitrust agencies, too. Consequently, 'restrictions on the exchange of confidential information remain a significant impediment to effective cooperation'[104], but these restrictions could be solved in the future in order to support effective cooperation and coordination.[105] The status quo is especially problematic with regard to anti-cartel investigations and abusive business practices where the involved companies mostly do not cooperate with the investigating antitrust authorities so that it is unlikely to get the consent of the parties involved to communicate confidential information.

In case of a merger or acquisition, the involved companies who have notified the proposed merger or acquisition to their domestic competition authority often agree to waive confidentiality restrictions. In this case, the competition authorities can share substantive and confidential information and analysis. This is especially important in case that the companies do not have to submit a premerger notification to the foreign competition authority, because, according to the confidentiality provisions of the US Hard-Scott Rodino Act, US competition agencies themselves are not allowed to make public the fact that domestic companies have submitted a premerger notification.[106] But also in case that the companies have to notify their merger plans to other jurisdictions, competition agencies can encourage the merging parties to help coordinating the timing of the different merger reviews and to waive confidentiality to speed the multiple agency review process and to enhance the possibility of complementary rather than inconsistent remedies.

---

[104] Zanettin (2002) p. 279.

[105] The 1994 US International Antitrust Enforcement Assistance Act (IAEAA) authorizes US antitrust authorities to sign antitrust cooperation agreements which include the exchange of confidential information – especially antitrust evidence about domestic firms.

[106] Cf. Parisi (1999) p. 17.

2.2.5.2 Regional and Multinational Cooperation

In addition to bilateral cooperation, there are also regional and multinational cooperation initiatives in antitrust enforcement. As regards their relation to the existing bilateral agreements, which are presently dominating international antitrust cooperation, there are some differences. While some multilateral initiatives explicitly recommend or even require additional bilateral agreements, others either try to compensate the limits of bilateral cooperation or they probably could turn out to become a future alternative to bilateral cooperation.

Regional Cooperation. *Regional* cooperation agreements have a special position in international antitrust. Although they are primarily focused on regional trade liberalization, i.e. the creation of a free trade area or a common market of the participating economies, some of them also help to reduce anticompetitive conduct in international business so that they have procompetitive effects beyond the borders of the regional integration zone. The more ambitious regional trade agreements like the European Union and the ANZCERTA include far-reaching provisions on antitrust because they intend to prevent any kind of constraints to competition which could harm regional integration.[107] Therefore, they partly could serve as a model for an international agreement on antitrust although one has to take into account that these regional trade agreements pursue more ambitious aims like the total integration of the national markets so that one has to make concessions as regards a transfer into an international competition policy regime.

Less ambitious regional trade agreements like the North American Free Trade Agreement (NAFTA) rather underline the sovereignty of the parties as regards competition law and antitrust enforcement. Therefore, most of them only include some general provisions on antitrust which are mostly non-binding and at best similar to those of bilateral agreements or necessitating further bilateral agreements between the signatories. For instance, the NAFTA[108] provides in Article 1501 that '(1) Each Party shall adopt or maintain measures to proscribe anticompetitive business conduct and take appropriate action with respect thereto, recognizing that such measures

[107] For more information about the supranational antitrust provisions of the European Union and its degree of centralization, see Chap. 2.3.2.2. As regards the decentralized approach of harmonization in the ANZCERTA, see Chap. 2.3.2.1.

[108] North American Free Trade Agreement (NAFTA) between Canada, the United States and Mexico, signed on December 17, 1992 and made effective on January 1, 1994.

will enhance the fulfillment of the objectives of this Agreement. To this end the Parties shall consult from time to time about the effectiveness of measures undertaken by each Party. (2) Each Party recognizes the importance of cooperation and coordination among their authorities to further effective competition law enforcement in the free trade area. The Parties shall cooperate on issues of competition law enforcement policy, including mutual legal assistance, notification, consultation and exchange of information relating to the enforcement of competition laws and policies in the free trade area. (3) No Party may have recourse to dispute settlement under this Agreement for any matter arising under this Article.' Consequently, the parties of the NAFTA have entered into additional bilateral antitrust agreements in order to meet with the general antitrust provisions of Article 1501.[109] In conclusion, less ambitious regional cooperation agreements like the NAFTA could be taken as a model for an international antitrust framework which commits the parties to cooperate on issues of antitrust both on the basis of some binding multilateral rules which build a common framework and on the basis of non-binding bilateral agreements which give scope for more flexibility.

Multilateral Cooperation. Multinational fora on international antitrust matters are a further legally non-binding approach to promote cooperation in international antitrust enforcement and to generate more convergence and coherency between the approximately one hundred jurisdictions that have already implemented a competition law.[110] Many governments, competition authorities and multilateral organizations have opened or entered into multilateral competition fora which facilitate dialogue on experiences in antitrust enforcement, convergence towards best practices and cooperation for more effective international antitrust policy by means of so-called 'soft law'. The most important multilateral fora are the ICN, the WTO Working Group on the Interaction between Trade and Competition, the OECD, the UNCTAD, and regional organizations such as the Asia-Pacific Economic Cooperation (APEC).[111]

International organizations like the OECD and the UNCTAD have focused both on dialogue, technical assistance, on developing know how, on proposing common non-binding principles (e.g. non-discrimination and transparency) and standards (e.g. the prohibition of hard core cartels) for bilateral and multilateral cooperation, and on recommendations for en-

---

109 The United States have signed a bilateral agreement both with Canada and Mexico, furthermore Canada and Mexico have signed a competition law enforcement agreement.

110 Tritell and Kraus (2006) p. 4.

111 Cf. ibid.; cf. Melamed (1999) p. 430.

tering into more intensive (bilateral) cooperation. In 1967, the OECD has published its *Recommendation on Cooperation between Member Countries in Restrictive Business Practices Affecting International Trade* for the first time.[112] The current recommendation, amended in 1995[113], encourages the OECD member countries to cooperate on case-specific law enforcement, i.e. to notify and consult one another when their antitrust enforcement activities affect other member countries′ important interests.[114] These OECD provisions mainly work as a (minimum) reference for the negotiation of non-binding bilateral agreements and MLATs between OECD members. The 1998 OECD *Hard Core Cartel Recommendation*[115] even calls upon the OECD member countries to implement national provisions that 'effectively halt and deter hard core cartels' and to sign MLATs on the bilateral level in order to foster cooperation against these criminal anticompetitive strategies.[116] Furthermore, it recommends the exchange of confidential information and to practice positive comity.[117] The 2005 *OECD Recommendation on Merger Review*[118] intends to support efficient, effective, timely, fair, non-discriminatory, and transparent merger review procedures, especially by means of international cooperation and coordination and by identifying international best practices as a result of periodic reviews. In conclusion, the OECD has taken a leading position in fostering international cooperation in antitrust although it offers just a forum and non-binding recommendations.

In 1980, the UNCTAD has endorsed a *Set of Multilaterally Agreed Equitable Principles and Rules for the Control of Restrictive Business Practices* (UN-RBP) as a model for common basic rules.[119] In contrast to the OECD who also wants to promote notification, consultation and cooperation, the RBP especially works towards an international harmonization of competition law.

Both the OECD and the UNCTAD recommendations are non-binding but useful instruments to support cooperation between competition authorities. Though it has to be underlined that neither the OECD nor the UNCTAD are potential candidates to serve as an institution or framework for international antitrust cooperation. This is because none of them can

---

112 OECD (1967).
113 OECD (1995).
114 Basedow (1998) p. 33; Winslow (2001) p. 118.
115 OECD (1998).
116 Cf. Melamed (1999) pp. 430f.
117 Cf. ibid. p. 430.
118 OECD (2005a).
119 UNCTAD (1980).

represent all nations that should take part in international antitrust cooperation. While the OECD is focused on the industrialized countries, the UNCTAD rather looks after the interests of developing countries, demanding a preferential or differential treatment for them.[120]

In contrast to this, the WTO and the ICN are potential candidates to become themselves the central institution for future multilateral cooperation, either on the basis of binding supranational provision and elements of centralization (WTO) or by means of non-binding provisions within a decentralized approach to international antitrust (ICN). In 1996, the WTO has decided to establish its Working Group on the Interaction between Trade and Competition, especially at the instigation of the European Union who underlined the effectiveness of an integration of binding international competition rules into the existing WTO framework. The WTO Working Group had to study on trade related aspects of anticompetitive practices and antitrust in order to identify issues that may merit further consideration in the WTO framework, for example the clarification of core principles (non-discrimination, transparency, and procedural fairness), provisions on hardcore cartels, modalities for voluntary cooperation, and support for progressive reinforcement of competition institutions in developing countries.[121] The idea to entrust the WTO with international antitrust and to develop an international antitrust law has been discussed intensively in economic literature and is still favoured by several scientists (see Chap. 2.3.2.2), but as regards the political dimension, there is no progress. On the one hand, the transatlantic trade disputes concerning the EC import regimes with regard to bananas and hormone beef have led to a more critical view of an internationalization of competition rules by the EC.[122] The United States still view the WTO as just a forum for discussing international competition policy.[123] Furthermore, the WTO General Council has decided in 2004 to suspend the proceedings on this issue during the Doha Round so that the WTO Working Group has been set inactive.

Although the discussion about the scope of competition policy within the WTO goes on, a more promising and realistic approach to international antitrust cooperation could be the ICN, though it is just a non-binding cooperative process among antitrust enforcement agencies.[124] The United States, who are generally sceptical about multilaterally binding competition rules, have initiated and established this network in 2001 as a counter-

[120] Cf. Immenga (2004) p. 12; cf. Section C.(iii) of the UN-RBP.
[121] WTO (2003).
[122] Meessen (2000) p. 6.
[123] Basedow (1998) p. 86; cf. Meessen (2000) p. 6.
[124] Graham (2003) p. 970.

reaction to the more ambitious WTO approach of developing supranational competition law. Meanwhile, the ICN has become a worldwide discussion platform for almost all national and multinational competition authorities, finding acceptance also at competition authorities that originally preferred the WTO approach (e.g. the European Commission and Germany).[125] Membership is voluntary and open to any national or multinational competition authority. The annual conferences and the working groups provide for regular contacts among the national antitrust experts for addressing practical competition concerns, improving national antitrust, fostering worldwide cooperation and enhancing bottom-up convergence through dialogue and the adoption of commonly recommended best practices (soft harmonization), for example as regards issues like merger notification procedures and merger remedies.

Despite the present dynamics and the success of the ICN, there are several problems to be identified. Besides its legally unbinding nature – which could result in a lack of implementation or an inadequate implementation and application of its recommendations – the ICN is likely to run into problems of legitimacy and reliability.[126] Furthermore, the ICN could be monopolised by the most powerful industrialized countries, both as regards the discussed issues and the final outcome.[127]

2.3 The Proponents of International Competition Rules

Many authors claim the necessity of international competition rules or at least a harmonization of national competition laws. They underline the role of international competition rules as a tool against restrictive business practices[128] (monopoly positions, horizontal agreements, international cartels, cross-border mergers, tacit collusion, vertical restraints, unfair strategies like refusals to deal and technology agreements), against a race to the bottom or a 'deregulation race'[129], and against the fears and claims of those who criticize the economic globalization and the undemocratic power of international enterprises.[130]

---

125 Cf. Monti (2004) p. 2.
126 Graham (2003) p. 970.
127 Todino (2003) pp. 283ff.
128 Cf. Meiklejohn (1999) p. 1237; Graham (2003) pp. 947ff.; Immenga (2004) pp. 17ff.; Guzman (2004) pp. 355ff.
129 See Sinn (1999).
130 Cf. Jens (2002) pp. 13ff.; cf. Meiklejohn (1999) p. 1241.

2.3.1 The Central Arguments in Favour of International Competition Rules

This chapter describes the main arguments that have been produced in favour of international competition rules. A critical reply to these claims follows in Chap. 2.4.

2.3.1.1 Globalization as a Challenge for National Competition Policy

The economic globalization is undoubtedly one of the most important challenges for national competition policy. The globalization of markets is a very dynamic structural change of national economies and international trade, requiring new and innovative strategies of national and international competition policy. Competition authorities have to take a fresh look on the relevant markets, they have to learn how to handle international mega-mergers and cartels in new and changing markets and they have to observe and assess a multitude of business activities in foreign countries. This internationalization of markets and business activities automatically leads to an internationalization of competition policy, which could overtax national competition authorities and cause many inefficiencies and international conflicts. Therefore, Jacquemin states that 'the globalization of markets, the rapid diffusion of modern technology and the multiplication of global actors adopting global strategies call for a coherent transnational regulatory framework. Cartels and concentration processes produce more and more substantial effects within several jurisdictions. Without some co-ordination and harmonization of competition policies, this inevitably increases the potential for conflict and insecurity for corporations.'[131] Guzman observes an over- and underregulation of antitrust at the international level which cannot be eliminated by soft cooperation.[132] The overregulation results from parallel investigations and certain forms of applying laws extraterritorially.[133] This leads to 'a more restrictive and burdensome set of substantive rules than exists under the legal regime of any single state'[134], for example in case of parallel merger investigations by the United States and the EU. The underregulation results from a lack of competition laws and applying them extraterritoriality, especially in developing countries.[135] Drexl underlines the interdependencies between international economic freedom, international property rights and international competition policy,

---

[131] Jacquemin (1993) p. 92.
[132] Guzman (2004) pp. 359ff., 370.
[133] Also confer Sedemund (2002) p. 111.
[134] Guzman (2004) p. 359.
[135] Ibid. pp. 360f.

which necessitate – in accordance with the maintenance of a long-term framework-consistency ('Ordnungspolitik') – an international competition law.[136]

Although competition policy is undoubtedly confronted with new challenges in the course of further globalization, it is necessary to be careful with the call for an international competition policy regime, because such statements could be interpreted as a value-judgement. Consequently, it is important to take a close look at the individual arguments of the proponents and opponents.

2.3.1.2 Negative Effects of National Competition Policy

Problems of national competition policy could result from two reasons. On the one hand, there could be natural limits of national competition policy as regards international competition restraints. In this case, national competition policy would be *unable* to deal effectively and efficiently with restraints of competition resulting from increasing transnational anticompetitive business practices (see Chap. 2.3.1.2.1). On the other hand, national competition policy could be abused like a strategic industrial or protectionist policy. In this case, national competition policy would be *unwilling* to deal with certain competition restraints (see Chap. 2.3.1.2.2).

2.3.1.2.1 Limits and Inefficiencies

There are at least two aspects which have to be considered as regards the natural limits of national competition policy in a globalized world economy. Possibly, national competition authorities are not in a position to deal with certain forms of international anticompetitive behaviour which are out of the control of any single nation.[137] Independent of their legal competences, their administrative and financial resources, and the existing forms of bilateral cooperation, they would be simply overtaxed with antitrust enforcement as regards certain forms of international cartels, market power abuse, or transborder mergers and acquisitions. Secondly, their attempts to deal with international competition restraints could cause inefficiencies and international conflicts that only could be settled by means of further international cooperation, coordination, or centralization.

The Increasing Danger of International Private Restraints of Trade. The international liberalization of markets for goods and capital investments has ambivalent effects on the intensity of competition on national

---

[136] Drexl (1998) p. 43.
[137] Tarullo (1999) pp. 445ff.

and international markets. On the one hand, globalization promotes national and international competitive pressure.[138] National enterprises are confronted with new international competitors because a market entry from abroad has become much easier. Consequently, in most cases national cartels and monopolies and other forms of anticompetitive business conduct cannot be maintained. The intensified national and international competition between enterprises is generally considered one of the most important positive effects of globalization. Consequently, the effects of free trade and globalization on international competition cannot simply be taken as an argument for international competition rules because they also could serve as an argument for even less competition policy. Liberal trade policy could be considered the best competition policy so that the demand for national and international competition rules would become increasingly irrelevant in the course of further globalization.[139] Furthermore, free trade can be considered an effective instrument to overcome the well-known trade-off between the effectiveness of competition and the generation of scale economies, i.e. between allocative efficiency and productive efficiency.[140] In global markets, enterprises have more scope to build up their optimal size without getting into conflict with a competition authority that is sceptical about a further concentration if this could cause *national* economic inefficiencies.

Blackhurst poses the question what competition-related problems would remain in a world of completely free trade in goods and services. He considers – besides the danger that new private uncompetitive practices might be stimulated – the alternative thought that 'if the United States were to practice complete free trade vis-à-vis the rest of the world, virtually all forms of uncompetitive behaviour in the domestic market would disappear or be severely curtailed'[141]. Furthermore, he underlines that 'it would not be enough to know what kinds of uncompetitive behaviour can be controlled by free trade, and which cannot', because 'we also need estimates of the current costs to society of each of the forms of uncompetitive behaviour'[142]. In case that free trade eliminates the most severe and costly categories of uncompetitive private behaviour, there would be no need for an international competition policy governed by a multilateral jurisdiction.

---

138 Cf. Christl (2001) p. 77; cf. Neven and Seabright (1997) p. 382.

139 Lloyd (1998) p. 1135; cf. Blackhurst (1994) p. 224. Also cf. Bloch who provides a differentiated position on this issue (Bloch (2001) p. 105).

140 Cf. Lachmann (2004) p. 196.

141 Blackhurst (1994) p. 224.

142 Ibid. p. 225.

Many economists doubt this optimism. Some economists generally state that trade liberalization and economic integration does not always intensify competition because cuts in tariffs do not automatically reduce the market power of domestic enterprises.[143] To the contrary, in certain cases economic integration could give an incentive to monopolize and cartelize.[144] Furthermore, the pro-competitive effects of free trade and foreign competition on domestic markets could be ruined by new private restraints of trade and competition.[145] Some economists refer to the increase in the number of cross-border activities of private enterprises, especially mega-mergers[146] and international cartels[147]. These activities could restrict both international competition and trade. Globalized markets are typically riskier for producers.[148] Many enterprises fear globalization, especially if they made much of a profit from former protectionism. They could try to compensate the removal of public restrictions to competition (e.g. former tariffs and import quotas) by erecting private restrictions to competition (e.g. import and export cartels, exclusive arrangements, market foreclosure, and dumping practices by market-dominating firms) in order to exploit domestic and foreign markets. It is possible that private enterprises erect higher trading restrictions compared to the former public protectionism.[149] Therefore, competition policy remains an important task.

---

143 Cf. Lachmann (2005) p. 124; cf. Khemani (1998) pp. 144ff.; cf. Anderson and Khosla (1995) pp. 15f.

144 Cf. Fung (1992) pp. 837ff. Fung provides a simple model in which trade liberalization, i.e. a reduction of tariffs 'can either promote or retard competition, depending on specific industry characteristics and the magnitude of the tariff cuts' (p. 838). This model analyzes the effects of liberalization from the viewpoint of the domestic country. The central assumption is that high cost-differences between firms reduce the probability of joint monopolization. Tariff cuts reduce or increase the inter-firm cost differences. In case that the domestic firm is the high cost firm and the foreign competitor is a low cost producer, tariff cuts would aggravate these cost-differences and this would reduce the home firm´s incentive to participate in joint monopolization. In this case, economic integration would promote competition. 'But if the home firm is the low cost producer, then economic integration retards competition if the initial tariff is low, but still promotes competition if the initial tariff level is sufficiently high' (p. 845). Consequently, economic integration is not in any case an adequate substitute of competition policy.

145 Cf. Meessen (2000) p. 7; cf. Immenga (2004) p. 17.

146 Cf. Budzinski and Kerber (2003); Lenel (2000) pp. 1ff.; Lenel (1999) pp. 7f.; Globerman (1990) pp. 80ff.

147 Cf. Monti (2004) pp. 2ff.; cf. Immenga (2004) p. 17; cf. Tarullo (1999) p. 447.

148 Lachmann (2001) pp. 1ff.

149 Ross (1988) p. 522.

One of the most important reactions of enterprises to globalization and the new international framework is the increase in the number and extent of mergers and acquisitions, especially so-called international mega-mergers, and a growing incentive to organize international cartels. For instance, the antitrust and merger control cases investigated by the US-Department of Justice (DoJ) and the US-Federal Trade Commission (FTC) increasingly have an international dimension. Partly they require contact with foreign enforcement authorities and can not be decided without information from abroad if the evidence that is needed both to discover and to prove the existence of an international cartel is dispersed in different countries.[150]

The same experience of international anticompetitive conduct has been made *within* the European Union: the integration of the Common Market has led to an increase in the total and relative number of cross-border cases, more than expected. Consequently, regional free trade associations like the EU and the NAFTA generally combine their initiatives to liberalize trade with additional measures with respect to competition policy.[151] As regards world trade, the post-war efforts of the United States and the United Nations to establish an International Trade Organization (ITO) also included an attempt to complete the gradual elimination of state-induced restraints to trade by an international cooperation 'to prevent, on the part of private or public commercial enterprises, business practices affecting international trade which restrain competition, limit access to markets, or foster monopolistic control, whenever such practices have harmful effects on the expansion of production or trade' (Art. 46 Havana Charter 1948). According to Art. 46 III, the ITO would have been given an extensive authority to decide on restrictive business practices like 'fixing prices, terms or conditions to be observed in dealing with others in the purchase, sale or lease of any product; excluding enterprises from, or allocating or dividing, any territorial market or field of business activity, or allocating customers, or fixing sales quotas or purchase quotas; discriminating against particular enterprises; limiting production or fixing production quotas; preventing by agreement the development or application of technology or invention whether patented or unpatented; extending the use of rights under patents, trade marks or copyrights granted by any Member to matters which, according to its laws and regulations, are not within the scope of such grants, or to products or conditions of production, use or sale which are likewise not the subject of such grants; any similar practices which the Organization may de-

---

150 Lloyd (1998) p. 1130; cf. Fullerton and Mazard (2001) p. 406; Graham (2003) pp. 947f.; Tarullo (1999) p. 447; WTO (1998).

151 See Chap. 2.2.5.2.

clare, by a majority of two-thirds of the Members present and voting, to be restrictive business practices'. But in contrast to the GATT agreement, the relevant articles of the Havana Charter have not been ratified so that the establishment of international competition rules has never been put in concrete terms and has not been realized up to now.

Consequently, as a result of international trade liberalization and a lack of international antitrust cooperation, national competition authorities are increasingly confronted with mega-mergers, global monopolies, oligopolistic pricing and other significant international antitrust-cases which could overtax their resources and exceed their competencies so that international cooperation seems to be necessary. These limits of national antitrust enforcement can only be overcome by more international cooperation. More cooperation would be necessary especially with regard to the possibility to secure necessary evidence from abroad and to share confidential information. The exchange of confidential information could help to compensate the limits of the existing bilateral agreements on positive comity. For instance, the positive comity agreement between the United States and the European Community only deals with anticompetitive business practices which also harm the markets and violate the competition laws of the requested party. The requested party is not allowed to start investigations and to assist the requesting party in case that business practices only affect the interests of the requesting country, even in case that these practices were – either wholly or in part – implemented in the territory of the requested party. This problem could be weakened by the exchange of confidential information, but most existing cooperation agreements are very restrictive in this respect.

The Danger of International Conflicts and Economic Inefficiencies as a Consequence of Applying the Effects Doctrine. Theoretically, the effects doctrine could work well because the market conduct of an enterprise on different markets generally can be dealt with under different jurisdictions and different competition laws. International companies are generally able to comply with different standards in foreign competition law[152] although this leads to additional financial, time and staff expenditures, especially in case of multiple notifications of merger transactions to national competition authorities.[153] Furthermore, the effects doctrine is – like the

152 Cf. Hauser and Schoene (1994) p. 211.

153 Heckenberger (2002) pp. 89ff. Also cf. Becher (2002) p. 77ff.; cf. Bär-Bouyssière (2002) pp. 104ff. These authors especially describe problems which result from international differences in formal law, but they also mention the lack of transparency and legal uncertainties as regards differences in substantive law.

principle of territoriality – accepted by international law because every sovereign country should have the right to protect itself against anti-competitive practices from abroad. Nonetheless, there are still some problems as regards the implementation of the effects doctrine, which could result in international conflicts and inefficiencies.

Firstly, the application of the effects doctrine frequently leads – in cases where the domestic market is affected by competition restraints of foreign enterprises – to *conflicts of extraterritoriality*, especially as regards investigations by the domestic antitrust authority and the enforcement of its decisions against foreign enterprises. According to international law, national competition authorities cannot enforce their decisions within foreign countries.[154] Consequently, a foreign enterprise even cannot be forced by the domestic competition authority to supply any information relevant for the investigation. Nevertheless, the investigating competition authority could be tempted to obtain relevant information by violating the other countries sovereignty and to enforce its antitrust decision by risking trade conflicts. In case that the accused foreign firm owns a branch, a subsidiary, or other investments within the domestic territory, a corporate group liability and financial recourse practiced by the domestic competition authority could lead to interjurisdictional conflicts.[155] In order to avoid international conflicts, competition authorities may shrink from applying the effects doctrine and refrain from antitrust enforcement.[156] Companies could try to take advantage of this legal vacuum.

Secondly, there could be a need for international cooperation and coordination because of conflicts and economic *inefficiencies* which result from inconsistent decisions or a cumulative competition policy by different national competition authorities, for example if a planned merger or an international cartel has to be investigated by several national competition authorities. The inefficiencies or additional (transaction) costs, caused by multiple notifications and time-consuming parallel antitrust investigations under several national laws, have to be carried both by the investigating nations and by the involved enterprises, but the main emphasis has to be put on the companies′ expenditures and their international competitiveness. Regarding this, further economic inefficiencies and even international political conflicts could arise as a consequence of opposing decisions by the national competition authorities. This could happen, for instance, in case that one of the involved antitrust authorities is responsible for a significant delay or even a failure of a planned merger, for example

[154] Cf. Fuchs (2000) p. 362.
[155] Cf. ibid. p. 362; cf. Scherer (1998) p. 16.
[156] Cf. Fuchs (2000) p. 362.

by setting relatively severe or cumulative merger conditions.[157] Countries become increasingly sensitive to the decisions of foreign competition authorities because the international competitiveness of their companies could be endangered. Hence enterprises sympathize with the idea of an international harmonization and closer cooperation of competition authorities as regards merger control. They are interested in simple procedures and fast decisions – if necessary by means of an international dispute settlement mechanism – because a long period of uncertainty about the permission for a merger or inter-firm cooperation causes additional costs and could endanger the planned business model.[158]

Further conflicts and inefficiencies could result from a nation's unwillingness to practice a fair and strict competition policy. This problem will be described in the following chapter.

2.3.1.2.2 The Unwillingness of Nations to Protect Competition on the International Level

The liberalization of world trade has led to some evasive strategies, applied by national governments, in order to protect the own economy. Besides the explicit, exceptional clauses and safeguard measures in the GATT (for example waivers, anti-dumping, emergency protection, countervailing duties, protection of the balance of payments, infant industry protection), further non-tariff trade barriers, industrial policy, and a misuse of competition policy have become more important instruments of foreign trade policy in the course of further globalization. The unwillingness of a national competition authority to practice a competition policy that produces positive external effects instead of negative spillovers expresses itself in discriminatory, protectionist, or too permissive practices. In a worst-case scenario, this unwillingness to stop international violations could be-

[157] Cf. Immenga (2000) p. 1059. The probably most prominent merger case which was characterized by transatlantic tensions because of a significant delay and the opposing position of the European Commission was the Boeing/McDonnell Douglas merger in 1997 (European Commission (1997) pp. 16-47). According to Sedemund, especially developing and transitory countries like Brazil and Mexico have attempted to block international mergers that have already been permitted by the United States and the European Union. These developing or transitory countries either fear a too high national market concentration – because they do not refer to the global market as the geographically relevant market – or they intend to protect domestic industries (Sedemund (2002) p. 110).

[158] Cf. Immenga (2000) p. 1059.

come a widespread strategy and result in a so-called race to the bottom and a prisoners′ dilemma situation.

The Danger of Discriminatory Competition Policy. National competetion authorities and governments are sometimes unwilling to protect international competition and to treat foreign enterprises without any discrimination based on their nationality. The application of the effects doctrine is for the most part egoistically motivated. Countries applying this unilateral strategy generally follow their own national interests. In contrast to a strict application of the principle of subjective territoriality, countries making use of the effects doctrine are not interested in cases where domestic enterprises restrict competition in foreign markets. Furthermore, they have no sufficient incentive to use the available tools to fight private restraints on competition, if domestic enterprises derive an advantage from anticompetitive behaviour. Therefore, the effects doctrine could lead to *discriminatory antitrust-policies*, treating foreign enterprises more severely than domestic firms. In terms of game theory, countries could be tempted to misuse the effects doctrine as a policy of protectionism and retaliation so that they could be trapped into a prisoners′ dilemma, characterized by a Pareto-inefficient Nash equilibrium. For instance, export cartels are often excepted from national anti-trust law because they do not affect the domestic market but a particular foreign market.

Furthermore, the governments of industrialized countries are interested in creating so called national champions which have a strong position in global markets. National competition authorities would implement a rather permissive strategy because strict competition policy could become a risk for the national economy. But this strategy is a danger for international competition and free trade because it can cause market foreclosures, e.g. by supporting mergers between national companies to prevent mergers with foreign companies, especially so-called hostile takeovers. Consequently, the concentration on national markets increases and a new protectionism, including strategies like dumping, could arise. In contrast to this rather permissive antitrust-strategy, the national competition authorities could be very sensitive to restrictive business practices from abroad. In this case, a strict application of national competition law to cross-border restraints of trade could cause international tensions, conflicts and inefficiencies, too. International tensions or conflicts especially arise if the sovereignty of foreign countries is affected (extraterritoriality conflicts). If that is the case, the international enforcement of national competition policy becomes difficult or even impossible.

In addition to this, in many countries competition policy is subdued to the influence of industrial policy considerations and industrial policy is viewed to be a better instrument to strengthen international competitiveness than strict competition policy. Generally, this is a likely scenario in countries which do not possess an independent competition authority. As a result of this, competition policy would become an instrument for national governments in order to pursue diverse other political aims, especially the aim to win elections. In this case, competition policy becomes a political instrument like trade policy so that an international competition policy could be a good way to protect national and international competition.[159] Many politicians would even approve a transfer of national competencies to an international institution because this would shield them from the pressure of interest groups.

Finally, it has to be taken into account that even positive developments in applying strict competition rules and abolishing anticompetitive industrial policy on the national level can not solve the fundamental problem of international conflicts, because in globalized markets even slight distortions of competition can cause profitable advantages in favour of domestic enterprises. Foreign countries could regard this as an unfair restraint of trade. As a consequence, international conflicts could become ubiquitous. The more intensive international competition gets, the stronger will be the effect of slight competitive advantages. Increasing liberalization and globalization could be accompanied by many new forms of protectionism.

The Danger of a Race to the Bottom. Some economists fear that a so-called race to the bottom could be the result of uncoordinated national competition policies, leading to a bottom-up convergence that offers only little protection for national and international competition.[160] They say that international regulatory competition is an incentive for governments to lessen national standards, for example to practice an increasingly permissive and protectionist competition policy because the international competitiveness of both the national economy and the domestic enterprises could be increased by doing this. The final outcome of this process would be a prisoners′ dilemma and a self-destruction of the regulatory competition. The standards would be internationally converged, but at a low level. World competition and trade would be at risk if this kind of convergence occurs to competition policy. All countries would lose welfare and only international coordination and harmonization could prevent this race to the bottom.

As regards the likeliness of this hypothesis in case of a continued predominance of national competition policy, Chap. 4.2.5 will revert to this

159 Cf. Meessen (2000) p. 11.

160 Cf. Sinn (1999).

theme by considering the limits of an international regulatory competition with regard to national competition policy.

2.3.2 Concepts to Intensify International Antitrust Cooperation

Chapter 2.2 has given an overview of the status quo of international competition policy. As regards international cooperation, we have seen that international cooperation is, with few exceptions, still limited to voluntary information-sharing agreements.[161] The proponents of a more extensive internationalization of competition policy say that there are problems in international antitrust which cannot be solved by this form of soft cooperation, but they vary in their answers to the question how to cooperate more intensively on the international level. The theory of integration has developed many alternative approaches for implementing more cooperation, focusing both on the degree of harmonization, the extent of centralization, the relation between national and international competition law, and the institutional embedding. Besides the question as to whether national competition rules should be internationally harmonized or even substituted by supranational competition rules, there is a debate of who should apply and enforce these harmonized national or international competition rules. Both the decision about the degree of harmonization, i.e. the creation of international substantive law, and about the allocation of law enforcement and agenda-setting competencies have significant consequences for how international cases are going to be decided, and this finally has consequences for the international competitiveness of nations.

The diverse concepts of international competition policy can be sorted according to the degree of cooperation, i.e. by increasing harmonization and centralization. Table 2.3 provides a simplified, schematic diagram of international antitrust concepts. The following two chapters offer more details.

[161] Cf. Guzman (2004) p. 369.

		Centralization		
Harmonization	International Competition Rules Applied by an International Antitrust Authority	International Minimum Standards Applied by an International Antitrust Authority	National Competition Rules Applied by an International Antitrust Authority	**Systems Competition**
		Lead Jurisdiction System One-Stop Shop System International Dispute Settlement		
	Multi-Level-System Applying International Competition Rules	Complex Multi-Level-System of Competition Laws	International Court Monitoring the Decentralized Enforcement of National Competition Rules	
		Twin-Track Approach of the van Miert Report (Bilateral and Multilateral Agreements)		
		Multilateral Fora like the ICN Bilateral Cooperation (Positive Comity)		
	Decentralized Application of International Competition Rules	Decentralized Application of International Minimum Standards	Decentralized Application of National Competition Rules (Effects Doctrine)	
		Decentralization		

Table 2.3: International Competition Policy and its Degree of Centralization and Harmonization

2.3.2.1 Decentralized Approaches with Different Degrees of International Harmonization

Compared to a total centralization of competition policy with regard to internationally relevant competition restraints, the basic advantage of decentralized approaches is the maintenance of a relatively high degree of national legislative competence, national enforcement activities, democratic control, and national sovereignty. These approaches put an emphasis on the principle of subsidiarity, they try to refer a case to the most appropriate competition authority and seek to assign cases to *national* competition authorities as long as this does not lead to intolerable distortions of international competition. But this advantage of decentralized approaches is at the same time a central disadvantage because national activities automatically produce a heterogeneity of law enforcement and the allocation of competencies remains to some extent open and conflictive.

There are several alternative models of decentralized international competition policy which disapprove a total international harmonization and centralization of competition policy and who therefore try to realize the lowest level of international antitrust cooperation that is apt to deal with the main deficiencies of the status quo of international antitrust.[162] These models of a decentralized international competition policy try to maintain the significant role of national competition authorities and national competition laws to a more or less degree. In general, they intend to allocate competences to the *national* competition authorities, but there are different approaches as regards (a) the specific case allocation, for instance with regard to the identification of the right and most competent *national* competition authority in any particular case; (b) as regards the determination of the degree of international harmonization; and (c) with regard to the assignment of the (national or international) law which has to be applied and enforced. Consequently, one characteristic of decentralization approaches is the strict differentiation between the assignment of the responsible competition authority on the one hand and the applied competition law on the other hand.

The range of international competition policy regimes starts with a decentralized approach based on the unilateral application of the effects doctrine and the status quo of bilateral or multilateral exchange of information as a first step to cope with international anticompetitive behaviour by private enterprises. Some economists and countries prefer these forms of soft cooperation and propose an *extension of bilateral agreements* – both geographically and as regards the content of these agreements – before im-

[162] Cf. Guzman (2004) p. 369.

plementing more radical steps of harmonization.[163] For instance, the United States of America traditionally reject claims for legally binding commitments as regards competition rules on a multinational level, especially within the WTO-framework.[164] They prefer bilateral agreements between competition authorities because their dominant position and power in world economy allows them to be reserved with respect to multilateral steps. This is also why the United States could start the so-called Structural Impediments Initiative (SII) involving bilateral talks between the United States and Japan in order to solve structural impediments in both economies that hinder international trade. Nevertheless, the United States acknowledge the importance of an internationalization of competition law as regards international merger control.[165]

Similar to the United States, a European Union's expert group[166] (so-called van Miert report) proposed in 1995 the creation of a dense net of bilateral agreements, including a gradual intensification of cooperation and coordination, especially by allowing the exchange of confidential information and introducing more far-reaching forms of positive comity. In addition to this, the experts group suggested that this net of bilateral agreements should be transferred into a plurilateral or multilateral agreement within the WTO-framework, hoping that the negotiation and development of a multitude of bilateral agreements would produce a sufficient degree of international convergence so that the next step, i.e. the implementation of a plurilateral or multilateral agreement on the basis of some common substantive and procedural provisions, could be taken.[167] Similarly, Graham says that bilateral cooperation could be seen as an 'interim partial solution to the problem of how to achieve an international competition policy'[168], i.e. he also proposes to transfer the bilateral agreements into a (more binding) multilateral agreement some day.

Another possibility to reach a higher level of international antitrust cooperation is to combine the existing forms of soft cooperation with a multilateral agreement on the international division of labour between national competition authorities. This division of labour is characterized by a 'procedural cooperation on choice-of-law rules, with an eye toward restricting the number of legal systems claiming jurisdiction'[169]. *Choice-of-law rules*

---

[163] Cf. Klein (2002) pp. 335ff.

[164] Jens (2002) pp. 13ff.; cf. Immenga (2000) p. 1059; cf. Swindle (2001).

[165] Immenga (2000) p. 1059; cf. Drexl (1998) p. 43.

[166] European Commission (1995) pp. 11ff.

[167] Ibid. pp. 11ff.

[168] Graham (2003) p. 970.

[169] Guzman (2004) p. 369.

assign jurisdiction to one or more states, for example by implementing a *one-stop shop system* or a *lead jurisdiction system*. In both cases, international antitrust investigations preferably take place under the leadership or sole responsibility of only one national competition authority in order to achieve faster antitrust decisions and to reduce international conflicts. Both models, the one-stop shop principle and the lead jurisdiction model, are something between a centralized and a decentralized antitrust enforcement system and they both require a certain degree of harmonization, at least some minimum standards and core principles, because otherwise the decisions of the assigned competition authority hardly would be acceptable for the other countries involved.[170] This necessity of minimum harmonization must not be regarded as a disadvantage of these models because there is already a relatively high degree of convergence between the national competition laws of the most important industrial countries. Furthermore, these models could be adequate because in many antitrust cases, only few economies are involved; sometimes only one national market is predominantly affected. Consequently, it could make sense to allocate the case by a choice-of-law rule to one of the most affected national competition authorities instead of referring it to an international institution. Especially in case of mergers whose consequences affect many countries, it could be recommendable to authorize only one national competition authority in order to avoid inconsistent results of international merger review.[171] As a further advantage, choice-of-law models would especially help countries that cannot apply their laws extraterritorially because of a lack of political and

[170] The lead jurisdiction model also could be combined with an agreement on international competition rules so that the leading jurisdiction would have to apply these international competition rules instead of national competition law.

[171] A one-stop shop system in merger control has been implemented for the first time by the European Merger Regulation (1990) according to which the European Commission deals with mergers and acquisitions exceeding certain worldwide and European turnover thresholds, giving the Commission the control over all major cross-border mergers and acquisitions. This one-stop shop concept has been made more flexible by the new merger regulation in 2004, introducing a pre-notification referral procedure by which some cases – according to certain criteria – can be referred to a national competition authority (cf. Chap. 2.3.2.2): 'The streamlining of the system of merger case referrals is aimed at ensuring that merger cases are normally handled by the competition authority best placed to deal with them, while at the same time keeping to a minimum the number of cases requiring multiple clearances from several agencies. In particular, the new rules include a possibility for the merging companies to request a referral to or from the Commission, prior to any formal notification being made.' (European Commission (2004a) p. 13).

economic power or because of certain legal requirements.[172] In this case, an antitrust investigation would be assigned to an antitrust authority in another country where the antitrust activity has been initiated or where the participating firms do a lot of business. Consequently, the choice-of-law rule 'would give injured plaintiffs a remedy against the actions of foreign firms that target states whose laws do not apply extraterritorially, as long as the conduct was within a state with effective antitrust rules.'[173] Nonetheless, choice-of-law-rules like a one-stop-shop model could also cause inefficiencies and international conflicts because every country is affected differently by a certain anticompetitive behaviour so that it is unlikely that the entrusted national competition authority finds an absolutely balanced decision that all affected countries would agree with.

A more complex concept concerning the international division of labour in antitrust is the so-called *multi-level-system of competition laws*[174], an international regime with decentralized elements. Multi-level governance is a specific form of governance through networks, characterized by an incremental evolution of competence allocation rules within a hierarchy of institutions. Each hierarchy level would be differently involved in the cooperation and coordination of international competition policy. The design of an international multi-level-system is – like all decentralization and network governance concepts – an optimistic approach hoping to achieve and preserve consent between the participating institutions and furthermore to generate efficient solutions. Up to now, there exists no elaborated concept of a multi-level-system, but the possibility to install a superior institution, which could, in case of need, force the system to produce a solution, is a pragmatic advantage of a multi-level-system. In the early nineties, an international experts group had elaborated the so-called Draft International Antitrust Code (DIAC) which was designed as a plurilateral WTO agreement and contained a simple model of a multi-level-system.[175] Besides some basic principles like the application of this code only on cross-border cases, the transfer of international minimum standards into national law and the application of the principle of national treatment, the DIAC proposed the

---

[172] Guzman (2004) p. 371.

[173] Ibid.

[174] Proponents of this view are Budzinski (2002) pp. 234ff.; Budzinski (2002a) pp. 469ff.; Kerber and Budzinski (2003) pp. 411ff.; Kerber and Budzinski (2004) pp. 53f.; Kerber (2003); Stearns-Bläsing (2004) pp. 325ff.; Worm (2004) pp. 227ff.

[175] Cf. Fikentscher and Immenga (1995); cf. Phillips (1994) pp. 327ff.; cf. Voß (2000).

implementation of an *international procedural initiative*.[176] This proposal was characterized by the demand to establish an International Antitrust Authority (IAA). This authority would not have any decision-making power but it would be allowed to file a suit before the national courts in case that the international minimum standards, which have been transferred into national law, are not applied adequately by the national competition authorities. Consequently, the international minimum standards would have to be applied by sovereign national competition authorities and courts. Only in case that a member country violates the Code, for instance because of an inadequate implementation of the international minimum standards into national law, an additional International Antitrust Panel would have to decide on the issue.[177] Consequently, this multi-level-system includes an element of centralization, but it still mainly characterized by the attempt to strengthen the decentralized forces.

Like the other concepts which are based on an international division of labour between national competition authorities and on choice-of-law rules, a multi-level-system also demands at least some minimum standards in antitrust in order to make cooperation possible. This aspect leads us to the next step towards a higher level of internationalization, focusing on the international *harmonization* of substantive and procedural law, either by unilateral action (bottom-up convergence) or by intergovernmental cooperation (multilaterally or bilaterally), including the adoption of internationally harmonized minimum standards in national competition law as a possible intermediate aim and culminating either in totally harmonized national competition rules or in the establishment of international competition rules as a final aim of international competition policy. This form of substantive cooperation and coordination 'imposes on states more or less demanding requirements in terms of their domestic substantive rules'[178], but it helps to prevent local favouritism and other discriminatory antitrust enforcement practices. The harmonized international competition rules could be implemented in different ways. On the one hand, they could be a rather non-binding self-commitment of the participating countries (for example similar to the GATT, which only provides for a dispute settlement mechanism), but they also could be transformed into national law (for example like the TRIPS agreement) so that national competition authorities and national courts would be obliged to enforce them in case of cross-border competition restraints, i.e. when at least two countries are affected by the restraint. In order to avoid a too heterogeneous application of harmo-

176 Cf. Immenga (2004) p. 19.
177 Cf. ibid. pp. 20f.
178 Guzman (2004) p. 370.

nized minimum standards, these rules would have to follow the rule of law approach. A rule of reason approach could be misused by national competition authorities so that international conflicts would emerge.

The ANZCERTA has implemented a far-reaching form of decentralized cooperation in antitrust which is legally binding and characterized by a high degree of harmonization of antitrust law. Since 1994, the competition laws of *both* countries are valid in the common economic area. The competition authorities of both countries are allowed to extend their jurisdiction to the territory of the other and both countries permit complainants in either country to initiate complaints for abuse of dominant position by firms in the other country.[179] This approach is especially helpful in case of market foreclosure, so that foreign exporters could file a lawsuit against domestic import restricting companies.[180] Furthermore, the ANZCERTA antitrust-cooperation also includes the mutual permission to hold hearings in the other country and serve a subpoena on persons located in the other country.[181]

Such a far-reaching model of cooperation and harmonization is probably only possible between a small number of countries which have close and friendly relations, similar competition laws, a similar competition culture, and a longer tradition of closer cooperation in other political fields. Nonetheless, as regards the global level, a similarly intensive form of cooperation could be established by means of a common (supranational) institution which would be allowed to take decisions that are binding for the member countries. This brings us to the second important organizational feature of international competition policy: the centralization of international antitrust enforcement.

2.3.2.2 Centralization with Different Degrees of International Harmonization

As already mentioned above, a first step towards a binding and centralized international antitrust regime could be the establishment of a choice-of-law system, a multi-level-system or an international competition agency which supervises national competition authorities. Such approaches would still mainly include elements of decentralization, favouring a *national* antitrust enforcement by applying national competition laws. Nevertheless, a multi-

---

179 Cf. Cadot et al. (2000) p. 16; cf. Shelton (1999) p. 68.

180 In other antitrust cases, like mergers and international cartels, this approach would not solve the problems which arise from conflicting antitrust investigations and decisions.

181 Cf. Basedow (1998) pp. 36f.; cf. Shelton (1999) p. 68.

level-system and an *international procedural initiative* would demand a certain degree of centralization and harmonization, starting with some minimum standards, both with regard to substantive and procedural law. In its extreme form, centralization would result in a total harmonization of procedural and substantive law or in the creation of supranational competition rules. These rules would be applied by an international or supranational competition authority which combines both the investigative, prosecutorial and adjudicative function in order to enforce the supranational competition law.[182] This most far-reaching concept of internationalization would include all significant cross-border cases.

Economic research has not yet developed detailed concepts for centralization. Though, the European competition policy could probably serve as a model for centralization.[183] The following explanations give an overview of the status quo of competence allocation in European competition policy, starting with some general characteristics of centralization and then presenting more detailed features of competence allocation with regard to Art. 81 and 82 EC Treaty (anticompetitive inter-firm agreements and the abuse of market power) and merger control. Several crucial features of this competence allocation system could be transferred into a far-reaching international competition regime.

The European Union has developed a supranational competition policy which exists parallel to the national competition policies of its member countries (so-called parallel competences). The coordination of these parallel competences is organized within a network of European competition authorities, finally aiming at a consistent and effective application of the supranational competition rules.[184] Despite this system of *parallel* competences and close cooperation, the European Community has developed a dominance of both the European Commission and European supranational competition law in the course of time. Firstly, the so-called 'Interstate Commerce Clause' ('Zwischenstaatlichkeitsklausel'[185]), which originally has limited the application of European competition law to those anticompetitive practices which affect the interstate commerce between the EU

[182] Meiklejohn (1999) pp. 1241f.; cf. Meessen (2000) p. 7. As regards the forms of intergovernmental cooperation and the difference between intergovernmental cooperation on the one hand and supranational governance and international integration on the other, see for example Risch (1998) pp. 19ff.; cf. Wils (2004) pp. 201ff.

[183] Sedemund pleads for an international antitrust authority that deals with international mega-mergers. Such an institution could follow the central characteristics of European merger control (Sedemund (2002) p. 108).

[184] See European Commission (2004).

[185] Cf. Emmerich (2001) pp. 374f.

member countries, has been construed extensively by the European Court of Justice. Consequently, even those cases which just have the *potential* to distort interstate commerce and competition, either directly or indirectly, fall under the legislation of European competition law, too.[186] This leads to an increase in the number of cases that come under parallel competences. Secondly, the so-called 'double restraint theory' ('Zwei-Schranken-Theorie'[187]), which formerly has been interpreted in such a way that both the European and the national competition laws had equal rights and that the stricter law had to be applied[188], has been abolished in the course of time, too. European supranational competition law has gained priority over national competition law. Consequently, parallel proceedings on the national and European level have to be coordinated as far as possible because, in case of conflict, European competition law has priority.[189]

As regards anticompetitive inter-firm agreements and the abuse of market power, the Commission is allowed to take over each case that affects interstate commerce and is within the scope of Art. 81 and 82 EC Treaty (Art. 11 VI of the Cartel Regulation).[190] In these cases, the European Union has gained control over all major cross-border competition restraints which have the potential to affect trade and competition on the common market. Nevertheless, the European competition policy maintains the possibility of decentralized legal proceedings, too. On the one hand, the European Cartel Regulation[191] maintains the system of parallel competence and the element

[186] Cf. ibid. pp. 374f., cf. Schmidt (2001) p. 226; cf. Fischer (2005) p. 237.

[187] Cf. Emmerich (2001) p. 377.

[188] Cf. Schmidt (2001) p. 226.

[189] Cf. Emmerich (2001) p. 378.

[190] According to Point 14, 15, and 54 of the Commission Notice on Cooperation within the Network of Competition authorities, the European Commission preferably could take over the antitrust investigations 'if one or several agreement(s) or practice(s), including networks of similar agreements or practices, have effects on competition in more than three Member States (cross-border markets covering more than three Member States or several national markets); moreover if the case 'is closely linked to other Community provisions which may be exclusively or more effectively applied by the Commission, if the Community interest requires the adoption of a Commission decision to develop Community competition policy when a new competition issue arises or to ensure effective enforcement'; furthermore if network members envisage conflicting decisions in the same case, if a decision will obviously be in conflict with consolidated case law, and if (a) network member(s) is (are) unduly drawing out proceedings in the case (see European Commission (2004) Point 14f. and 54; cf. Fuchs (2005) pp. 95 and 97).

[191] European Council (2002).

of decentralization so that member countries are still allowed to deal with cases capable of affecting trade and competition between EU member countries as long as the European Commission has not opened legal proceedings (Art. 11 VI of the Cartel Regulation). On the other hand, the member countries are obliged to apply Art. 81 and 82 EC Treaty 'whenever they apply national competition law to restraints of competition within the scope of Art. 81 and 82 EC Treaty'[192] (cf. Art. 3 I of the Cartel Regulation). Consequently, national *substantive* competition law has been marginalized because European competition law has priority over national competition law. The national influence on cases which touch the scope of Art. 81 and 82 EC Treaty is – for the most part – reduced to the application of national *procedural* law and the interpretation of European substantive competition rules.[193] This leads to a further harmonization of antitrust enforcement in the European Union. In addition to this, parallel investigations in multiple jurisdictions concerning the same case shall be avoided. The EC regulation[194] favours a one-stop shop concept. The fact that one national competition authority is already dealing with a case shall be sufficient grounds for the other member countries to suspend their own proceedings or to reject the complaint (Art. 13 of the Cartel Regulation).[195] To sum up, an exclusive competence of national competition authorities and courts is limited to those cases which are not within the scope of Art. 81 and 82 EC Treaty.[196] Only in these local cases which do not affect trade between the EC member states, the national competition authorities and courts can practice an exclusive application of national substantive law; they are not obliged to apply European substantive competition rules, but they are allowed to do so.[197]

As regards merger control, Art. 1 of the ECMR[198] defines clear turnover thresholds which decide on the community dimension of a merger or acquisition. The European Union has reinforced the one-stop shop approach in order to prevent multiple notifications and parallel investigations.[199] In general, the competition authorities and the courts of the member states are responsible to deal with a market concentration and to apply national merger control laws only in case that a merger or acquisition does not exceed

[192] Cf. Klees (2006) p. 400.
[193] Cf. Fuchs (2005) p. 115.
[194] European Council (2002).
[195] Cf. Fuchs (2005) p. 95.
[196] Cf. Lässig (1997) pp. 33ff.; 42ff.; cf. Klees (2006) pp. 400f.
[197] Cf. Wißmann (2000) p. 128; cf. Schmidt (2001) p. 244.
[198] European Council (2004).
[199] Cf. Díaz (2004) pp. 179, 181; cf. Mische (2002) p. 28.

the thresholds which assign a case to the European Commission. Otherwise, the Commission has exclusive competence to assess the case and national merger law is irrelevant. Nevertheless, there are exceptions because the European Union also intends to assign each case to the most appropriate competition authority.[200] Consequently, the merger regulation includes some built-in flexibilities and elements of decentralized enforcement: a pre-notification referral system and a post-notification referral system.

Firstly, Art. 4 IV, V ECMR establishes a pre-notification referral system making a referral possible at the request of the notifying parties, both in the direction from the Commission to a member state (Art. 4 IV) and from a member state to the Commission (Art. 4 V).[201] In the first case, the companies are allowed to 'inform the Commission, by means of a reasoned submission, that the concentration may significantly affect competition in a market within a Member State which presents all the characteristics of a distinct market and should therefore be examined, in whole or in part, by that Member State' (Art. 4 IV). In this case of Art. 4 IV, the Commission can decide to refer the case if all member states agree (veto right); the assigned member state has to apply European Competition law because 'no Member State shall apply its national legislation on competition to any concentration that has a Community dimension' (Art. 21 III ECMR). In the second case concerning Art. 4 V, the firms may, before any notification to the competent authorities, inform the Commission by means of a reasoned submission that the concentration should be examined by the Commission although the concentration does not have a community dimension (Art. 4 V). This request is possible when the concentration is capable of being reviewed under the national competition laws of at least three EC member states. In this case of Art. 4 V, the Commission has to examine the case if all member states that would be competent to review the case agree (veto right).[202]

Secondly, under Art. 9 and 22 ECMR, the EC has established a post-notification referral system. According to Art. 9, a notified case – which exceeds the turnover thresholds and therefore normally would have to be allocated to the Commission – can be assigned to a national competition authority if the concentration threatens to affect significantly competition in a market within that member state, which presents all the characteristics of a distinct market (Art. 9 II, III ECMR). It is the affected member state that has to inform the Commission about these consequences of a merger or acquisition, but the Commission decides autonomously whether the case

[200] Cf. Díaz (2004) p. 179.
[201] Cf. ibid. p. 182.
[202] Cf. ibid. p. 183.

shall be referred or not. Conversely, for referrals from member states to the Commission according to Art. 22 I ECMR, 'one or more member states may request the Commission to examine any concentration as defined in Article 3 that does not have a Community dimension within the meaning of Article 1 but affects trade between Member States and threatens to significantly affect competition within the territory of the Member State or States making the request.' Again, it is the Commission who decides autonomously if it wants to examine the case (Art. 22 III).

This European competence allocation system could be a model for the establishment of an international competition system, though not unlimited. On the one hand, it has to be taken into account that the European efforts to establish an efficient and transparent competence and case allocation system that attains its aims are still in progress. The history of European Competition Policy shows that there has often been a need for institutional and legal reforms, either because of deficits of the established system or because of new challenges caused by further European integration, globalization, and other factors. Furthermore, it has to be considered that the European integration, the creation of a Common Market, is a more ambitious project than the present economic globalization. Hence a global competition regime probably could do without such a high degree of harmonization and centralization. Indeed, a far-reaching centralization of international competition policy and the creation of supranational competition law is a rather unlikely scenario for the near future.[203] There seems to be a consensus that the establishment of an international competition regime will be a long path with many small steps ('piecemeal-engineering').[204] For several economists and jurists, an integration of supranational competition rules into the WTO, especially with regard to those competition restraints which have negative effects on global free trade, would be an adequate first step towards centralization.[205] They highlight the close relation between trade policy and competition policy in globalized markets and point to the competition-related provisions that have already been im-

203 Cf. Fuchs (2000) p. 357; cf. Graham (2003) pp. 970f.

204 Jens (2002) p. 17; cf. Epstein and Greve (2004) pp. 333ff.; cf. Neugebauer (2004) pp. 179ff.; Kerber (2003) p. 271.

205 Proponents who prefer an integration into the WTO are, for example, Basedow (1998); Drexl (1998) p. 44; Graham (2003) pp. 947ff., 969ff.; Immenga (2000) p. 1059; Fikentscher and Immenga (1995); Fikentscher (1994) pp. 281ff.; Mitchell (2001) pp. 343ff.; Gerhardt (2001) pp. 49ff.; cf. Zanettin (2002) pp. 229ff., 279ff.

plemented into the WTO agreements.[206] Furthermore, they underline that the WTO already offers an elaborated framework which might be appropriate to incorporate an additional WTO agreement on Trade Related Antitrust Measures (TRAMs).[207] The WTO framework includes a dispute settlement and law enforcement mechanism that is already applicable to all WTO member countries. This juridification of international trade is supposed to be beneficial especially for small and developing countries and could be beneficial in international antitrust policy, too.[208] On the other hand, one has to take into account that, according to the present philosophy of the WTO, 'a competition code in the WTO would process competition problems principally as market access problems'[209]. Consequently, the implementation of supranational competition rules and centralized enforcement competences with regard to anti-cartel policies, merger review and abusive market conduct would necessitate a far-reaching reorganization and extension of the WTO.

2.4 Arguments Against International Competition Rules

Though many economists emphasize the necessity for an international harmonization (e.g. minimum standards) or even centralization of competition rules to protect international competition and trade, there are nevertheless some economists who reject the claim for international competition rules and who conclude that the current shortcomings mentioned above are rather insignificant so that they cannot be taken as a justification for far-reaching measures of international harmonization.[210] Competition policy is not considered to be the core problem of international trade and competition.

---

206 See, for instance, Art. 8 II and 9 GATS, Art. 40 TRIPS, and Art. 9 TRIMS; cf. Tritell and Kraus (2006) p. 406; cf. Wins (2000) pp. 161ff.; Drexl (1998) p. 13; cf. Bliss (1996) p. 315.

207 Cf. Meessen (2000) p. 7.

208 As regards the opinion of developing countries with respect to international competition rules, see Chap. 4.3.2.3.

209 Tarullo (1999) p. 445.

210 Economists who take a negative view of international competition rules are, for instance, Moeschel (2005) p. 479; McGinnis (2004) pp. 126ff.; Meessen (2000) pp. 5-16; Rosenthal and Nicolaides (1997) pp. 355-383; Stephan (2004) pp. 66-98; Hauser and Schoene (1994) pp. 205-222; cf.; Koopmann (2000) p. 32.

2.4.1 The Status Quo Is No Danger for International Competition

Two questions arise in view of the debate about an international competition policy regime. Firstly, one has to consider whether there are really such forms of restrictive business practices which have a significant negative effect on foreign countries and which can not be dealt with by national competition rules and existing forms of international cooperation. Does the present system of national competition policy and international cooperation – which is characterized by the application of the effects doctrine, bilateral agreements and an international regulatory competition – work so bad that we are confronted with massive inefficiencies, discriminatory antitrust-policy, international jurisdictional conflicts and private competition restraints on international markets which can not be eliminated and which lead to significant welfare losses?

Secondly, one has to ask whether an international competition authority would achieve significantly better results for international competition so that the expenditures and disadvantages which come along with an absolutely new system, characterized by international harmonization or even centralization, can be justified.[211] Some opponents of international competition policy conclude that most restraints to trade are still caused by strategic trade policy (e.g. export subsidies, voluntary export restrictions, and anti-dumping) and strategic industrial policy.[212] According to Rosenthal and Nicolaides, 'differences in antitrust enforcement between nations do not significantly impede the functioning of open markets' so that 'harmonizing national antitrust laws with each other is a less urgent concern'. Instead, five other law and policy sectors *directly* restrict national and global competition: '(1) protectionist trade measures, (2) measures intended to attract or exclude categories of foreign investors, (3) nonborder regulations that confer a competition advantage on local products or firms, (4) industrial policies intended to promote national champions and save jobs, and (5) overly broad protection of intellectual property rights in some nations'[213]. Antitrust authorities have little impact on these policies[214], which

---

211 Cf. Vaubel (1992) p. 34.

212 Jens (2002) pp. 13f.; Rosenthal and Nicolaides (1997) pp. 356f.; cf. Christl (2001) p. 80.

213 Rosenthal and Nicolaides (1997) pp. 356f., 360ff. The authors describe the role of these five policy sectors in the European Union and underline the limited role of EU competition policy to influence them. Also cf. Khemani who, from an opposite perspective, describes several anti-competitive practices and trade barriers which cause 'the insufficiency of trade liberalization as a guarantor of competition' (Khemani (1998) pp. 144ff.). Khemani views competition law as

sometimes have an *indirect* negative effect on global competition, too. For instance, protectionist trade restrictions which intend to cut off domestic markets from foreign enterprises could cause an anticompetitive reaction by these foreign enterprises, for example the forming of a defensive export cartel to maintain their access to similar markets.[215] Instead of pleading for an international harmonization of competition policy in order to avoid such problems and promote international competition, Rosenthal and Nicolaides demand a *national* harmonization of competition policy with other national policy sectors, i.e. a harmonization of national policy processes in each major country in order to break down domestic barriers that separate national competition policy from trade policy, investment policy, deregulation policy, intellectual property policy, and industrial policy.[216] An effective joining of competition policy with trade policy and other areas of national politics could promote competition in protected sectors although the competition authority would have to be willing to make concessions and give way to other legitimate policy concerns, too.[217]

According to Hauser and Schoene, it is useful to distinguish the following two forms of internationally relevant anti-competitive behaviour: restrictive business practices by import competing firms and by exporters. On the one hand, the anti-competitive strategies of import competing enterprises, which intend to shield their traditional domestic markets from foreign competitors, can be considered a significant threat to international trade and competition. Furthermore, globalization has led to an increase of export activities and competition on export markets so that there are significant incentives for exporters to apply anti-competitive strategies in order to exploit foreign markets.

2.4.1.1 Restrictive Business Practices by Import Competing Companies

The problem of market foreclosure against foreign imports is characterized by a 'mix of public and private actions that limit access of foreign firms to

complementary to trade liberalization, but he does not vote for international competition rules. Instead, he underlines the role of *national* competition policy to be a 'cornerstone of government economic framework policies' and 'to play an advocacy role to ensure that the competitive process is properly taken into consideration in broader economic policy-making' on the national level (Ibid. p. 151).

[214] Rosenthal and Nicolaides (1997) pp. 360ff.

[215] Ibid. p. 372.

[216] Ibid. pp. 377ff.; also cf. Khemani (1998) pp. 144ff.

[217] Rosenthal and Nicolaides (1997) pp. 378f.

domestic distributions systems'[218] and by an interplay between trade laws and antitrust laws because both laws could be ...

1. ... misused to shield domestic markets from foreign competitors. According to economic mainstream, trade law plays the dominant role to protect import competing firms whereas 'competition policy plays a comparatively tiny role in influencing access to markets'[219]. Calkins states that an 'international coordination of vertical restraint standards is unlikely to play an important role in facilitating transnational market access'[220], whereas horizontal restraints – like, for instance, standard-setting abuses, customer or market division, boycotts of foreign companies, and collective exclusive dealing[221] – 'may well be more important'[222].
2. ... used to protect competitive markets: '... the exporting country may seek to use its own antitrust laws to protect competitive market access for exporters to another foreign country or it may seek to use trade law remedies (or the WTO trade dispute mechanism) to penalize the importing country for not using its antitrust laws to protect import access'.[223]

Nevertheless, the status quo of international antitrust shows that in certain cases which are located at the crossroads of trade and competition policy, neither competition law nor trade law are effective and efficient instruments to deal with restrictive business practices by powerful import competing firms in foreign countries.

As regards competition law, competition authorities generally are not able to open up foreign markets. The application of the effects doctrine by the exporting country is difficult to realize and could easily affect the importing countries' sovereignty and cause international conflicts.[224] Furthermore – although the possibility to start lawsuits against domestic subsidiaries of the foreign cartelists becomes increasingly relevant in times of globalization and internationalization of enterprises[225] – this approach does not necessarily solve the problem of market foreclosure in foreign countries. In spite of this limited workability of competition policy against for-

218 Tarullo (1999) p. 454.
219 Calkins (1998) p. 211.
220 Ibid. p. 211.
221 Cf. Hawk (1996) p. 9.
222 Calkins (1998) p. 211.
223 Baker and Miller (1997) pp. 83; 107.
224 Cf. Anderson and Khosla (1995) p. 87.
225 Cf. Hauser and Schoene (1994) p. 218; cf. Fox and Pitofsky (1997) p. 265.

eign market foreclosure, there would be no need for international competition rules if all national competition authorities implemented a modern competition law and applied it consistently against domestic companies, too. Every national competition authority is generally able to fight domestic import cartels and other forms of market foreclosure – like for example vertical integration and exclusive rights – within its territory in order to protect import access. This solution would correspond to an application of the principle of territoriality according to which every national competition authority fights against competition restraints caused by domestic import competing enterprises on domestic markets. But as already mentioned above, sovereign states normally have no sufficient external incentive to prosecute competition restraints whose negative effects only affect foreign competitors or foreign markets.

As regards trade law, one could consider the role of the GATT – or the modalities of an new international antidiscrimination antitrust code incorporated within the WTO framework[226] – which could deal with the problem of market foreclosure without creating an absolutely new and far-reaching international competition policy regime and without causing an extensive loss of national competences. In case that a national competition authority deliberately does not deal with domestic market foreclosure, for example with the intention to protect domestic enterprises instead of domestic consumers and competition, then the GATT framework, which deals with governmental trade restrictions, could be an adequate solution because 'restrictive business practices by import competing firms distort international trade and restrict market access like traditional trade barriers'[227]. Currently, the GATT cannot be applied on these competition restraints caused by private agents[228], because – according to the Kodak-Fuji-Case[229] – import restricting practices by private enterprises which go conform with their national laws and which are characterized by an absence of continuing government involvement in restricting market access can not be viewed as a state-induced trade distortion.[230] Nevertheless, certain cases of market foreclosure could in future be covered by violation complaints (Art.

226 Cf. McGinnis (2004) pp. 126, 136ff. McGinnis rejects far-reaching approaches of harmonization. Instead, he pleads for an antidiscrimination antitrust regime that is integrated within the WTO system and that is 'limited in scope, incremental in application, and sensitive to issues of institutional design' (p. 137).

227 Hauser and Schoene (1994) p. 207.

228 Meessen (2000) pp. 5f.

229 WTO (1998a).

230 Meessen (2000) pp. 5-7; Tarullo (1999) pp. 448f. This rule protects the national sovereignty to define certain national exemptions from private competition.

III GATT) and by non-violation complaints (Art. XXIII GATT) if the complaints concern governmentally promoted, encouraged, approved, or at least tolerated private restrictions of import competition.[231] In many cases it would be difficult or impossible to prove the involvement of the government. Therefore, it would be necessary to qualify even the passive toleration of private import-restricting business activities – for example the deliberate failure to apply national competition policy against domestic import restricting companies or the decision to exempt such business activities from competition law – as a GATT-relevant governmental support of discriminatory practices against foreign exporting enterprises. A supplementary plurilateral or even multilateral agreement to the GATT, which obliges the member countries to enact appropriate national competition rules according to the principle of non-discrimination, could cope with this topic.[232] Such a solution could be translated into action more easily than the establishment of an absolutely new international competition regime.[233] In order to avoid a too centralized approach for removing private market foreclosures, the affected countries could be obliged by the GATT to find a bilateral solution within a certain period of time. The Structural Impediments Initiative (SII) between the United States and Japan could serve as a model for such bilateral consultations although the SII is no adequate substitute for sound competition policy.[234] US enterprises had complained that they were unfairly excluded from the Japanese market. The US Department of Justice could have initiated lawsuits against the Japanese import cartels because the cartelists′ behaviour was also illegal in Japan and Japan refrained from enforcing its competition law.[235] Instead, the United States and Japan started a common working group in order to identify and solve the existing structural impediments which limit trade on both sides. An agreement has been reached in 1990 granting concessions to each other in

[231] Evenett et al. consider two forms of 'privately-orchestrated and trade-related cartels' which could be covered by a WTO agreement: 'First, laws which permit recession cartels, where firms under considerable competitive pressure – potentially from imports – to engage in market division, could be banned on the grounds that the WTO has already well-established safeguard mechanisms. Second, disciplines could be placed on legally-sanctioned export cartels' (Evenett et al. (2001) p. 1243). The second aspect of export cartels will be taken up again in the following Chap. 2.4.1.2).

[232] Cf. Hauser and Schoene (1994) pp. 207ff., 218; cf. Meessen (2000) pp. 7f., 16; cf. Fuchs (2000) pp. 359f.

[233] A rather sceptical view with regard to the possible role of the GATT can be found in Blackhurst (1994) pp. 225f.

[234] Cf. Stearns-Bläsing (2004) pp. 319f.

[235] Fox and Pitofsky (1997) p. 265.

order to achieve trade and balance-of-payments adjustments. In case that a bilateral agreement does not eliminate the impediments to trade, the WTO regime could deal with the problem, based on a new plurilateral or multilateral agreement.

Nevertheless, such an additional agreement would not solve all problems. On the one hand, there would have to be room for exceptions, e.g. in case that superior national interests are responsible for the market foreclosure. Secondly, the present WTO negotiations about a further opening of national markets for goods and services show how difficult it is to achieve an international consent within the WTO framework. An expansion of WTO responsibilities with regard to antitrust matters even could aggravate these problems. Thirdly, the WTO mechanism generally is confronted with charges of 'legal imperialism', giving the more powerful countries more possibilities to enforce their interests.[236]

Last but not least, before signing an internationally binding agreement on international competition rules and giving up national sovereignty, countries should be willing to implement national competition rules against such restrictive business practices and to enforce these rules. They would pay a higher price if they consent to an international agreement which forces them to eliminate domestic market foreclosures and, in addition to this, causes the transfer of national competences to an international competition regime. This transfer of national competences to an international institution can be considered an even more problematic loss of national sovereignty than the negative impact of the extraterritorial application of competition law (effects doctrine) on the national sovereignty of foreign countries. Consequently, from this point of view, a national enforcement of national competition rules against domestic market foreclosure would be a more adequate practice to deal with restrictive business practices by import competing firms. For instance, this aim could be achieved by allowing foreign exporters to file a lawsuit against market foreclosing business practices or the abuse of dominant position caused by domestic import competing firms. Such a regulation could be arranged, for instance, by binding bilateral cooperation agreements, but it is doubtful whether all countries would be willing to modernize their competition laws correspondingly on their own initiative and allow foreign enterprises to file a lawsuit against domestic enterprises. If not, then it is unlikely that they would be willing to agree to an international agreement, which would force them to reach the same aim by means of even more harmonization and less influence on the exact modalities.

---

[236] Cf. Baker and Miller (1997) pp. 83f.

2.4.1.2 Restrictive Business Practices by Exporters

As regards competition restraints by exporters like cartels, international mergers, and the abuse of market power which, for instance, lead to discriminatory practices or monopolistic pricing strategies, there are no international rules like the GATT which could be applied, though national governments are often involved in such restrictive business practices, for example by explicitly allowing export cartels.

Consequently, these deficiencies could be taken as an argument for additional international rules and harmonization claims. Nevertheless, there are at least two arguments against international competition rules in this field of restrictive business practices. Firstly, if countries sincerely and seriously wanted to fight restrictive business practices by exporters, then they should start unilaterally with a prohibition of export cartels in their national competition law instead of pleading for international competition rules.[237] It is doubtful that countries permit export cartels only because they allegedly find themselves trapped in a prisoners′ dilemma. Secondly, a consequent application of the *effects doctrine*[238] could be a good basis for international antitrust progress as regards restrictive business practices by foreign exporters. Furthermore, competition restraints by exporters are generally directed towards a particular foreign market so that these anti-competitive strategies 'should be part of the jurisdiction of this particular export market'[239].

Although there are several limits as regards the application of the effects doctrine, one can conclude that a national antitrust authority applying both its own strict competition law and the effects doctrine is able to protect national competition against a large number of anti-competitive business practices from abroad.[240] The limits of the effects doctrine concerning investigative competencies (for example in case of blocking statutes) and enforcement power (for example in case of clawback statutes[241]) are, in most

[237] Epstein and Greve (2004) p. 349.

[238] Cf. Chap. 2.2.3.

[239] Hauser and Schoene (1994) p. 211.

[240] Cf. ibid. pp. 217f.

[241] Clawback statutes authorize local suits to recover damages already paid in connection with a foreign judgment, i.e. domestic companies have a domestic right of recovery against parties that had won antitrust damages in a foreign country. Consequently, a clawback statute gives national courts the power to reverse foreign judgements. The clawback statute generally only applies in case of multiple damages, the domestic company can recover the amount that exceeds the part attributable to compensation (cf. Fullerton and Mazard (2001) p. 408; cf. Tarullo (1999) p. 448; cf. Neuhaus (1981) p. 1097).

cases, either not too restrictive or they are rather temporary so that a comprehensive international competition regime is not indispensable. For instance, at the beginning of the 1990s, the USA were taking aggressive action against international cartels by applying the effects doctrine; this has been criticized by some foreign countries 'as an improper extraterritorial application of domestic antitrust law'[242] so that they passed blocking statutes. These problems have been solved without international harmonization or centralization, because 'several high profile enforcement actions have convinced policymakers in other industrial countries that stronger measures against international cartels ought to be taken. Consequently, corporate leniency programmes have been revised or introduced in several countries, international norms for and reforms of cartel enforcement have been proposed at the OECD, and bilateral cooperation developed between selected jurisdictions'[243].

The third aspect, the development of bilateral cooperation, is only relevant for the more complex and conflictive cases of foreign competition restraints which can not be dealt with in a satisfactory manner by means of the effects doctrine. It is mostly possible to remedy these cases by using the existing and future forms of bilateral cooperation between the *industrial* nations because the persons responsible for cartelisation are primarily located in the firms′ headquarters in industrial nations.[244] Evenett et al. remind of the 1994 US case against General Electric. The company was charged by the US Department of Justice with international conspiracy to fix prices for industrial diamonds, along with the South African diamond mining and trading corporation De Beers and several European firms. This case 'collapsed with the trial judge citing the inability of US enforcement authorities to secure the necessary evidence from abroad'[245]. Bilateral cooperation which focuses on these limits of national anti-cartel enforcement would have been sufficient to fight against cartels which are located outside the direct jurisdiction of the domestic competition authority. Meanwhile, it has become more unlikely that important competition authorities like the US Department of Justice and the European Commission stop any significant antitrust proceedings because of difficulties in collecting evidence if these anticompetitive activities have significant effects within their territory.[246]

---

[242] Cf. Evenett et al. (2001) p. 1238.
[243] Ibid. p. 1238.
[244] Ibid. p. 1240.
[245] Ibid. p. 1237.
[246] Tarullo (1999) p. 451.

Furthermore, in order to protect the domestic market, it is not always necessary to enforce antitrust decisions abroad (for example by imposing antitrust fines or damages) because in many cases it is sufficient to 'punish' foreign enterprises under threat of severe trade restrictions and other retaliatory measures for the future.[247] Moreover, international enterprises and exporters are increasingly represented in importing countries by a permanent branch or subsidiary so that an antitrust enforcement can be carried out more easily within the domestic territory.

The limits of the effects doctrine with regard to restrictive business practices by exporters also concern business activities like international mergers and acquisitions. Merger control is one of the most difficult and controversial areas of competition policy, because there is no academic and political consensus as regards the evaluation of merger activities, especially with respect to a harmonization of substantive law.[248] Furthermore, merger control has a significant influence on market and industry structures so that the nation states are interested in keeping their competencies. Therefore, international conflicts are likely as a consequence of applying the effects doctrine. In conclusion, bilateral agreements seem to be an adequate approach to deal with international mergers and acquisitions so that the involved nations can keep their competencies and find an individual bilateral solution. Such bilateral or international agreements could 'support

---

[247] The strategy to threaten with trade restrictions as a retaliatory measure, for example to forbid the import of goods produced by the accused foreign company, can only be applied effectively by countries which constitute an important export market for the foreign company. Especially developing countries do not have the market power to threat with severe trade restrictions. Nevertheless, they can apply the effects doctrine to protect their markets against competition restraints from abroad, but in doing so, they often would harm themselves. Nevertheless it is doubtful to what extent international competition rules would be favourable for developing countries (cf. Chap. 4.3.2.3).

[248] The academic debate on the application of competition policy originally had a focus on cartels and monopolies because there was a dangerous cartelization and monopolization in world economy since the second half of the 19th century and the beginning of the 20th century. Nowadays, there is an international consensus as regards the fight against hard core cartels and the supervision of monopolies, but there is an ongoing debate on the evaluation of mergers which has produced some prominent but conflicting approaches like the Austrian Tradition (Ludwig von Mises, F. A. von Hayek, Israel Kirzner), the Harvard School (Workable Competition), the Chicago School of Antitrust Analysis, the concept of the optimal intensity of competition in a wide oligopoly (Kantzenbach), and the Contestable Markets Theory (cf. Hauser and Schoene (1994) p. 215; cf. Campbell (1997) pp. 89-126; cf. Campbell and Trebilcock (1992) pp. 5-37).

the application of national antitrust law according to the effects doctrine'[249]. This approach is both more likely to be realized and more apt to take into consideration the particular interests of the affected countries. Multinational agreements, leading to an international harmonization or centralization, are not necessary and cannot be justified on the grounds of potential interjurisdictional conflicts. International ex ante rules could even intensify international conflicts in particular cases if these rules are not suitable and flexible enough to deal with the tension between safeguarding competition on the one hand and controlling industry and market structures on the other hand.

Anyway, one has to take into account that merger control is not the central problem in international antitrust-cooperation although mergers often come into the focus of claims for international competition rules. As described above, the proponents of harmonization underline the inefficiency, legal uncertainty, and the potential for serious international conflicts as a consequence of cross-border spillovers, which result from parallel and controversial merger control investigations.[250] Nevertheless, it has to be underlined that mergers and acquisitions are not the main priority in international antitrust although most differences between existing national competition policies concern merger control regulation. The most serious threat for competition comes in the form of international cartels and government restraints of competition (cf. Chap. 2.4.1). The former EU competition commissioner Monti underlined that 'undoubtedly, international cartels are the most damaging distortions of competition. Their prosecution requires a combination of resourceful enforcement domestically and of effective cooperation internationally'[251]. In case of a merger, the involved companies automatically inform the affected competition authorities and they have an incentive to deliver the necessary information in order to receive a decision as soon as possible, whereas 'in cartel investigations, companies usually have no incentive to grant a waiver for sharing information'[252]. As already mentioned above, an international antitrust cooperation among national competition authorities should focus on this problem,

---

[249] Hauser and Schoene (1994) p. 218.

[250] Cf. ibid. p. 215; also cf. Budzinski and Kerber (2005) pp. 11ff.

[251] Monti (2004) pp. 2ff. Also see Evenett et al. (2001) pp. 1221ff., and Tarullo (1999) p. 450. As regards the prosecution of international cartels, the increase in the number of international cartels is sometimes taken as an argument to establish international competition rules. Though, on the other hand, the detection of a high number of cartels also could be taken as an argument for the effectiveness of the present antitrust regime.

[252] Monti (2004) pp. 2ff.

but it is doubtful whether these problems of international anti-cartel enforcement require a far-reaching harmonization or centralization of competition policy. A combination of strict national antitrust policy (effects doctrine) and bilateral cooperation could be sufficient. The 1998 OECD Anti-Cartel Recommendation already serves as a catalyst for more effective national anti-cartel programs.[253] Evenett et al. say that the negative effects of cartels on nations′ markets 'might not be a concern if national anti-trust laws provided a sufficient deterrent to international cartels'[254]. Therefore, they propose both 'reforms to national policies and to international cooperative agreements that will strengthen the deterrents against international cartels and reduce the strategic creation of entry deterrents'[255] As regards international cooperation against international cartels, the exchange of confidential information would be necessary in order to reduce constraints on the ability to secure necessary evidence from abroad against undiscovered and unproven national and international cartels. As a prerequisite for such more intensive forms of cooperation against cartels, the countries would have to relax their national laws which still ban the exchange of information between competition authorities.[256]

2.4.2 Inefficiencies and Delays Are Not a Decisive Criterion

Economic inefficiencies, which could result from multiple notifications, parallel investigations, and cumulative and contradictory remedies by several national competition authorities, especially in case of merger control, are a central argument of companies[257] and economists pleading for international competition rules. Though it is doubtful whether these aspects are that significant that they necessitate and justify an international competition policy regime.

In general, considerations as regards the costs for the affected enterprises and the public administration should not become a decisive criterion in competition policy. Especially private efficiency interests, i.e. a reduction of transaction costs for firms that are subject to antitrust investigations, should not overrule the allocative efficiency considerations of com-

---

253 Winslow (2001) p. 119.
254 Evenett et al. (2001) p. 1244.
255 Ibid. p. 1222.
256 Cf. Winslow (2001) pp. 120f.
257 Many enterprises support the intentions to establish international competition rules not only for reasons of efficiency, but because they want to get rid of the strict competition policy of their country; this can be assumed at least for German firms (cf. Jens (2002) p. 15).

petition authorities. It has to be underlined that there is no justification for simple and cheap merger control procedures and quick decisions of the competition authority, when the merger or acquisition causes difficult problems for antitrust authorities. A far-reaching streamlining of international merger control – for example by implementing an international one-stop shop system in order to reduce the workload for competition authorities and the costs for the companies – could conflict with the primary aim to protect competition. Furthermore, merging parties themselves are often responsible for inefficiencies and time-consuming merger reviews because they do not share significant information or they fail to grant waivers of confidentiality to speed the multi-jurisdictional review process and to enhance the probability of complementary rather than inconsistent decisions or remedies. This rather indicates that the costs of filing multiple pre-merger reviews are not too burdensome.[258]

Moreover, international competition rules would not be a guarantee for faster decisions and more transparent procedures. It is likely that an international competition authority would suffer under a growing workload and build up an enormous bureaucracy in order to monitor business activities all over the world, to review the competition policy of national competition authorities, and in order to satisfy the member countries′ demand of participation and collaboration, for example on the staff level. Consequently, the decisions of an international institution could take a long time, too. In case of conflict, the decision of an international antitrust regime could even take longer and cause more inefficiencies and further conflicts than the final decisions of independent national competition authorities.[259]

These arguments show that the efficiency argument is not convincing with respect to an alleged necessity of international competition rules. In order to reduce inefficiencies for the affected enterprises, for example merging companies, it would be a more adequate measure to harmonize the national notification systems and to standardize the timetable required to deal with the investigations and the decision finding process.[260]

---

[258] Tarullo (1999) p. 449.
[259] Cf. Meessen (2000) p. 14.
[260] Ibid. p. 14.

2.4.3 International Conflicts: Extent and Appropriate Approach for a Consensual Settlement

As already mentioned, unilateral competition policy and the application of the effects doctrine can cause international tensions or even conflicts because of conflicting decisions or incompatible remedies. But all in all, an extraterritorial application of competition law does not lead to a danger of severe international conflicts, because in most cases the anti-competitive behaviour of an exporting firm in foreign markets has no repercussions on its domestic market, so that an extraterritorial enforcement of competition law does not affect the domestic market of the accused (exporting) firm: 'States can keep control of their markets without far-reaching repercussions on other economies'[261]. Conflicts could rather arise with regard to important international mergers in case that one country is interested in this merger whereas the other country is sceptical about its effects on competition (confer, for instance, the conflict between the United States and the EU as regards the merger between the US-American aircraft manufacturers Boeing and McDonnell Douglas in 1997[262]). Also cases of market foreclosure, supported, encouraged, or tolerated by national governments, could lead to international conflicts, but as already described above, these conflicts could be settled within the framework of the WTO.[263] Hauser and Schoene propose that an 'international court or tribunal could be designed to supervise the non-discriminatory application of national antitrust laws. This would not require any harmonization or centralization of antitrust-policy.'[264]

Nevertheless, recent historical experience gives evidence that modern open economies are in a position and willing to settle their bilateral trade disputes. The growing economic interdependencies between nation states in the course of further globalization and internationalization of enterprises even forces the nation states to settle arising conflicts in order to profit from further common trade. Otherwise, they could be trapped into a prisoners′ dilemma, and third countries could profit from this situation. While the 1970s and the 1980s were characterized by 'the controversial use of the effects doctrine by the United States, and the international conflicts it caused'[265], the 1990s were a decade of bilateral cooperation so that, compared to the bitter conflicts of the 1970s, the present situation is 'quite

261 Hauser and Schoene (1994) p. 218.
262 European Commission (1997) pp. 16-47.
263 See Chap. 2.4.1.
264 Hauser and Schoene (1994) p. 212.
265 Zanettin (2002) pp. 279f.

calm'[266]. Despite the existing international differences in formal and substantive antitrust law, the vast majority of international antitrust cases result in compatible decisions by the involved national antitrust authorities.[267] As regards international mergers and conflicts between the USA and the European Community, the following record of mergers from about 1991 to 2001, given by US-FTC Chairman Muris, is instructive (table 2.4):

The EC decided over 1,700 merger cases, of which approximately 400 involved at least one U.S.-based firm. The EC required undertakings as a condition of clearing a deal in about 9 percent of those cases (36 of 402). In about four percent of those cases (17), the parties withdrew from the proposed transactions in the face of a likely antitrust challenge (e.g., *Time Warner/EMI*). The EC prohibited mergers of U.S.-based firms in only two cases – *WorldComMCI/Sprint* and *GE/Honeywell* – the former of which was also challenged by the DOJ. The EC has blocked 16 other mergers, none of which involved a U.S. firm. Another case involving U.S. firms, *Boeing/McDonnell Douglas*, generated much controversy despite the EC's ultimate conditioned clearance. Finally, in approximately 75 of those cases there was significant trans-Atlantic communication and cooperation.

Table 2.4: Merger as a Source of Conflict between the USA and the EC[268]

Moreover, an international competition policy would not be a guarantee for a significant reduction of international conflicts. Depending on the exact organizational features of an international competition regime, international conflicts could be internalized within the organizational structure, and they also could occur as an open intergovernmental dispute. This can be observed by the example of the WTO, where even an elaborated dispute settlement mechanism can not totally prevent severe international trade disputes. Furthermore, while the experts of independent national competition authorities could – by means of intensive dialogue and cooperation – absorb and reduce the potential for conflict, an internationally centralized antitrust regime could lead more directly to disputes and animosities on the political level between the involved governments who want to take in-

266 Tarullo (1999) p. 448.

267 Becher (2002) pp. 80f.; cf. Muris (2001) p. 5; cf. Stearns-Bläsing (2004) p. 166; cf. Klodt (2001) p. 879; cf. Baron (2005) p. 125.

268 Muris (2001) p. 5.

fluence on the international competition authority.[269] This form of cooperation could lead to unreliable, politically influenced international enforcement mechanisms. In contrast to such political disputes, contradictory decisions of independent national competition authorities are not as dangerous. In the long run, they even could lead to a better understanding of each others′ judgements and approaches and to a bottom-up convergence (i.e. a selection of best practices) as a consequence of an international systems competition between the national experts. Therefore, it is a problematic aim to avoid every international conflict between national competition authorities; such conflicts can be of valuable use for the further development of competition policy and bilateral cooperation.[270] It would be an overreaction to demand an international competition policy regime just because of the transatlantic tensions in the course of the Boeing/McDonnell Douglas and the Honeywell/General Electric merger cases which were 'the exception to the rule of productive consultation'[271]. Furthermore, bilateral agreements can help to find individual solutions in case of conflict and to push ahead a bottom-up convergence; such a bilateral consensus is more likely and probably more efficient than a multinational ex ante consent as a prerequisite for an international harmonization of antitrust policy.

2.4.4 Allowing an International Bottom-up Convergence of National Competition Law

Economic history shows that beginning with the second half of the twentieth century, there has been in many countries a development towards better competition policy.[272] This development began parallel to the negotiations and failure of the Havana Charter 1948 and started with the implementation of a new competition policy in Germany and Japan under the supervision of the United States and the other allies.[273] The US American competition policy, which was the most modern and advanced one in that postwar period, had a strong influence and acted as the model for many na-

---

[269] Cf. Guzman (2004) p. 368.

[270] Cf. First (2003) pp. 49f.; McGinnis (2004) pp. 131, 137. McGinnes emphasizes the evolutionary function of conflicts and focused criticism on the substance of antitrust law. Especially open debates and conflicts that 'focus the attention of the press and other elites outside government circles on the wisdom of government antitrust intervention' can prompt changes in competition regimes (p. 131).

[271] Tarullo (1999) p. 448.

[272] Cf. Rosenthal and Nicolaides (1997) p. 358.

[273] Cf. ibid. p. 359.

tional competition laws. In fact, all national competition laws were still relatively weak because several economic sectors and regulated enterprises were exempted from the rules. During that period, competition authorities had modest resources and weapons so that the laws could not act as a deterrent.[274]

The fight against anticompetitive practices made progress in the late fifties under the influence of the *Harvard School of Workable Competition* in the United States and the establishment of the first multinational competition law by the European Community. In that period, Germany was developing a relatively strict competition policy whereas many other industrialized countries practiced a rather weak antitrust enforcement.[275] The European competition policy made progress but was focused on the integration of the single European market by opening national markets for the member states. The next step of modernization which had a strong influence on many national competition laws and EC competition policy was the US deregulation policy (*Chicago School of Antitrust*) in the seventies and eighties of the twentieth century. In addition to this deregulation, the last two decades of the twentieth century were characterized by a 'globalization' of competition and national competition laws. Several developing and newly industrializing countries in Asia, Latin America, and Eastern Europe, for example the East Asian tigers South Korea, Taiwan, and Hong Kong, have modernized their competition policy or introduced a competition law for the first time.[276] The transformation of the former socialist countries into free market economies has led to an increase of open markets and modern competition law in many countries, often closely following the competition laws of the European Union or the United States.[277]

This positive development towards more competition, better national competition policy and international bottom-up convergence is still in progress. The number of countries implementing a modern competition policy and signing bilateral antitrust cooperation agreements has increased and will go on growing in future.[278] Moreover, the implemented substantive

---

[274] Cf. ibid. p. 359.

[275] Ibid. p. 368.

[276] Cf. Meessen (2000) pp. 11f.; cf. UNCTAD (1997) Annex Table A.22; cf. WTO (1997) p. 46; cf. Lachmann (1997) pp. 202ff., 211ff.; cf. Liang (2004) pp. 72ff.; cf. Lin (2002) pp. 27ff.

[277] Fullerton and Mazard (2001) p. 407.

[278] Cf. Rosenthal and Nicolaides (1997) pp. 355f. Interestingly, this welcome increase in the number of countries implementing modern antitrust regimes also has given rise to claims for more international centralization in antitrust. Especially enterprises would prefer a smaller number of antitrust authorities who

rules of national competition laws show a high degree of international convergence.[279] As regards the European and the US American competition laws, they are largely congruent: 'All oppose monopolies that abuse monopoly power, and all oppose mergers that create monopolies. They all oppose cartels that are price-fixing, supply-restricting, or market-allocating. They all oppose extending exempted monopolies beyond the boundaries of their legal exemption. They all proscribe group boycotts and attempts to monopolize through predatory practices.'[280] Furthermore, recent years have led to a bottom-up convergence of enforcement practices, for example as regards the implementation of leniency programmes.[281] Especially the bilateral agreement between the United States of America and the European Community in 1991 has initiated 'some genuine convergence of the substantive competition laws of the United States and the European Union, although it is perhaps too early to say how extensive and durable that convergence will be.'[282]

The question arises whether one should allow this bottom-up convergence to go on, maybe leading by itself to a sufficient degree of harmonization of competition policy, or whether it is necessary to promote this process of convergence by means of an international top-down harmonization. On the one hand, one could say that the international convergence of competition law is an argument in favour of an international harmonization and centralization. If national competition laws converge, this could be taken as an evidence of an international interest in common standards so that it would be helpful to support this process by a top-down-harmonization-strategy.

At least two arguments can be put forward against this view, i.e. the bottom-up convergence of competition law also can be taken as a counter-argument against a top-down harmonization. Firstly, if competition laws are already converging, then there is no need to harmonize them, neither ex ante nor ex post of the convergence process. The bottom-up convergence

investigate international mergers (cf. Becher (2002) p. 77ff.; cf. Bär-Bouyssière (2002) pp. 97ff.).

279 Cf. Meessen (2000) pp. 5f.; Basedow (1998) pp. 5f., 7f.; cf. Neumann (2001) pp. 30-46; cf. Rosenthal and Nicolaides (1997) p. 366; Anderson and Khosla (1995) pp. 77ff. Despite this convergence of national antitrust policies, there are still differences remaining as regards the fundamental aims of national antitrust and the relevant substantive and procedural antitrust rules (Bär-Bouyssière (2002) p. 98; Becher (2002) pp. 80f.; Kennedy (2001) pp. 181ff.).

280 Rosenthal and Nicolaides (1997) p. 366.

281 Cf. Scott (2004) pp. 7f.; Levy and O'Donoghue (2004) pp. 75ff.; Motta and Polo (2003) pp. 347ff.; cf. Wils (2003) pp. 578ff., 586f.

282 Zanettin (2002) pp. 279f.

could be seen as a substitute for a top-down harmonization and it is likely that a slow, open and dynamic process of convergence, resulting from the actual market developments, leads to better results than a top-down harmonization. One has to take into account that an international harmonization would stop the process of steady modernization, which is a result of the present international systems competition (cf. Chap. 4.2.5). The opponents of harmonization point to the fact that competition policy is a complex and dynamic issue which cannot be harmonized as easily as trade law has been harmonized by the WTO agreement.[283] Consequently, it appears to be doubtful whether international competition rules would lead to a significant improvement of international competition, especially in a long-term perspective. It could be more likely to achieve a convergence of substantive and procedural law and of enforcement activities by a gradual and dynamic bottom-up convergence, resulting from an international regulatory competition and professional dialogue which produces internationally acknowledged best practices. Professional but non-binding initiatives like the ICN are endorsed by the governments of the participating antitrust agencies and they could produce a more intelligent and efficient form of convergence and cooperation than a top-down strategy.

Secondly, it is important to take into consideration that a top-down convergence of formal and substantive law does not automatically include a convergence as regards the application of law and the law enforcement by the national competition authorities. Apart from the fact that many countries, especially poor countries, still do not possess a competition law or that they do not enforce it adequately[284], there are still differences between national antitrust policies, especially as regards enforcement practices. Furthermore, national competition authorities always have the power to apply competition laws rather leniently or rather strictly so that even a total convergence and harmonization of national competition laws would not lead to identical enforcement practices.[285] In order to solve this problem, it would be necessary to combine the international harmonization of competition rules with an international *centralization* of enforcement activities. Though, such far-reaching measures of top-down harmonization and centralization also could undermine international cooperation between national antitrust authorities and prevent further convergence and mutual understanding. Instead of developing international relations based on mutual cooperation and trust, the countries could develop rather hostile attitudes

[283] Meessen (2000) p. 10.
[284] Cf. Basedow (1998) p. 7; cf. Rosenthal and Nicolaides (1997) pp. 366f.
[285] Cf. Zanettin (2002) p. 280.

towards each other as a consequence of being disputing parties before an international antitrust authority like the WTO panel.[286]

2.5 Conclusion: Benefits, Limits and Problems of the Status Quo

The discussion about the necessity, workability, modalities and institutionalization of international competition rules results in an ambivalent situation. The existing forms of international cooperation in antitrust – i.e. the so-called effects doctrine, the bilateral agreements which have been signed to deal with the deficiencies of the effects doctrine, and the multilateral fora – are successful, but they do not solve all problems of international antitrust arising from the globalization of competition. Nevertheless, the necessity to implement any kind of a single and comprehensive international agreement – which might lead to international harmonization, supranational competition rules, or the establishment of an international competition authority allowed to interfere more or less directly with enforcement activities in national jurisdictions – is still disputed.

On the one hand, the establishment of a net of bilateral agreements between the leading economies during the 1990s – based on the effects doctrine and partly resulting from former multilateral recommendations by the OECD and other international organizations – has been successful in reducing international conflicts and inefficiencies stemming from unilateral antitrust enforcement ('effects doctrine') or inconsistent and cumulative multi-jurisdictional antitrust enforcement activities, especially in merger review. The application of the effects doctrine has become less conflict-ridden and retaliatory measures like blocking and clawback statutes have been reduced, too. Furthermore, a new generation of bilateral cooperation agreements has – compared to the positive effects of former informal cooperation – created further provisions which help to promote a common understanding on substantive antitrust principles and an international convergence of best practices. In isolated cases, international conflicts on specific antitrust cases like the Boeing/McDonnell Douglas merger case still could become an endurance test for bilateral cooperation. Nevertheless, the danger of severe international conflicts is limited. In general, the 1991 agreement between the United States of America and the European Union on the application of their competition laws has 'exceeded all the most op-

[286] Tarullo (1999) p. 452.

timistic expectations'[287], both as regards the cooperation between the US and EC antitrust authorities and its influence on other countries' willingness to enter into bilateral agreements. Nevertheless, there are certain limits of bilateral cooperation:

1. Bilateral agreements are limited as regards their contents. Although the conclusion of bilateral agreements has as a prerequisite a certain degree of convergence in procedural and substantive antitrust norms, there is no general harmonization of competition laws. Hence there are still deficiencies in national competition law – for example as regards legal exceptions for export cartels and market foreclosing practices. Furthermore, bilateral agreements have no binding force in law and no dispute settlement mechanism so that many results of bilateral cooperation probably also could be reached by informal cooperation. Many problems of international antitrust caused by national law and national interests can not be solved by the existing agreements when the parties are not willing to give up control or their national interests, especially as regards the exchange of confidential information. For instance, according to the (positive comity) agreement between the United States and the European Community, the parties are not allowed to start investigations and to assist each other in case that business practices only affect the interests of the requesting country.

2. The limited number of parties of a bilateral agreement could cause problems. On the one hand, it is likely that the parties of a bilateral agreement primarily take into account their own interests in antitrust enforcement so that third parties' interests could be harmed. In practice, this has not become a significant problem yet. To the contrary, bilateral antitrust cooperation is likely to have pro-competitive effects on third countries' economy, too. Furthermore, some authors fear incompatibilities between a multitude of bilateral agreements and that there is too little chance to enhance the effectiveness of international cooperation by international convergence.[288] At least two arguments can be put against this point of view. Firstly, heterogeneity does not necessarily prevent effective cooperation. To the contrary, heterogeneity allows to take into account special circumstances and this could even improve international antitrust cooperation. In addition to this, a comparison of the existing bilateral agreements shows that they often contain the same or similar provisions. Although national activities and bilateral agreements automatically produce a certain degree of

[287] Zanettin (2002) p. 1.
[288] Cf. Fuchs (2000) p. 364.

heterogeneity, it is likely that future advances in bilateral and multilateral cooperation will lead to even more convergence. Secondly, a total convergence of bilateral agreements is necessary mainly from the point of view of those authors who claim that, in the long run, there is a need for 'some sort of an internationally negotiated agreement that goes beyond the creation of more national laws, enforcement agencies, and cooperation among them'[289]. As already mentioned above, this claim as regards the necessity to implement a single and comprehensive international agreement is disputed and doubtful.

3. The present forms of non-binding cooperation and the existing net of bilateral agreements primarily favour the interests of the industrialized countries. Although developing and transitional countries partly also enter into bilateral agreements with the industrialized countries – confer the agreements of the United States and Canada with Mexico – they do not have the economic and political power to enforce their interests in case of conflict and to protect themselves sufficiently against all kinds anticompetitive conduct from abroad. This structural asymmetry of power in negotiations, consultations, cooperation and coordination partly could be remedied within a legally binding international framework. Though, as can be seen by the example of the WTO, an international juridification can not entirely correct the international imbalance of power.

In sum, the necessity and workability of international harmonization, supranationalization, and centralization is still doubtful. Admittedly, it is tempting to demand the establishment of a global competition authority which is endowed with nearly unlimited rights so that many of the present deficiencies in international antitrust would disappear.[290] Nevertheless, one should not be too optimistic as regards the effectiveness and efficiency of international institutions. It is easy to claim that global problems within a globalized world economy need solutions on a multinational level, but according to the principle of subsidiarity, competences should not be transferred too early from the national to the international level. A far-reaching harmonization or even centralization could be like taking the proverbial sledgehammer to crack a nut. It has to be underlined that international competition and antitrust generally works well although there are some deficiencies. Extraterritoriality, combined with bilateral agreements, has been an effective instrument against most international anticompetitive business

[289] Graham (2003) pp. 970f.
[290] Cf. Evenett et al. (2001) p. 1241.

practices.[291] Although international competition problems could grow in future, they are presently fairly modest.[292]

In order to increase the effectiveness of antitrust policy in a globalized world economy, the first task should be to support the establishment of independent and well-endowed national competition authorities who practice a strict competition policy and apply the effects doctrine. Up to now, several countries do not even possess a modern competition law. At least the most important trading nations have to enact modern competition laws which fulfil certain minimum standards; these standards are likely to result from multilateral dialogue and the present convergence process. Several competition restraints and problems of international antitrust enforcement are caused on the national level and could be solved on the national level by well-endowed, modern competition authorities.

In case that this starting position still leads to a lack of antitrust enforcement, inefficiencies, or international conflicts, the independent national competition authorities should interact on a basis of *several* non-binding institutions, especially by means of more intensive bilateral cooperation (e.g. through the above mentioned MLATs), multilateral networking (ICN), multilateral non-binding recommendations (OECD), and bottom-up convergence.[293] Many countries have not signed (enough) bilateral agreements yet and in many cases these agreements are incomplete. There is 'probably considerable scope for further cooperation among competition enforcement agencies in critical areas such as merger review and regulation and control of international cartels'[294] and competition authorities are, for instance within the ICN framework, 'capable of harmonizing their regulations on their own initiatives, without revising provisions of respective competition laws'[295]. This is because 'substantive provisions ... usually use abstract terms and phrases to sufficiently cover diversified and changing economic realities'[296]. Furthermore, there is potential 'to enhance the international law organizing the competition of competition laws so as to fill gaps and to deal with the frictions as they arise from time to time'[297]. For instance, the cooperation agreement between the United States and the

[291] Zanettin (2002) p. 2.

[292] Tarullo (1999) p. 446.

[293] According to Vaubel, even the aim to create a common market in the European Union could be achieved by networking and subsidiarity. Therefore, he states that the role of the European Commission as a dominant competition authority is rather unnecessary (cf. Vaubel (1992) pp. 34f.).

[294] Graham (2003) p. 970.

[295] Kurita (1995) p. 373.

[296] Ibid. p. 373. As regards the role of abstract terms, confer Chap. 4.3.2.1.

[297] Meessen (1989) p. 29.

European Communities focuses on merger review and could be intensified with regard to anti-cartel enforcement.[298] More cooperation would be necessary especially because of constraints on the ability to secure necessary evidence from abroad and to share confidential information (thereby countries could compensate the limits of present positive comity) or in case that a unilateral law enforcement would lead to inefficiencies or international conflicts – for example in case of time-consuming parallel merger control investigations. Instead of implementing a single, comprehensive and far-reaching 'solution' like one of the models presented in Chap. 2.3.2, *different* instruments and fora, built upon national regulatory systems, might be an appropriate way to different problems of international antitrust.[299]

These forms of cooperation partly could be combined with a minimum harmonization as regards enforcement practices and procedural aspects.[300] But attempts to practice a top-down harmonization should be limited to a minimum. For instance, the international antitrust enforcement could be improved by an implementation of leniency programmes into national competition law; though, this aim also could be reached by means of an uncoordinated international convergence of best practices in antitrust enforcement. Furthermore, non-efficient merger control could be reduced by an internationally harmonized timetable and notification system. This would eliminate a large part of the cumulative costs for the concerned companies. Just to give an example, international law could rule that if a national competition authority does not meet the internationally agreed deadlines for the assessment of a merger, then the overdue decision could be interpreted as permission. In case of contradictory decisions, for example as regards the approval of a merger or the calculation of fines against cartel members, an international expert panel or dispute settlement mechanism could act as a mediator to find a common solution.

In conclusion, a far-reaching harmonization of competition law or the establishment of an omnipotent global competition authority is not necessary; though, in case of market foreclosing practices of private companies, it could be recommendable to establish an additional antidiscrimination antitrust regime that is integrated within the WTO system and that is 'limited in scope, incremental in application, and sensitive to issues of institutional design'[301]. But even if there were a necessity for international competition rules, the importance of *national* competition policy for the international competitiveness of a nation possibly could be taken as a justification for a

[298] Fullerton and Mazard (2001) pp. 415ff.
[299] Cf. Tarullo (1999) pp. 453ff.
[300] Cf. Evenett et al. (2001) p. 1241.
[301] McGinnis (2004) p. 137.

keeping up of national competition policy despite the alleged necessity of international competition rules. This question will be discussed in the following Chaps. 3 and 4.

3 The International Competitiveness of Nations

The question about the international economic competitiveness of nations has received a lot of attention in recent years, not only in academic literature. In times of economic globalization, open economies are concerned about a possible loss of international competitiveness.[302] Furthermore, international organizations and fora like the WTO, the United Nations Industrial Development Organization (UNIDO), the Organization of Economic Cooperation and Development (OECD), the International Monetary Fund (IMF), the UNCTAD, and the World Economic Forum are interested in the international competitiveness of nations and their industries and financial markets, too.[303] They try to assess national economies in order to prevent fundamental problems for the growth and stability of world economy, to support the integration of developing countries into global trade and to forecast future developments on global markets.

This multitude of publications about the international competitiveness of nations contrasts with the uncertainty about its exact meaning and the lack of its theoretical foundation, so that the aim to strengthen a nation´s international competitiveness could be misused as a justification for diverse political and legislative aims and projects. Despite these theoretical and practical problems, the concept of international competitiveness shall be taken as a theoretical basis of this investigation. Therefore, in order to be able to analyze the role of national competition policy for the international competitiveness of nations in Chap. 4, it is necessary to get clear about the concept of international competitiveness.

The following Chap. 3.1 gives a short description of several historical economic concepts and theories about the sources of national and international welfare and about the benefits of international trade. These theories offer an historical introduction into the debate about the concept of international competitiveness. Afterwards, Chap. 3.2 presents the current debate concerning the fundamental and controversially discussed issues whether

---

302 See, for example, European Commission (2006); European Commission (2004d); Gelauff and Lejour (2006).

303 See, for example, OECD (2005); UNCTAD (2002); UNCTAD (2001); Lopez-Claros et al. (2006); cf. Boltho (1996) p. 1.

international competitiveness is solely a microeconomic concept or in addition to that also a macroeconomic concept. Furthermore, Chap. 3.2 will present some approaches to define the international competitiveness of a nation and to identify the relevant indicators and factors of international competitiveness.

3.1 The Historical Development

The subsequent short history of economic thoughts on trade, welfare and competitiveness describes some approaches which have passed the way to the present competitiveness debate although these historical concepts are generally too simple and too unbalanced to explain the complexity of international competitiveness in modern industries. This is because the focus of these historical ideas was set on the structure and the benefits of international trade as a main factor of national welfare, not on the explanation of international competitiveness of nations.

3.1.1 Mercantilism

The so-called mercantilism is the generic term for the dominant schools of economics in the period from the beginning of the 16th century to the 18th century. In the time of absolutism in Europe, countries like England, France and Germany were striving for political and military power by enhancing the prosperity of the nation, mostly thinking that they only could achieve this aim at the expense of other countries.[304]

As regards international trade, many early mercantilists were holding that trade was a zero-sum game, i.e. that the global amount of prosperity, which was measured in precious metal like gold and silver, was restricted. According to this position, a crucial factor for enhancing national prosperity, which was held by the state, was governmental interventionism. The state was governing international trade, trying to support economic growth and to increase the national amount of money and precious metal by achieving an active balance of trade and by prohibiting the export of bullion.[305] Furthermore, governments and merchants aimed at enhancing domestic production and reducing domestic consumption.[306] Consequently, mercan-

304 Cf. Schmidt (2002) p. 41; cf. Lachmann (2006) p. 48f.; cf. Born (1989) pp. 98ff., 108f.; cf. Pribram (1998) pp. 82f., 99f., 110, 171f.

305 Cf. Kolb (1997) pp. 19f.

306 Cf. Stapelfeldt (2001) pp. 43ff.

tilism was characterized by a general supremacy of the state over the economy although some economists and merchants tried to reduce governmental interventions.[307] This led to a protectionist trade policy, encouraging exports – for example by granting subsidies and lowering taxes – and restricting imports of goods – for example by using tariffs – so that precious metal flowed into the state treasure.[308] This type of early protectionist mercantilism, which set the focus on international trade, was especially characteristic for the economic policy of England.[309] The central aim was an increase of the state treasure (Bullionism) by means of protectionist legislation (for example by the Navigation Acts of Oliver Cromwell). France followed similar aims and similar politics, but compared to England, France practiced more interventionism with regard to domestic industries. To achieve an increase of exports, the French government started to organize and regulate the domestic industry in order to promote domestic production (Colbertism).[310] As regards competition policy, national and state-controlled monopolies were seen as an adequate instrument to reach these aims, both in England and in France.[311]

Mercantilism could be regarded as an early concept of international competitiveness, because mercantilism emphasized the idea that national economies or nation states were competing against each other, striving for the same aims. The assumption that international trade and increasing national wealth amounts to an international zero-sum game has created intensive competition between the European nation states. It is through these central views that mercantile economic policy has introduced several aspects into economic thinking that still belong to the modern competitiveness debate: the aim to increase national productivity, to enhance exports, to attract workers from foreign countries, to increase national wealth by underlining the rivalry between nations – but nowadays not necessarily within a zero-sum game – and the central and active role of national governments to achieve the envisaged aims. Pointing out these similarities between mercantilism and the modern debate on international competi-

[307] Pribram (1998) pp. 83f.

[308] Some mercantilists (especially Thomas Mun) had a more differentiated view on imports and exports. They underlined the positive effects of certain imports (e.g. as regards raw materials and natural resources) and they even allowed the export of precious metal in order to finally promote the export of industrial products and to maximize the country's overall trade surplus (cf. Schmidt (2002) p. 43; Pribram (1998) pp. 105ff.).

[309] Cf. Stapelfeldt (2001) pp. 86f.; Pribram (1998) pp. 99ff.

[310] Cf. Kolb (1997) pp. 26ff.; cf. Born (1989) pp. 99f., 106ff.; Pribram (1998) pp. 109ff.

[311] Born (1989) p. 100; Pribram (1998) pp. 90f.

tiveness, it has to be emphasized that there are significant differences with regard to the instruments which are applied in order to become internationally competitive. Protectionist instruments played a central role in mercantilism whereas the modern debate on international competitiveness focuses on instruments which do not restrict free trade but, quite the reverse, have to show their effectiveness in a competitive business environment.

3.1.2 The Theory of Absolute Advantages

In opposition to the export-orientated trade policy of the so-called mercantilists, Adam Smith presented his classical thoughts about absolute advantages in his 'Inquiry into the Nature and Causes of the Wealth of Nations' in 1776: 'If a foreign country can supply us with a commodity cheaper than we ourselves can make it, better buy it of them with some part of the produce of our own industry employed in a way in which we have some advantage.'[312] This means that if one country is able to produce a certain product with less cost and to sell it more cheaply than other countries, then it has an absolute advantage. An absolute advantage can be the result of a better production technology or a better factor endowment. According to Smith, a greater division of labour would lead to productivity gains and technological improvements. Furthermore, every nation should specialize itself on products with an absolute advantage and export these goods so that all countries can profit from these absolute advantages and increase their national wealth. Accordingly, Smith′ trade theory of absolute advantages does not adhere to the mercantilist idea that international trade results in a zero sum game, but in economic growth and a positive sum game.[313] It is remarkable that Smith did not title his work '... the wealth of the nation', but '... the wealth of nations'. He underlined that *all* countries could profit from international specialization and free trade. This specialization and greater international division of labour increases the productivity so that the absolute advantages even grow.

The theory of absolute advantages is an approach to the concept of international competitiveness. A nation is competitive if it possesses an absolute advantage so that it can produce certain products less costly compared to other countries. Absolute advantages still play an important role for the structure of international trade and for the international com-

[312] Smith (1776) Book IV, Chapter II; cf. Schmidt (2002) p. 38; cf. Kurz (1990) p. 244; cf. Brown (1994) pp. 154ff., 216; cf. Pribram (1998) p. 255.

[313] Schefold and Carstensen (2002) p. 69; cf. Recktenwald (1989) p. 149.

petitiveness of firms. Some even suggest that 'competitive advantage is a synonym for absolute advantage: some natural or policy-induced superiority (such as lower taxes or greater labour-market flexibility) which reduces costs for all home sectors'[314]. Nevertheless, there are deficiencies with regard to the present competitiveness debate. The concept of absolute advantages is too simple and too static to explain the modern debate on international competitiveness. Although Smith also considered the division of labour and the national technology, Smith mainly started from the assumption that absolute advantages are primarily *natural* advantages, that they result from the natural factor endowment of a country: 'The natural advantages which one country has over another in producing particular commodities are sometimes so great, that it is acknowledged by all the world to be in vain to struggle with them.'[315] This concept of natural advantages reveals at least two deficiencies.

Firstly, *long-term* natural advantages cannot explain intra-industry-trade and the international competitiveness in modern industries. The competitiveness of firms and countries increasingly depends on temporary and dynamic factors like superior technology, modern design, product differentiation, services, infrastructure, economies of scales, effective sales and marketing practices etc. These factors permanently generate *new* competitive advantages which cannot be guaranteed for a long-term period so that it is not in vain for firms to compete with the present owner of absolute advantages. By focusing on the so-called natural advantages, Smith underestimated the influence of good governance and especially the active role of good management for improving the international competitiveness of the nation or its firms.

Secondly, the concept of natural advantages focuses on the production costs as the determinant of absolute advantages. This approach seems to be too unbalanced because phenomena like intra-industry-trade make it doubtful that the international competitiveness of countries or firms mainly depends on cost functions. Furthermore, Smith′ model would not work in case that trading countries or their firms have the same cost function so that no country has an absolute advantage.[316] Moreover, the theory of ab-

---

314 Cf. Neary (2003) p. 457.

315 Smith (1776) Book IV, Chapter II.

316 The theory of absolute advantages and other historical concepts of competitiveness and trade stress the differences between countries to explain trade. In contrast to this, the new trade theory 'stresses similarities between countries rather than differences' in order to explain trade patterns (Neary (2003) p. 458). Therefore, product differentiation and economies of scale are taken as significant factors which also can explain intra-industry-trade.

solute advantages would stop trade between two countries in case that one of the trading countries has no absolute advantage at all.

Thirdly, as regards the role of government, Smith holds an ambivalent and partly contradictory position. On the one hand, he criticized governmental interventions during the period of mercantilism (import restrictions, national monopolies, export subsidies, wage regulation etc.). While the mercantilists strived for national self-sufficiency, Smith thought that free trade and competition would lead to international specialization and economic growth so that governmental (protectionist) interventions become unnecessary and should be reduced to a minimum, for example to erect and maintain certain public works and institutions which would never be erected by individuals.[317] Although this view has preference over mercantilist ideas, Smith neglects two aspects. On the one hand, certain additional governmental activities could be advantageous for economic growth, international welfare, and international competitiveness. Furthermore, a far-reaching specialization of nations as intended by Smith only could be realized by strict governmental interventions and regulation and this would be incompatible with the aim to protect international competition.

3.1.3 The Theory of Comparative Advantages

The theory of comparative advantages is an extension of the theory of absolute advantages. It was first described by Robert Torrens in 1815 and by David Ricardo in 1817.[318] This theory explains in a simple model with two countries, two goods, and only labour as input, why it is beneficial for these two countries to start foreign trade even though one of the trading partners is able to produce the two traded goods with less absolute production costs than the other.

Whereas the theory of absolute advantages compares the absolute production costs of two countries, the theory of comparative advantages compares the domestic opportunity costs. These opportunity costs can be defined as the value or the benefits that could be received from producing the other good. More generally speaking, in a model with more than two goods, the opportunity costs would be determined by the next best opportunity to use the production factors for generating welfare. According to Ricardo´s model, every economy should produce and export the one product which causes lower opportunity costs compared to the other country.

[317] Cf. Cho and Moon (2000) p. 6; cf. Kolb (1997) p. 59.

[318] Kolb (1997) p. 67; Torrens (1815); Ricardo (1817); cf. Ellis (1989) p. 200; cf. Pribram (1998) p. 315.

This means that the two trading countries specialize on the production of the one good where they give up less of the other product compared to the foreign country. Consequently, global production of both products can be increased by this kind of international specialization and division of labour. Furthermore, the welfare in both trading countries would increase if adequate terms of trade lead to intense free trade.

The most important result with respect to the competitiveness debate is that every country is internationally competitive, because every country has a comparative advantage in at least one industry.[319] If the first country has a comparative advantage in producing one good, then the second country must have a comparative advantage in the other good. No country can lose its comparative advantage in everything if the other country achieves technological progress. Simultaneously, no country can possess a comparative advantage in all its industries, even if it generates more technological advances in all its industries compared to other country. This theory of comparative advantages is still important in foreign trade theory to justify international trade as an instrument to increase overall welfare, but it does not provide a comprehensive framework for analyzing the entire competitiveness phenomenon. Quite the reverse, the theory of comparative advantages rather stops the discussion about the international competitiveness of nations because of its simple answer that every country is internationally competitive. Furthermore, Ricardo's model includes several deficiencies making it inapplicable on modern industries and open and free markets.

Firstly, the model cannot explain why there are different comparative advantages between modern industrialized countries.[320] Similar to Adam Smith, Torrens and Ricardo had used a model in which comparative advantages result from the natural factor endowment of a country and from a different (factor) productivity.[321] In his *Principles*, Ricardo explicitly mentions the capitalist who makes the discovery of a machine or who first usually applies it to get an additional advantage.[322] According to these factors, certain domestic industries achieve a comparative advantage over foreign industries because of lower opportunity costs. Even developing countries

---

319 Cf. Lachmann (2001) p. 4, 6. By generalizing Ricardo's approach to international competitiveness, Dornbusch, Fischer, and Samuelson have shown that each nation will always have industrial sectors that are able to compete with foreign companies, but possibly at the expense of a loss of national welfare because of a cut in wages or a devaluation of the domestic currency (cf. Dornbusch et al. (1977) pp. 823ff.; cf. Lachmann (2001) p. 7).

320 Cho and Moon (2000) p. 1.

321 Cf. Daniel (2000) pp. 418ff.

322 Cf. Ricardo (1817) Chapter 31 ('On Machinery').

that are lacking behind in productivity and technology have a comparative advantage. Assuming an international immobility of production factors, the national production conditions result in long-term comparative advantages.[323] In contrast to this model, natural and long-term production conditions are not the decisive factor in the majority of modern dynamic industries which are confronted with international competition and intra-industry-trade. Most present comparative advantages permanently have to be developed or attracted by firms and nations. Though, one has to appreciate that – similar to Smith′ concept of *absolute* advantages – Ricardo′s basic idea also could be transferred into more complex, more realistic concepts of competitiveness which underline the role of technological and entrepreneurial differences to determine *comparative* advantages.

Furthermore, Ricardo′s model does not work in case that both countries have the same opportunity costs in producing a certain good so that no country has a comparative advantage. This is not an unlikely scenario, because modern industries are increasingly characterized by intra-industry-trade and a fast transmission of new technologies and know-how. Moreover, an international convergence and harmonization of technological standards, human capital, wages, capital costs, standard of living, laws etc. could make it more likely that countries′ opportunity costs converge, too. But although this process of convergence and harmonization could level opportunity costs, it is likely that countries would still possess a more or less different degree of international competitiveness because the international competitiveness does not only depend on different opportunity costs.

Thirdly, the theory of comparative advantages would necessitate an international governmental coordination of trade and production in order to achieve a far-reaching international specialization. This would lead to a globally planned economy, a supremacy of the state over the economy. For instance, if one of the trading countries has absolute advantages in both industries, then the government would have to determine that the one of these internationally competitive industries which does not have the *comparative* advantage would have to give up its business and start producing the other product. The government would have to carry through a strict specialization on the one product where the economy possesses a comparative advantage. Such governmental interventions are not compatible with nowadays dynamic industries and international competition. Ricardo′s model is too static, i.e. it applies to an economy where governmental interventions and international specialization prevent international competition, where international competitiveness is a rather static concept. In contrast to this, in present world economy a movement towards free trade is automati-

---

[323] Cf. Pribram (1998) p. 315.

cally combined with a dynamic concept of competitiveness and welfare based on international competition instead of specialization.

3.1.4 The Heckscher-Ohlin-Model

Smith and Ricardo did not provide a thorough explanation why a country has an absolute or a comparative advantage. The Heckscher-Ohlin-Model[324] intends to offer a solution for this problem by focusing on the *relative* factor endowments of countries.[325] The neoclassical model starts from Ricardo´s theory of comparative advantages, but it rejects Ricardo´s basic assumptions and introduces some new assumptions. Firstly, the Heckscher-Ohlin-Model introduces a second factor (capital) so that it includes two production factors (labour and capital). Secondly, the model assumes that there are no international factor movements and that all countries use the same technology so that differences in productivity only arise from differences in factor endowments and from the resulting different combinations of labour and capital.[326] In contrast to this, Ricardo´s one-input-model explains the generation of comparative advantages and different labour productivities with the existence of different technologies in the trading countries. By means of these alterations compared to Ricardo´s theory, the Heckscher-Ohlin-Model highlights the role of different factor endowments for differences in national productivity and for the resulting international division of labour. According to Heckscher and Ohlin, every trading country focuses on the production of those goods where it possesses a relative abundance of the needed inputs because this relative abundance causes low production costs and by this the comparative advantage (so-called factor proportions theorem). Consequently, patterns of trade can be predicted by analyzing the relative factor endowment of all trading nations.

As regards the discussion about the international competitiveness of nations, the Heckscher-Ohlin-Model has made an important contribution by turning the attention to a special factor of competitiveness. The international competitiveness of a nation is considered to depend on its relative factor endowment. It is still undisputed that the factor endowment is an important factor of international competitiveness, but it cannot explain the whole problem.[327] The Heckscher-Ohlin-Model is too simple and one-sided

---

324 Heckscher (1919) pp. 273ff.; Ohlin (1933).

325 Heckscher (1919) pp. 277ff.; Neumann (2002) pp. 279f.

326 Heckscher (1919) pp. 274ff.; Cho and Moon (2000) p. 10.

327 Cf. Venables (1996) p. 52.

to explain the different competitive advantages between countries. Several deficiencies of the model have to be mentioned.

Firstly, the empirical evidence has put into question the model by discovering the so-called Leontief Paradox. According to the Heckscher-Ohlin-Model, the United States of America were supposed to export capital-intensive products and to import labour-intensive commodities. In 1954, Leontief tested the Heckscher-Ohlin-Theory and found that the empirical evidence was contradictory to the theory.[328] The United States, well equipped with capital, exported rather labour-intensive goods and imported capital-intensive products, i.e. the exported goods had a lower capital-intensity than the imports. This paradox mainly has been tried to explain by the following two considerations. On the one hand, the paradox revealed the necessity to differentiate between normal labour and highly skilled labour. Some economists underlined the role of highly skilled labour for the US exports industry. Highly skilled labour could be introduced as a third factor or it could be viewed as capital, including human capital. Another approach to cope with the Leontief Paradox was Vernons'[329] product cycle model. Vernon argued that many new marketable goods go through a product cycle of introduction, growth, maturation, standardization, and decline.[330] This model stated that the United States' comparative advantage was characterized by its ability to innovate new products which – during the introduction stage – had to be produced at home by using relatively labour-intensive production methods. In the following stage of growth and maturity, the new products have been standardized so that the production became more capital-intensive; the new capital-intensive production facilities partly have been located abroad.[331] Although both approaches could not entirely explain the Leontief Paradox, the identification of these two possible factors (i.e. human capital and the product cycle) put into question the Heckscher-Ohlin-Model. The assumption that competitive advantages do not depend on technological differences but only on factor endowments became doubtful because highly skilled labour and innovativeness are closely connected with high technology so

[328] Leontief (1953).

[329] Vernon (1966) pp. 190ff.

[330] Cho and Moon (2000) p. 14.

[331] Ibid. pp. 14f. This kind of international labour division along the product cycle might have been valid at that time, i.e. in the 50th and 60th. Meanwhile, globalization has led to an internationalization of many R&D and production processes so that the product cycle model is no more apt to explain the international division of labour (Vernon (1979) pp. 255ff.).

that both the degree of skilled labour and the existing technological differences between countries became relevant for the competitiveness debate.

Secondly, the Heckscher-Ohlin-Model also follows the idea of *long-term* natural advantages, on the basis of *natural* factor endowments and a locational immobility of production factors. On this point, Heckscher and Ohlin did not go beyond the static approaches of Smith and Ricardo. Therefore the Heckscher-Ohlin-Model also cannot explain the factor endowment and the international competitiveness of modern industries. The competitiveness of most firms and countries essentially depends on factors which have become internationally footloose in times of economic globalization. Capital and highly skilled labour are increasingly mobile in search of higher profits and better locational conditions.

Thirdly, trading countries often have a similar factor endowment and sometimes even similar factor costs in their industries. Nevertheless, they trade with each other and they compete on global markets, trading similar products (intra-industry-trade) and trying to achieve economies of scale.[332] Therefore, the factor endowment and an optimal international specialization cannot be the crucial factors to explain the international competitiveness of countries and the structure of trade. Although it has to be conceded that many factors of competitiveness are closely linked to the factor endowment, many decisive factors of competitiveness do not depend on the factor endowment, for example the size of the domestic market, economies of scale, product differentiation, and domestic demand conditions. Heckscher and Ohlin did not acknowledge the role of these factors for trade patterns and competitiveness.[333]

Moreover, the Heckscher-Ohlin-Model leads to a win-win-situation through trade liberalization. If all trading countries specialize on the production of those commodities where they have a relative abundance of inputs, then the commodity prices fall and all countries profit from this specialization by cheap imports. This is an optimistic view, depending on strict assumptions and simplifications. In the real world, there is no guarantee that every country gains from trade liberalization. Some economists even emphasize that the ability to gain from free trade and to enhance national welfare is an essential feature of international competitiveness. Countries have to strive for a position in which they profit from free trade, the benefits of free trade do not come to all countries automatically. Especially developing countries are in danger to fall into the so-called Heckscher-Ohlin-Trap which could result in a poverty trap. In this case, a country has specialized too much on those goods which suffer from decreasing

---

332 Neumann (2002) p. 280; Cho and Moon (2000) pp. 18f.

333 Cho and Moon (2000) p. 18.

terms of trade, for example on goods which are produced by unskilled labour force because of a relative abundance of this input. Consequently, in the long run the country would not participate equally in technological progress and welfare because of falling terms of trade (also confer both the Prebisch-Singer hypothesis and the theory of immizerising growth[334]). The inflow of foreign direct investments into these incumbent industries could even reinforce this situation.

3.1.5 Conclusion

The historical (classical and neoclassical) theories and models of foreign trade which have been touched on in the preceding exposition were not designed as concepts of international competitiveness but as models to explain the pattern and the benefits of international trade and specialization (inter-industry-trade) as a main factor of national welfare. Therefore, they have turned out to be too simple and restrictive to explain the phenomenon of international competitiveness, especially as regards intra-industry-trade. Ricardo´s theory of comparative advantages even would result in the conclusion that every country is competitive somewhere so that there would be no need for a theory of international competitiveness.[335]

Nevertheless, these historic theories have provided the first aspects to the explanation of international competitiveness, especially with regard to the factors of competitiveness, especially with regard to the factor endowment, product-process innovations, and entrepreneurial activities.[336] The aspect of international specialization even has experienced a growing importance in the course of multinational enterprises´ strategy to internationalize the production ('slicing up the value added chain'). Furthermore, the historic theories have passed the way to a macroeconomic view on the concept of competitiveness. This is important to state because the present debate on competitiveness especially concerns the question as to whether it is economically legitimate to talk about an international competitiveness of *nations*.

---

[334] Bhagwati (1958) pp. 201ff.; Lachmann (1994) pp. 133ff.

[335] Cf. Preusse (2001) p. 1.

[336] Daniel (2000) p. 424.

3.2 The Modern Controversy

In economic literature, there are different views and definitions with regard to modern concepts of international competitiveness. One of the fundamental and controversially discussed issues is whether it is solely a microeconomic concept (international competitiveness of *enterprises*) or in addition to this also a macroeconomic concept (international competitiveness of *nations/economies*). This debate also includes the question whether free trade increases welfare in all participating countries or whether globalization has increased economic rivalry between all open economies.[337] Furthermore, the proponents of a macroeconomic concept of international competitiveness vary in their concepts how to define, measure, and improve the international competitiveness of a nation so that there are many further questions to be answered.

It is undisputed that every enterprise and even every national industry is characterized by a certain degree or indicator of international competitiveness – e.g. the ability to make sufficient profits on foreign markets – and by certain crucial factors of competitiveness – e.g. the ability to rapidly react on business activities of business partners and competitors; to recognize and to develop new and advanced technologies and to integrate them swiftly and reliably into existing or new marketable products; the ability to permanently improve manufacturing processes and the capability to meet customers′ demands. Enterprises and industries that are not able to keep up with the dynamic developments on national and international markets lose their competitiveness and, in the long run, they would have to leave the market.

With regard to the international competitiveness of nations, the question arises as to whether anything similar could happen to national economies, too. The debate about the macroeconomic competitiveness is a very interesting one because of the extremely diverging points of view among economists. By observing this debate, one may ask whether one of the two disputing parties is absolutely wrong or whether both parties are talking at cross purposes so that both positions could be reconciled by clearing up the existing misunderstandings.

[337] Cf. Lachmann (2001) p. 2.

3.2.1 The Critic Against the Concept of an International Competitiveness of Nations

An early and well-known critic of using the concept of international competitiveness with reference to nations is Krugman[338]. His point of view is characteristic for many opponents of the concept of macroeconomic competitiveness who state that a macroeconomic competitiveness of nations does not exist. The concept is rejected because of the following reasons.

Firstly, according to the Ricardian theory of comparative advantages, every country always has 'a comparative advantage in something'[339] so that competitiveness of nations is a largely meaningless concept.[340] Chapter 3.1.3 has shown the weak points of this argumentation.

Secondly, nations can not go bankrupt. While firms have to go out of business when they do not fulfil their liabilities to pay, countries only become poorer: 'Countries ... do not go out of business. They may be happy or unhappy with their economic performance, but they have a well-defined bottom line'[341].

Thirdly, the international competitiveness of domestic enterprises can have a negative influence on the competitiveness of other domestic enterprises, for example in case that the increasing competitiveness and productivity of a certain national industry leads to an upward revaluation of the exchange rate or an increase of wages so that other domestic industries, which do not achieve the same productivity gains but also have to pay increased wages and sell at higher prices, become less competitive.[342]

Fourthly, countries do not economically compete against each other.[343] Instead, at the end of the day, only companies do compete in a zero-sum game because they are judged on their performances on global markets so that the competitiveness debate finally should be given up in favour of a mere microeconomic productivity concept. Besides the fundamental assumption of economic theory that 'trade between a country and the rest of the world tends to be balanced, particularly over the long term'[344], global trade can be regarded as a positive-sum game. This means that, in most cases, countries benefit from the welfare gains of foreign countries so that there is no rivalry and competition between countries, except for status and

[338] Krugman (1994) pp. 1-17; Krugman (1995); Krugman (1996) pp. 17-25; Krugman (1997).

[339] Krugman (1996) p. 20.

[340] Krugman (1994) p. 14.

[341] Ibid. p. 4.

[342] Cf. Monopolkommission (2005) p. 76.

[343] Krugman (1994) p. 7.

[344] Bloch and Kenyon (2001) p. 4.

power.[345] Indeed, quite the reverse, modern open economies′ welfare depends on the positive economic development of other countries, especially in times of economic slowdown or crisis. If a certain country grows, possibly faster than the others, then the global markets will expand and all foreign trading partners will benefit from the availability of better or cheaper products and from more favourable terms of trade.[346] Consequently, there are neither winners nor losers. The false and illogical idea to increase the welfare and international competitiveness of a country by means of national policy is based on the wrong idea that world economy would amount to a *zero-sum game* so that every country would have to increase its welfare and competitiveness at the expense of other countries. Krugman explicitly warns that this could cause the return of a 'dangerous obsession', which means protectionism, industrial policy, and other kinds of bad governmental policy, based on false and negative political attitudes and ideas against free trade and resulting in the waste of money. This would cause harm both to consumers, tax-payers, and to the development of the domestic economy. There are at least two reasons for these negative effects. Firstly, governments do not know which industries or companies have good prospects for the future. Furthermore, even in case that the government knew about the future prospects of industries and companies, all attempts to support their international competitiveness would have negative and selective effects. Secondly, every form of strategic trade and beggar-thy-neighbour policies would harm international competitors and result in retaliatory measures. This would finally end in a negative-sum game.

These arguments against the term 'international competitiveness of nations' have not convinced all economists because of several shortcomings. The following chapter will criticize these arguments by describing the proponents′ view on international competitiveness.

3.2.2 Modern Views Supporting the Concept of Macroeconomic Competitiveness

A systematic approach to define and understand the concept of international competitiveness of nations has to pay attention to the following aspects. Firstly, it has to be analyzed whether there is something like a macroeconomic competitiveness that is not just an aggregation or an average of the microeconomic competitiveness of domestic companies. The national welfare or the locational attractiveness of nations for foreign and do-

345 Krugman (1994) p. 8.

346 Cf. Boltho (1996) p. 4; Krugman (1994) pp. 7f.

mestic investors probably could be taken as an example for this kind of *macro*economic competitiveness. In this way, the theory of 'good governance', which is also a rather nebulous concept, could be relevant (see Chap. 3.2.2.1).[347]

Secondly, it is important to distinguish between the factors (independent variables) and the indicators (dependent variables) of international competitiveness and whether they belong to the microeconomic or macroeconomic sphere (see Chaps. 3.2.2.2 and 3.2.2.3). Just as several factors of (micro- or macroeconomic) competitiveness belong to the macroeconomic sphere, indicators of (micro- or macroeconomic) competitiveness partly also are macroeconomic quantities. In this respect, it is of special importance to identify factors which are important for the (microeconomic) international competitiveness of domestic enterprises or industries and – and this is important – which are substantially determined by the macroeconomic or political sphere. This approach deals with the interface between microeconomic and macroeconomic competitiveness. The focus would still be on the (microeconomic) competitiveness of enterprises, but because of the crucial influence of the state on some factors, it could be adequate to complete the picture by also taking into account a macroeconomic concept of international competitiveness. Consequently, it could be more appropriate to talk about an international competitiveness that is influenced both by microeconomic and macroeconomic factors so that both the state and the domestic enterprises are responsible for the international competitiveness of the economy as a whole. Though, apart from the fundamental features of a free market economy which have to be installed and guaranteed by the state, the state probably would play the minor role within such an approach, compared to other (microeconomic) factors of international competitiveness.

3.2.2.1 Definitions of International Competitiveness

The debate about the competitiveness of nations still goes on but has not led to a consensual definition of international competitiveness and its interpretation yet.[348] Furthermore, a generally accepted theory of international competitiveness is still missing.[349] Consequently, the existing lack of

---

347 Cf. Preusse (2001) p. 16.

348 Lachmann (2001) p. 5f. For a survey of different definitions, also cf. Reichel (2002) pp. 16ff.

349 According to Bofinger, a central reason for this lack of theoretical foundation is a general lack of research on the interface between international trade theory on the one hand and international monetary economics on the other. He states that the concept of an 'International Competitiveness of Nations' is located

theory and consensual definition results in a multitude of concepts which partly even do without any explicit theoretical foundation. These concepts vary from each other as regards their (political) point of view, i.e. their intention and argumentation, and with regard to the provided indicators and factors of international competitiveness. Therefore, the different concepts are even partly contradictory, especially because many factors and indicators of international competitiveness stand in a conflict relation with each other. The inner tensions and contradictions can be shown by some examples. For instance, one could highlight the role of FDI inflow as a factor or indicator of international competitiveness, especially with regard to the locational attractiveness of the economy. Though, on the other hand, there are also good reasons to take into account the FDI outflow as a factor and indicator of international competitiveness. As a second example for inner contradictions, it is possible to refer to relatively low labour costs as an important factor for international competitiveness, although a relatively high real wage also could be taken as an indicator of international competitiveness.

At a quick glance, these inner tensions and contradictions could be viewed as a fundamental theoretical problem because, in order to establish a consistent definition and theory of competitiveness, it would be helpful if all factors and indicators were standing in a complementary relation with each other. Instead, the international competitiveness of nations rather seems to be a complex phenomenon that touches a multitude of economic aspects which cannot be captured easily within one overarching definition or theory.[350] Hence the factors and indicators of international competitiveness, each representing a hypothesis on international competitiveness, would have to be analyzed more closely – especially with regard to their combination, interaction, and their case-specific weight and meaning – in order to generate a complex theory of international competitiveness that is able to reconcile aspects that seem to be contradictory at first glance.[351] This task would go far beyond the scope of this examination. Therefore, the following explanations only present an overview of the different definitions, indicators (see Chap. 3.2.2.2) and factors (see Chap. 3.2.2.3) of international competitiveness in order to give a representative insight into the debate and to achieve a theoretical basis for the subsequent investigation in Chap. 4.

---

within this interface region and that the real exchange rate is an important indicator of international competitiveness (Bofinger (1995) pp. 467ff.; cf. Reichel (2002) p. 11).

[350] Cf. Bloch and Kenyon (2001a) p. 32.

[351] Cf. Preusse (2001) p. 16.

The Dynamic Welfare Approach: Locational Attractiveness and Good Governance. In a rather simple and static approach to the phenomenon of macroeconomic competitiveness, international competitiveness could be taken as a concept of the relative economic welfare and prosperity of regions, including both their existing, accumulated wealth (savings, assets etc.) and the wealth that results from current market activities (especially consumers′ and producers′ rent). All regional units are characterized by different degrees of economic activities and resource endowments, frequently just by chance or because of certain historical events. Consequently, differences in welfare can not necessarily be seen as the result of competitive behaviour and an outstanding political or managerial performance.

In contrast to this static welfare approach, many economists like, for instance, Siebert[352] and Berg[353] emphasize the active role of competitive behaviour. Siebert differs between *three* 'levels' of international competitiveness who 'attempt to maximize their own utility', but who are interdependent so that they can be subsumed under one single, broadly used concept of locational competition[354]:

1. Firms compete in product markets.
2. Geographical territories and countries compete for mobile production factors.
3. Immobile production factors (primarily less-qualified labour) compete for their income level and for the security of their jobs.

The competitiveness of enterprises is a similar concept like that of cities, metropolitan regions, nations etc., because they are all confronted with competition, having the chance to gain competitiveness or to lose it. But there is a difference between the competitiveness of firms and that of a national economy or a free trade zone. Regions differ from enterprises with respect to the object of competition. While companies compete for market shares, cities, regions and countries compete against each other for the mobile factors of production. It is the government′s permanent task to 'take into account the exit option of capital and of other mobile factors'[355], to attract new mobile factors, and to make a cost-benefit analysis, i.e. 'to weigh the advantages of the supply of public goods against the burden of

352 Siebert (2000) pp. 3ff.; cf. Siebert (2005) pp. 2ff.
353 Berg (1983) pp. 4ff.
354 Siebert (2000) pp. 3f.
355 Siebert (2005) p. 20.

financing them'[356]. The criterion used to determine 'whether the inflow or the outflow of mobile factors is beneficial is the welfare level'[357].

This competition between locations is, according to Siebert, 'a powerful concept in the theory of the division of international trade'[358]. Similarly, Huovari et al. underline the interstate competition for mobile factors. They state that 'regional competitiveness is the ability of regions to foster, attract and support economic activity so that its citizens enjoy relatively good economic welfare. Competitive regions have build [sic!] a production environment with high accessibility that perpetuates and attracts mobile production factors, and results in fostering the economy. These mobile factors include skilled labour, innovative entrepreneurs and footloose capital. Success in attracting these factors creates external economies, such as agglomeration and localisation benefits, that further enhance the economic fortune of a region.'[359] Though, it is doubtful to what extent international competitiveness could be seen as a self-reinforcing process so that competitive regions automatically become even more competitive because of agglomeration and localisation benefits.

Regarding this, it has to be emphasized that the existence of a locational competition between countries is even acknowledged by economists who generally support a purely microeconomic concept of international competitiveness and who therefore reject the macroeconomic concept of international competitiveness; they limit the concept of international competitiveness of nations to a mere concept of locational competitiveness and attractiveness.[360] Consequently, other dynamic and welfare-oriented macroeconomic concepts do not focus as much on the attraction of mobile factors; they support a more comprehensive approach and introduce some further aspects.

For instance, the European Commission generally focuses on the aim to *create* welfare: 'Competitiveness is a measure of an economy´s ability to create valuable goods and services productively in a globalising world so as to raise the standard of living and secure high employment'[361]. The OECD defines the international competitiveness of a nation as 'the degree to which it can, under free and fair market conditions, produce goods and services which meet the test of international markets, while simultaneously maintaining and expanding the real incomes of its people over the longer

356 Ibid. pp. 2, 9.
357 Ibid. p. 11.
358 Ibid. p. 4.
359 Huovari et al. (2001) p. 1; cf. Meessen (2000) p. 15.
360 Also cf. Straubhaar (1994) pp. 534ff.
361 European Commission (2004a) p. 3.

term'[362]. This dynamic welfare approach corresponds to the Global Competitiveness Report, published by the World Economic Forum, who wants to explain 'why some countries are much more successful than others in raising income levels and opportunities for their respective populations'[363]. The report is explicitly addressed to policymakers and business leaders in order to formulate improved economic policies and institutional reforms which go beyond the mere locational attractiveness of the nation.[364] Similarly, Boltho focuses on 'the longer-run aim of rising living standards' which could be achieved by 'the highest possible growth of productivity that was compatible with external equilibrium'[365]. Fagerberg concludes, that international competitiveness 'reflects the ability of a country to secure a high standard of living for its citizens, relative to the citizens of other countries, now and in the future'[366], especially 'without running into balance-of-payments difficulties'[367].

Two aspects have to be highlighted with regard to governmental activities to enhance welfare. Firstly, good governance does not neglect the role of entrepreneurial activities with regard to attracting mobile factors and generating relatively high income levels, but it focuses on the governments´ (initial) performance, especially to support the inflow of foreign direct investments and the immigration of highly skilled and entrepreneurial people, obviously also at the expense of other countries (so-called brain-drain). Secondly, theoretical approaches to macroeconomic competitiveness often focus on the supply side of domestic markets, underlining the necessity to improve the international competitiveness of domestic enterprises and to attract foreign production factors. But in order to indicate the welfare of the whole economy, it is important to take both the consumer´s rent and the producer´s rent into account when national welfare is to be indicated. Consequently, competitiveness does not only implicate a domestic firm´s ability to sell and earn on international markets but also a firm´s productivity which allows low consumer prices. This is an important aspect with regard to competition policy.

The Interstate Rivalry Approach. Prestowitz underlines the role of international trade as an essential concern of international competitiveness. By contradicting Krugman, Prestowitz states that international trade can become a zero-sum game between two trading countries. He says that

---

[362] OECD (1992) p. 237.
[363] Lopez-Claros et al. (2006) p. xi.
[364] Ibid. p. xi.
[365] Boltho (1996) pp. 2f., 15.
[366] Fagerberg (1996) p. 48.
[367] Fagerberg (1988) p. 355.

Krugman was only correct 'in case of trade between the United States and Costa Rica, where America imports bananas it does not grow and exports airplanes and machinery that Costa Rica does not make'.[368] In this case, both countries benefit from free trade and this result corresponds to the empirical evidence of economic history that international trade has promoted economic growth and welfare. But as regards, for instance, trade between the United States and the European Union, Prestowitz states that both economies produce similar products (intra industry trade) so that, instead of profiting from each others´ comparative advantage, they compete against each other for jobs and income.[369]

Consequently, while most economists agree that free trade generally generates welfare and amounts to a positive-sum game, it is doubtful whether there is no rivalry and competition between countries in a globalized world economy. The idea of international competitiveness of nations could be mainly associated with rivalry[370], especially because the term competitiveness is not about a country´s absolute performance, 'but how well it does relative to other countries'[371]. Theoretically, all countries could benefit from the rapid economic growth and increasing welfare of another country because a growing economy mostly increases its international demand and offers better and cheaper products for the rest of the world. Even if this country primarily grows because of high exports which successfully compete with industries in the importing country, the exporting country equally has to increase its imports in the long run because otherwise its reward for being so industrious would only be a high amount of paper money in foreign currency. Therefore, Krugman states that 'if foreigners become relatively more productive in a particular industry, then of course we will lose jobs in that industry. But that doesn´t mean that we lose jobs in the economy as a whole, or that foreign productivity growth hurts us'[372]. The economic growth of foreign countries often is a prerequisite for a nation´s own economic development. For instance, the European Union´s level of economic activity is positively correlated with the US American economy.

---

[368] Prestowitz (2000) p. 38.

[369] Ibid. p. 39. Prestowitz also states that the loss of economic competitiveness may have a negative influence on national security and on the 'vulnerability to political regimes and international cartels that may severely constrain a country´s economic potential' (p. 40).

[370] Cf. Boltho (1996) p. 2. Some economists even fear a so-called race to the bottom which could result from rivalry and countries´ attempt to become more competitive. This race to the bottom would decrease international welfare and amount to a negative-sum game.

[371] Fagerberg (1996) p. 40.

[372] Krugman (1996) p. 20.

Nevertheless, countries do not benefit automatically from foreign growth and welfare gains. They have to practice good economic policies, i.e. they have to protect competition, they have to open their markets, and they have to provide for locational conditions under which domestic enterprises become more competitive and which attract foreign investors, too. If that is not the case, countries could even lose welfare and competitiveness in spite of a worldwide increase of welfare. They can not go bankrupt like a private company, but countries can become impoverished, both absolutely and relatively.[373] Therefore it is too simplistic to think that all countries automatically have a comparative advantage in something and benefit from a positive-sum game. Some countries will even grow at the expense of foreign countries because of their better locational policy, a more intelligent competition policy, a sophisticated industrial policy and other forms of state-guided activities.

3.2.2.2 Indicators of International Competitiveness

Closely related to the task of finding a definition for 'international competitiveness of nations', it is necessary to identify adequate indicators that correspond to the chosen definition and that reliably show whether an economy is internationally competitive. As there is no generally accepted definition of the term 'international competitiveness of nations', it is also a disputed question which indicators reliably could measure the international competitiveness of nations. Consequently, there is a multitude of indicators which have been presented in economic literature and which are all controversial. This multitude of indicators is rather confusing so that it is useful to introduce a classification for these indicators.

A Classification of Indicators of International Competitiveness. The following table 3.1 shows a classification and gives an overview over the most important indicators.

In general, one has to distinguish between microeconomic and macroeconomic indicators, i.e. some indicators are focussed on macroeconomic quantities like the real exchange rate, while others refer to the microeconomic level (enterprises and industries), for example the number of innovations in certain industries. Though, the differentiation between micro- and macroeconomic indicators does not always have a good selectivity, i.e. some indicators could be used both as a microeconomic and macroeconomic indicator (for example the FDI inflow).

[373] Cf. Reichel (2002) p. 33.

	Microeconomic	Macroeconomic
Short-term	- Productivity, Prices and Costs: Unit Labour Costs in Labour Intensive Industries; Relative Price Index; Relative Cost Index - Exports and Export Market Shares (Ability to Earn and to Sell) - Revealed Comparative Advantage of Industries (RCA-Analysis) - FDI Outflow and Inflow (Ability to Invest and to Attract) - Technology; Innovations (Ability to Invent): Patents; R&D Expenditures;	- Total Factor Productivity (TFP): The Average TFP of Countries Could Indicate the Overall Competitiveness of the Nation. - Real GDP Growth Rate; Real Per Capita GDP; Real Personal Income; Real Wage Growth - Real Effective Exchange Rate: Terms of Trade; Purchasing-Power-Parity - Trade: Global Export Shares; Market Shares-Analysis - Capital Market Figures: Real Returns on Capital Employed in Industry; Tobin´s Q - External Macroeconomic Balance: (Sectoral) Current Account Balance; FDI Balance (Ability to Attract) - Internal Macroeconomic Balance: Employment Rate and Inflation Rate
Long-term	- Sustainable Growth of Profits and Company Capital	- Long-Term Real Effective Exchange Rate - Long-Term (Moderate) Interest Rate - Long-Term (Moderate) Inflation Rate - Long-Term Standard of Living: Human Development Index (HDI)

Table 3.1: Indicators of International Competitiveness

Furthermore, it is possible to distinguish between short-term and long-term indicators. Some indicators can be interpreted differently from a short-term perspective compared to a long-term perspective. This is because it is possible to promote the international competitiveness of a nation in the short run by means of political measures and conditions which would be a sign of low competitiveness in the long run. For instance, low wages[374] and a weak domestic currency can be interpreted differently from a short-term and a long-term perspective. They can be applied to strengthen the international competitiveness in the short run, but in the long run, low wages and a weak currency would rather indicate a lack of competitiveness. This problem will be described exemplary by means of the real effective exchange rate.

Besides the differentiation between 'short-term vs. long-term' and 'microeconomic vs. macroeconomic' indicators, it is possible to subdivide the *macro*economic indicators into those which refer to the commodity market (for example the current account balance, the share of global trade, the terms of trade, and the real effective exchange rate) and those indicators which refer to the international locational competition, i.e. the ability to attract (for example the balance of foreign direct investments, the balance of capital account, the international allocation of investments, and the attraction of human capital).[375]

This classification helps to get an overview of possibly relevant indicators, but it does not provide an order of rank as regards the hierarchical structure and the quality and validity of these indicators. Therefore, it is an additional task to analyze which indicators are most reliable and valid to indicate international competitiveness. There is a limited number of indicators which attract most attention among economists according to the above definitions of international competitiveness.

Most Favoured Indicators and the Search for a Final Outcome of International Competitiveness. As already described in Chap. 3.2.2.1, some define international competitiveness as the ability of regions, countries, industries or enterprises to perpetuate and attract mobile production factors ('ability to attract'). Consequently, the inflow or the balance of foreign direct investments (FDI) and the attraction of human capital could be taken as crucial indicators for international competitiveness. Though, the FDI balance is an ambivalent indicator. Firstly, an FDI inflow could result from barriers to trade which simultaneously reduce the international competitiveness. Secondly, a positive FDI balance could indicate that the economy is not as developed as the investor′s country so that foreign capital that is needed to develop markets and to foster economic growth is attracted by a relatively high yield. Thirdly, there are also good reasons to

---

[374] In the short run, low wages can increase the competitiveness of enterprises. In the long run, relatively low wages would indicate low competitiveness. As regards empirical evidence, 'growing market shares and growing relative unit labour costs tend to be positively associated' (Fagerberg (1996) p. 40).

[375] Cf. Stierle (2002) pp. 5ff.

take into account the FDI outflow as a positive factor and indicator of international competitiveness. An increase of FDI outflow does not necessarily result in a loss of domestic production, employment, and locational attractiveness; it also indicates the ability of domestic enterprises to internationalize, to grow, to generate economies of scale, to develop new markets, and to promote an international vertical integration. Since both the state and the private sector are able to influence the attractiveness of the economy and to attract FDI and human capital, this indicator could be applied on different aspects, i.e. one could establish different indicators of attractiveness, for example an indicator for the attractiveness of a certain region (e.g. resulting from relatively low taxes, relatively low factor costs, and a competitive environment) and for the attractiveness of a certain industry (e.g. with regard to an industrial cluster where innovative and competitive companies, that are already located there, attract further foreign investors and human capital). In practice, there could be significant interactions between public and private activities to foster the ability to attract so that it is doubtful whether the national 'ability to attract' internationally mobile production factors is dominantly determined by the government. Though, the government's efforts to increase the locational attractiveness could be regarded as a decisive factor or even as a prerequisite for domestic companies' ability to be more successful in international markets than foreign competitors and to generate a relatively high income level.

Furthermore, one could focus on the ability of domestic enterprises and industries to sell their products successfully and profitably on foreign markets ('ability to sell and earn').[376] Consequently, export market shares and profit rates of domestic enterprises or industries on foreign markets could serve as ex post indicators and these microeconomic indicators could be aggregated to macroeconomic indicators.[377] Furthermore, the balance of trade, the exchange rate, and the relative global trade and export shares could be taken as macroeconomic indicators of the 'ability to sell'.[378] This approach widely corresponds to a purely microeconomic concept of international competitiveness because it focuses on the *enterprises'* international performance. As regards the reliability and validity of these indicators, market shares and profit rates could be influenced or manipulated by problematic factors like, for instance, anticompetitive market conduct, export subsidies, exchange rate variations, cuts in wages, expansive mone-

[376] Cf. Balassa (1962) p. 29. It has to be taken into account that, according to Balassa, the 'ability to sell' on foreign markets indicates the international competitiveness only in case of fixed exchange rates (cf. Reichel (2002) p. 18).

[377] See Stierle (2002) pp. 78ff.

[378] Cf. Reichel (2002) pp. 135ff., 264ff., 313ff.

tary policy, or even protectionist measures.[379] This is why these indicators are not reliable as regards the indication of an increase in national welfare, especially in the short run. Correspondingly, as regards the competitiveness of domestic industries, the revealed comparative advantage (RCA) also does not indicate an increase in welfare because the RCA just compares the export quota of a domestic industry with the export quota of the whole economy, indicating the relative success of a domestic industry on foreign markets and the economy´s pattern of industrial specialization.[380] Furthermore, the trade balance is characterized by an ambivalent interpretation with regard to competitiveness and welfare, too.[381] The example of the USA shows that a high external deficit does not automatically indicate a lack of welfare and international competitiveness; the deficit simply indicates that the USA consume and invest more than they currently produce.[382] One could possibly even state that an external deficit indicates international competitiveness, as a sign of international credit worthiness, a high inflow of foreign capital, high investments, and a high standard of living.[383] Consequently, one should look more carefully on each individual case and focus on the long-term external balance because it is unlikely to achieve a long-term surplus despite a lack of international competitiveness. Though, in the long run, the balance of trade generally is characterized by its self-compensating mechanism, especially in case of flexible exchange rates which will be discussed below.

In order to exclude the above mentioned problematic influences and the ambivalence of interpretation, the international competitiveness could be defined more narrowly as a sustainable growth in productivity and innovativeness. In many industries, the 'ability to sell and earn' depends, for the most part, on the *technological* competitiveness of domestic enterprises. Therefore, a more reliable, though restricted approach to indicate international competitiveness could be to analyze the ability of domestic indus-

---

379 Lachmann (2001) p. 8.

380 Reichel (2002) pp. 242ff., 262f.

381 For a more comprehension discussion of the trade balance as an indicator of international competitiveness, see ibid. pp. 135ff.

382 In addition to this, the trade balance could be a misleading indicator for countries like the USA who conduct relatively little international trade compared to their gross domestic product so that national welfare is primarily a result of domestic productivity (Krugman (1994) p. 5).

383 For a critical view on this aspect, see Reichel (2002) pp. 136ff.; also cf. Krugman (1994, p. 4) who refers to the case of Mexico´s debt crisis era in the 1980s which forced Mexico 'to run huge trade surpluses in the 1980s in order to pay the interest on its foreign debt' and 'began to run large trade deficits after 1990 as foreign investors recovered confidence'.

tries and enterprises to innovate efficient production processes and new marketable products ('ability to innovate') and to adjust to new developments on international markets, for example to react quickly on economic shocks or to specialize on new (high tech) products whose global demand is much higher than global supply ('ability to adjust').[384] The number of (new) patents, the degree of specialization of domestic enterprises, the overall productivity rate, and the ability to change the specialization towards markets and products with a promising future could be measured and taken as an indicator because it is likely that countries whose enterprises are able to innovate and to adjust quickly and efficiently to new forms of specialization on new and growing markets are internationally competitive.[385]

The multitude of definitions and indicators is helpful to understand the complexity of the competitiveness debate, but it is doubtful whether there exists an order of rank among these indicators which would be important for establishing a more precise theory of international competitiveness. In practice, the multitude of indicators and the missing hierarchy rather leads to the construction of compiled and multidimensional indicators that allow a broader view on competitiveness.[386] Nonetheless, there are even attempts to identify one certain final outcome of competitiveness and to define one 'catch-all' indicator that is apt to measure international competitiveness.

Some adopt the view that as a final, long-term result of international competitiveness, the citizens should enjoy a relatively high economic welfare (see Chap. 3.2.2.1).[387] In this perspective, for instance, the real per capita income or the gross domestic product could be placed at the top of a hierarchy of indicators so that all other indicators only function as interim indicators, probably giving an early signal about the development of a country's international competitiveness. But it is doubtful whether the real per capita income or other indicators of economic prosperity are valid final results or indicators of welfare and international competitiveness. Eco-

---

384 Cf. Lachmann (2001) pp. 5f.

385 Cf. Gottwald (1992) p. 19.

386 The number of dimensions or indicators that are covered by an index varies dramatically among different concepts. For an index based on a small number of dimensions, see, for instance, Gapinski who focuses on microeconomic dimensions, defining competitiveness as 'the ability to provide internationally a quality product promptly at a reasonable price' (Gapinski (2001) pp. 36ff.). In contrast to this, the World Economic Forum publishes an index that includes over 100 indicators, both microeconomic and macroeconomic dimensions, that are grouped into nine pillars (see Lopez-Claros et al. (2006)).

387 Cf. Boltho (1996) p. 2.

nomic welfare also depends on other factors such as income distribution[388], savings, and natural resources.[389] These factors do not reliably indicate international competitiveness. Furthermore, economic welfare can also be the result of an excellent *national* market performance (while the *international* performance is of average degree)[390] and – as economic history has shown – high economic welfare also can be the beginning of economic decline or decreasing competitiveness so that welfare is an ambivalent indicator.

According to several economists, the real (effective) exchange rate could be the most favourable 'final' indicator of international competitiveness.[391] In order to prevent a misinterpretation of the exchange rate, one has to take into account some additional aspects because the exchange rate is characterized by some peculiarities. Firstly, the exchange rate also can be used as a *factor* of competitiveness so that this indicator could be deeply influenced by the government, at least in the short run.[392] In the long run,

---

[388] If a country increases its competitiveness, this does not necessarily mean that all sections of the population benefit. There could be winners and losers so that the social welfare function finally decides whether the national welfare has been increased or reduced.

[389] The role of a rich endowment of natural resources with regard to the international competitiveness is ambivalent. On the one hand, natural resources can serve to promote the international competitiveness, for example according to the Heckscher-Ohlin-Model. On the other hand, the mere existence of natural resources does not automatically strengthen the competitiveness of domestic firms and it does not significantly promote the locational attractiveness of the nation. To the contrary, natural resources could give false incentives and impede a further industrialization and modernization of the economy. Furthermore, problems like the so-called 'Dutch Disease' could occur in case of high exports of natural resources which revalue the domestic currency, harm other domestic industries′ international competitiveness, and reduce the inflow of foreign direct investments.

[390] Cf. Krugman (1994) p. 5.

[391] Cf. Reichel (2002) pp. 313ff.; cf. Bofinger (1995) pp. 467ff.; cf. Erlandsson and Markowski (2006) pp. 10ff. Also cf. Boltho (1996) pp. 2f. 13, who equates competitiveness in the short run with the value of the real exchange rate, 'defined as an index of relative unit labour costs in a common currency'.

[392] Berg states with regard to the Federal Republic of Germany during the Bretton-Woods-System of fixed exchange rates ('adjustable peg system'), that as long as Germany was able to avert or delay an overdue upward revaluation of its currency, there was no need for specific activities to promote the international competitiveness (cf. Berg (1983) p. 5). This formulation is inappropriate because a nation′s resistance against an upward revaluation within the Bretton-

the exchange rate should generate external balance and could serve as an endogenous indicator. Secondly, one should consider to which extent the exchange rate is controlled by the national government and to which degree international markets (international trade and foreign exchange markets) or foreign countries determine the exchange rate. The following explanations refer to a regime of floating exchange rates.[393]

A governmentally controlled depreciation and (temporary) undervaluation has the potential to increase the international competitiveness in the short run. Firstly, a depreciation of the national currency has the effect of an export subsidy and affects the price competitiveness of domestic products. This is especially important for countries whose products are mostly tradables so that they have a relatively high export quota. Secondly, it could promote the inflow of foreign direct investments. Thirdly, both a short-term and a long-term undervaluation controlled by the national government could serve as an *indicator* of international competitiveness because this underlines a country´s 'ability to control'.[394] Though, it has to be taken into account that there are many ambivalent and also negative effects that could result from a depreciation.[395] For instance, a reduced outflow of foreign direct investments, an increased inflation, and capital flight could reduce the international competitiveness of the nation. Furthermore, retaliatory measures of foreign countries are likely if these countries regard the depreciation as a form of protectionism or 'beggar-thy-neighbour' policy.

In contrast to a depreciation that is controlled by the government, a significant and long-term depreciation forced by the international (foreign exchange) markets (for example by international trade or speculative attacks) primarily indicates a loss of competitiveness and national welfare although, in the short run, the depreciation could help to maintain the international competitiveness. According to Lachmann, 'there is always an ex-

Woods-System can be viewed as a specific activity to promote the economy´s competitiveness.

393 In case of fixed foreign exchange rates, a country would lack international competitiveness 'if it runs a sustained balance of payments deficit. The country is internationally competitive if it has external balance or a balance of payments surplus' (Bloch and Kenyon (2001a) p. 22).

394 The currency policy of PR China possibly could be taken as an example for this. From 1994-2005, there existed a fixed exchange rate between the Chinese currency yuan and the US dollar. According to the USA, this de facto US dollar peg had led to a protectionist undervaluation of the yuan which distorted global trade and harmed the US economy. This example of China shows that even a long-term undervaluation could be seen as an indicator of competitiveness as long as the country has the ability to control its currency.

395 Cf. Boltho (1996) pp. 7ff.

change rate which helps a country to be internationally competitive for some sectors. There will always be an exchange rate, if we have flexible exchange rates, that matches exports with imports'[396]. Though, in the long run, inevitable depreciations are a sign of uncompetitiveness and a depreciation-inflation spiral could even result in a currency crisis and a macroeconomic crisis.

Analogously, an upward revaluation forced by the political pressure of other countries would reduce the international competitiveness, whereas a long-term upward revaluation of the domestic currency, caused by the markets or by deliberate exchange market interventions of the government, rather indicates a high international competitiveness of domestic products. A long-term strong currency indicates low inflation, relatively low production costs, and favourable commodity terms of trade, which means that domestic products are successful on foreign markets – in extreme cases because of a monopoly position or scarce natural resources – so that they can be sold at relatively high prices, compared to foreign import goods. This corresponds to an increase in national welfare. Nevertheless, such an upward revaluation simultaneously could weaken the international competitiveness so that the positive net effect on the international competitiveness and national welfare could be reduced or even eliminated by the upward revaluation. The exchange rate elasticities of exports and imports would play a decisive role in this respect, similar to the Marshall-Lerner Condition and the J-Curve which explain and describe the real exchange rate effects on the balance of trade.

To sum up, there is no indicator that can show at a first glance whether a country is internationally competitive or not. Both the long-term real per capita income and the long-term real effective exchange rate should be taken as main indicators, but it is necessary to look more closely on the specific national and international conditions and political activities which take influence on these indicators. A domestic currency that – in the long run – is not influenced by governmental distortions and that increases in value, combined with an external macroeconomic balance and a long-term increase of real per capita income, seems to be the most reliable indicator of international competitiveness.[397]

3.2.2.3 Factors of International Competitiveness

The indicators (dependent variables) of international competitiveness have to be distinguished from the determinants or factors (independent vari-

---

[396] Lachmann (2001) p. 7.

[397] Cf. Reichel (2002) pp. 313ff., 428f., 485ff.

ables) of competitiveness. An indicator validly and reliably has to depict and measure the effects that the factors finally contribute to the international competitiveness. An indicator has to react precisely and consistently on changes of the observed factors that are supposed to be essential for international competitiveness. But there is a fundamental problem. The differentiation between factors and indicators of international competitiveness does not succeed completely in practice because several factors could be taken as indicators, too. In other words, some results of economic competitiveness can be taken as a factor for future competitiveness, for example the inflow of foreign direct investments. Furthermore, some factors of competitiveness could be so important and decisive for the international competitiveness of the nation that they already signal international competitiveness. For instance, the unit labour costs and the real exchange rate could be taken both as factors and as indicators.

Classification and Concepts. Economic literature has gathered a multitude of possible determinants of competitiveness. In fact, many of these factors have a long tradition in economic growth theory. For instance, in an early study of the question why national growth rates differ, Denison had given an analysis about the sources of long-term differing growth rates of nine western countries in the postwar period.[398] The quantity and quality of over twenty factors like the level of income, capital and labour input, educational attainment, economies of scale, natural resources, advances of knowledge, lag in application of knowledge, and improved allocation of resources have been taken to explain why postwar growth rates of national income differed, though based on a number of assumptions and estimations. Denison himself described his analysis as a 'hazardous and speculative undertaking'[399] because the subject of economic growth is a comprehensive and complex issue. This problem also adheres to modern competitiveness literature. Factors of competitiveness vary from concept to concept so that they are equally controversial as the indicators of competitiveness.

Besides the two above mentioned fundamental questions as to whether there is such thing as an international competitiveness of nations and whether there exists a clear and unambiguous indicator, there is a third fundamental debate about the question, what role especially governments and what role primarily domestic enterprises can play in increasing the international competitiveness of the nation, both as regards the locational attractiveness of the nation and the international competitiveness of domestic

398 Denison (1967).
399 Ibid. p. 3.

enterprises. One may think that governmental activities primarily influence the locational attractiveness of the nation whereas the microeconomic environment and entrepreneurial activities mainly determine the international competitiveness of the domestic enterprises. Though, things do not seem to be so simple. The following table 3.2 shows that governmental and entrepreneurial activities take influence on both the locational attractiveness of the nation and on the international competitiveness of domestic enterprises, often simultaneously. This is especially true as regards governmental activities, i.e. when governments intend to promote the locational attractiveness of the nation, in most cases they simultaneously strengthen the international competitiveness of the incumbent domestic firms. Though, governments have a limited scope for selective political measures that exclusively favour foreign production factors, for example by establishing special economic zones like investment promotion zones or export processing zones.

Some economists rather underline the role of the state as the most important factor of international competitiveness, partly falling back upon the findings of growth and development theory.[400] In general, the discussion about state-induced factors of competitiveness is in danger to move in a wrong direction. Governmental activities to improve competitiveness could be misused as a pretext for other goals such as protectionism, interventionism, and lobbyism. For instance, lobbyists in Germany often direct the debate about the locational attractiveness of nations towards specific issues like supposedly too high labour costs, corporate taxes, and ecological standards.[401] In order to exclude protectionist and interventionist measures which could result from discretionary and direct political interferences, one should focus on the fundamental, long-term institutional, economic, and legal framework like, for example, an excellent public infrastructure (especially as regards the supply of public goods, an excellent education system, and an institutionalized public support of private R&D), relatively low taxes compared to other countries, low inflation, low costs of capital, supporting agglomeration (external scale economies[402]), envi-

[400] For a short survey, cf. Reichel (2002) pp. 92ff., 128ff.

[401] Cf. Müller and Kornmeier (2000) pp. 22ff., 122, 143ff.

[402] Cf. Venables (1996) pp. 52ff. Venables asks why 'the City of London [is] so heavily specialized in financial services, or Silicon Valley in electronics'. He states that the major patterns of specialization 'have no obvious basis in comparative advantage'. Instead, history or 'some small chance event' may have started some activity to be there, 'leading to a concentration of activity' – especially complementary activities – and higher profits or wages in this location. Though, the success of agglomeration in one sector could increase factor

ronmental protection, strict competition policy, and the accessibility of markets.

<table>
<tr><td></td><td></td><td colspan="2">Two Dimensions of the International Competitiveness of Nations</td></tr>
<tr><td></td><td></td><td>Locational Attractiveness of the Nation</td><td>International Competitiveness of Domestic Enterprises</td></tr>
<tr><td rowspan="3">Two Factors of the International Competitiveness of Nations</td><td rowspan="2">Government</td><td colspan="2">Fiscal Policy / Tax Policy
Monetary Policy: Low Inflation and Low Interest Rates
Currency Policy
Capital Market Regulation
Public Infrastructure
Social and Ecological Standards
Trade Policy and Competition Policy: Open and Free Markets
Education Policy
R&D Policy</td></tr>
<tr><td>Special Economic Zones for Foreign Investors</td><td>Industrial Policy for Domestic Firms, e.g. Export Processing Zones, R&D Policy
Promote Risk-Taking and Industriousness</td></tr>
<tr><td>Domestic Enterprises</td><td>Industrial Clusters
Pro-Competitive Behaviour
Readiness for Co-operation in R&D
Attractive Banking Services</td><td>Innovativeness
Pro-Competitive Behaviour
Productivity
Internationalization
Business Strategy
Management Capabilities
Firm Specific Human Capital
Export Orientation</td></tr>
</table>

Table 3.2: The Two Dimensions of International Competitiveness

prices and reduce the international competitiveness of another sector (Ibid. pp. 52, 60).

The creation of such an institutional framework which creates legal liability and low transaction costs has been the central aim of the ordo-liberal school of economics ('Ordnungspolitik') and the 'good governance' discussion. Though, the reason for the present interest in governmental strategies also lies in the positive historic experiences with the industrial policies in countries like Japan, South Korea, Singapore and PR China. These political measures primarily strengthened the international competitiveness of domestic enterprises, but some of them also had an influence on the locational attractiveness of the nation for foreign production factors.

Other economist rather emphasize the decisive role of enterprises – for example their innovativeness, productivity, technology, R&D efforts, their firm-specific human capital, their export orientation, their general business strategy or management capabilities – and other microeconomic factors like, for instance, factor conditions, demand conditions, and savings and investment rates. In many industries, factors like innovativeness and marketing have received a growing importance compared to the traditional price (Bertrand competition) and output competition (Cournot competition).[403] Furthermore, if the proponents of international harmonization would be successful in enforcing their many and diverse standardization claims (cf. Chap. 2.1), these microeconomic determinants of competitiveness would remain as the decisive factors of international competitiveness and locational attractiveness, besides some political and macroeconomic factors like education policy, health policy, family policy, and the endowment of natural resources, which would not or could not be harmonized.

Besides the differentiation between microeconomic and macroeconomic factors, it is also possible to distinguish between short-term and long-term factors, similar to the above discussion about the indicators of competitiveness. The following table 3.3 shows this classification and gives an overview over some of the most important factors:

403 Cf. Preusse (2001) pp. 7f.

	Microeconomic	**Macroeconomic**
Short-term	- Unit Labour Costs: Cut in Wages, Rationalization - Marketing: Price Policy, Advertising	- Currency Policy: Devaluation to Boost Exports - Monetary Policy: Interest Rates - Social Standards - Ecological Standards - Competition Policy: Market Accessibility - Trade Policy: Barriers to Foreign Trade - Capital Market Regulation - Fiscal Policy: Corporate Taxation - Labour Market Policy - Economic Laws: Bureaucracy etc.
Long-term	- Factor Conditions: (Firm-specific) Human Capital, Corporate Finance, Technology - Management and Business Strategy: Internationalization; Export Orientation; Specialization; Product Differentiation - Strategic Investments: New Technologies, FDI Outflows (Internationalization); R&D Investments for Innovativeness; Mergers and Acquisitions - Productivity: Process Innovations; EOS - Marketing: Reputation and Image (Brand Name etc.) - Demand Conditions	- Political System - Social and Moral Capital: Culture, Mentality, Ethics - Long-term/Potential Labour Force: Family Policy, Education Policy, Health Policy - Internationalization and Openness - Public Infrastructure - Size of Domestic Markets - Country Similarity - Efficiency of the Public Sector and Public Finance - Level of Agglomeration - Currency Policy - Monetary Policy: Inflation Rate

Table 3.3: Factors of International Competitiveness

As regards the differentiation between short-term and long-term effects of certain factors, there are two aspects to be underlined. Firstly, the short-term factors often also have long-term effects, whereas the long-term factors are not relevant for short-term competitiveness aims because long-term factors cannot be influenced significantly in the short run. Secondly, the differentiation between short-term and long-term factors involves a differentiation between a static and dynamic view as regards the effects of certain factors. Short-term competitive advantages finally can turn out to be long-term disadvantages. For instance, factors like low taxes, permissive competition policy, and low social and ecological standards could serve, in the short term, to reduce costs and to increase profits for enterprises so that these factors could be used to stop capital flight, to become an attractive location for foreign companies, and to increase the international competitiveness of domestic companies. Though, in the long run, low taxes and standards could reduce the international competitiveness of the companies and the locational attractiveness of the country. Low standards can reduce incentives to innovate whereas high standards induce factor substitution and innovations. Furthermore, low taxes could lead to a poor public infrastructure, and a too permissive competition policy could cause high prices and cartelized domestic industries which deter foreign companies from entering domestic markets.[404]

Most concepts of international competitiveness take into account both microeconomic market conduct and governmental influences, and they include both short-term and long-term factors.[405] In contrast to the debate on an adequate indicator of international competitiveness, there is a consensus that no factor *alone* can ensure international competitiveness. For instance, the Global Competitiveness Report 2006-2007 has classified Switzerland to be the most competitive country, taking into consideration both six macroeconomic factors – i.e. the institutional environment (e.g. the protection of [intellectual] property rights; transparency and stability of public institutions), the infrastructure, the national economy (e.g. the avoidance of macroeconomic imbalances), the health and primary education system, and the efficiency of markets – and three microeconomic factors – i.e. the technological readiness or status quo, the capacity for technological innovativeness (expenditures on R&D) of the firms, and the sophistication of busi-

---

[404] Cf. Scholz and Staehler (1999). As regards the long-term effect of factors like low taxes, the final outcome with regard to the international competitiveness generally is ambivalent. For instance, Switzerland was able to attract a lot of capital by means of low tax rates so that the total tax revenue increased.

[405] Though, many concepts do not explicitly differentiate between all these categories, especially as regards the short-term and long-term dimension of each factor.

ness culture.[406] These nine pillars of competitiveness are themselves based on a multitude of sub-factors.

One of the first concepts of international competitiveness, the so-called diamond model, developed by Porter[407], focuses on the microeconomic factors of international competitiveness but also includes the role of the state. Porter´s model explains the competitive advantage of a nation in a certain industry by means of six factors.[408] The four most important factors of competitiveness are the so-called determinants. They are endogenous factors because they belong to the characteristics of the national industry itself. These four determinants – (1) the factor conditions, (2) the demand conditions, (3) the related and supporting industries, and (4) the firm strategy, structure, and rivalry – are interrelated so that when they are illustrated schematically it looks like a diamond (see Fig. 3.1).

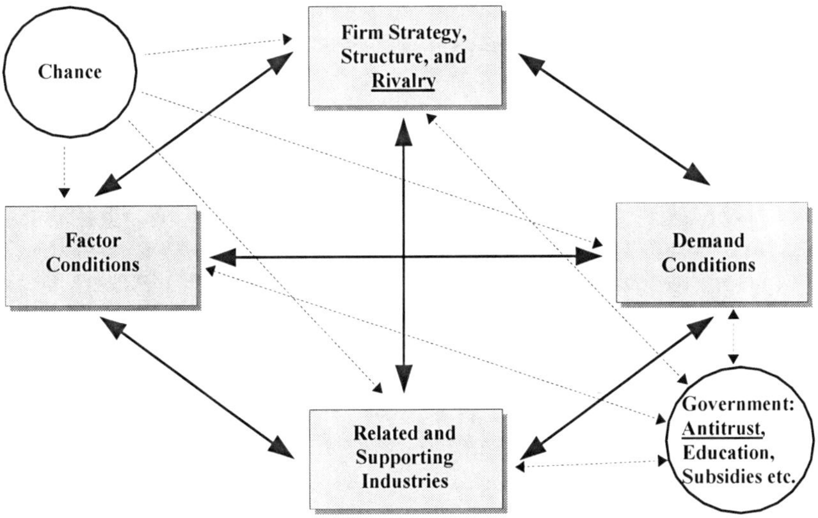

Fig. 3.1: Porter´s Diamond Model

[406] Lopez-Claros et al. (2006); cf. Frankfurter Allgemeine Zeitung (2006a) p. 14. As regards publications like the Global Competitiveness Report, they provide a lot of interesting data, but their conclusions and scientific foundation are disputed.

[407] Porter (1990).

[408] Ibid. pp. 69ff.

According to Porter, every national industry has its own 'diamond' which determines its international competitiveness. Porter completed this model by adding two exogenous factors, chance and government. The factor 'chance' influences the four endogenous factors spontaneously but naturally cannot be influenced by them. Porter says that chance events play a role as 'acts of pure invention', 'significant shifts in world financial markets' or 'discontinuities in input costs such as oil shocks'.[409] In contrast to this, the factor 'government' is interrelated with the four endogenous factors, i.e. 'government' can influence the four endogenous factors positively and negatively (for example by means of subsidies, education policy etc.) and the four endogenous factors themselves can influence the exogenous factor 'government', for example 'strong home demand for a product may lead to early introduction of government safety standards'[410]. As regards the role of governments, Porter acknowledged that many economists 'see it as a vital, if not the most important, influence on modern international competition' so that – especially with regard to the positive historic experiences with government policy in countries like Japan and South Korea – 'it is tempting to make government the fifth determinant'[411]. Nonetheless, Porter rejected this position, but he underlined the important role of 'government' by influencing the four determinants, 'though its role is inevitably partial. Government policy will fail if it remains the only source of national competitive advantage'[412]. The fault the critics find with the diamond model is that this model concentrates too much on industries and national microeconomic conditions so that it underestimates the role of government and multinational activities.[413] Consequently, Porter´s model cannot be applied on underdeveloped and small economies which actively have to utilize governmental intervention and international variables to enhance their competitiveness: 'In fact, Porter recognized the importance of international or global variables for a nation´s competitiveness, but his diamond model did not explicitly include these variables'.[414]

Despite these deficiencies, Porter´s concept is a helpful starting point for considering the relationship between (national or international) competition rules and the international competitiveness of nations. Porter explicitly mentions the role of domestic inter-firm rivalry as a determinant of com-

[409] Ibid. pp. 124ff.
[410] Ibid. p. 128.
[411] Ibid. p. 126.
[412] Ibid. p. 128.
[413] Ibid. pp. 67f., 617ff.
[414] Cho and Moon (2000) p. xv.

parative advantage.[415] Despite his focus on the microeconomic level of inter-firm rivalry, Porter also considered the role of competition policy as a governmental factor which influences the determinant 'firm strategy, structure, and rivalry': 'Government policy also influences firm strategy, structure, and rivalry, through such devices as capital market regulations, tax policy, and antitrust laws.'[416] Though, Porter did not explicitly differentiate between national and international competition policy.

Competition Policy as a Factor of International Competitiveness. The predominant factors in economic competitiveness literature, as regards the role of the government, are industrial policy, currency policy, capital market regulation, corporate taxation, labour market policy, trade policy, social and environmental standards, and education policy. Many authors do not explicitly integrate the role of (national or international) competition policy as a factor of international competitiveness.[417] Though, closely related to the theory of industrial policy and industrial organization, merger policy traditionally has been regarded as an important strategy to foster efficiency, innovation, and competitiveness of domestic *enterprises*, often at the expense of intensive competition. On the other hand, competitive markets are generally considered to enhance the innovativeness and international competitiveness of domestic *enterprises*.

For instance, according to the European Commission, 'empirical findings do not give conclusive support to the idea that market concentration and reduced competition is conducive to innovation. Evidence suggests that the likelihood of innovation is higher among firms in competitive industries. Fewer competitors and higher average profits are also associated with lower productivity growth.'[418] Hence the European Commission concludes that 'vigorous competition in a supportive business environment is a key driver of productivity growth and competitiveness. However, competition is not an end in itself. It is a vital market process which rewards firms offering lower prices, better quality, new products, and greater choice'[419]. This is true both for the domestic market and for international markets: 'There is also ample evidence that vigorous domestic competition promotes success in international markets ...; as a principal factor behind

---

415 Porter (1990) pp. 117ff.

416 See ibid. p. 128.

417 The following publications on international competitiveness do not explicitly mention the role of competition policy: Bofinger (1995) pp. 467-497; Fendel and Frenkel (2005) pp. 26-32; Müller and Kornmeier (2000); Reichel (2002); Siebert (2000) pp. 6ff.

418 European Commission (2004a) pp. 4f.

419 Ibid. p. 3.

increased innovation and growth in productivity, effective competition between firms in the enlarged internal market must be seen as one of the key elements of a successful strategy to build up a competitive Europe and reinvigorate the Lisbon Strategy.'[420] According to this strategy, the EU focuses on the innovativeness and productivity of domestic enterprises, whereas the locational attractiveness of the EU seems to be of secondary importance. Consequently, there is a danger to focus too much on industrial policy instead of providing for attractive locational conditions. In this way, the European Union uses the concept of international competitiveness as a justification of its competition policy, saying that the integration of the common market and the international competitiveness of the European industry require a strict and harmonized European competition policy.

Nevertheless, the EU and other authors fail to define precisely what international competitiveness is and how competition policy in detail takes influence on the international competitiveness. In particular, there is no differentiation between national and international competition policy and between the competitiveness of enterprises and nations. This is problematic because the transfer of antitrust competences from the national to the international level could be disadvantageous for the international competitiveness of nations. This issue will be discussed in the following Chap. 4.

3.3 Conclusion

The modern discussion about the international competitiveness of nations is characterized by different approaches to define this phenomenon and by a multitude of indicators and factors of competitiveness that have been collected by economic literature. In conclusion, the theoretical deficits as regards the definition, the indicators, and the factors of international competitiveness leave open the question what 'international competitiveness of nations' really is and to what extent the indicators really indicate international competitiveness and whether the observed factors really are the decisive factors of international competitiveness. Nonetheless, as regards a macroeconomic concept of international (locational) competitiveness, we have to recognize that – in times of economic globalization – national economic policy undergoes an international test. Governments can improve conditions for attracting foreign production factors and they can adjust politics to strengthen the competitiveness of domestic enterprises so that, as the final long-term outcome, the nation is characterized by a relatively

[420] Ibid. p. 4f.

high welfare and a strong currency. Therefore it seems to be adequate to define the international competitiveness of nations in two ways.[421]

On the one hand, the international competitiveness of nations is the ability of nations to foster successful economic activities by attracting new investors, mobile capital, and human capital. Consequently, the concept of international competitiveness of nations has to be located within the debate on the international locational competition and the relative attractiveness of a region for production factors which are characterized by mobility and a great international demand for them. Locational factors become increasingly important in global economics so that the governments have to focus on their role to create an attractive (macroeconomic) environment for production factors. They are confronted with an international locational competition that is – on the one hand – characterized by rivalry, but – on the other hand – international trade has the potential to result in a positive-sum game so that all countries can profit.

On the other hand, the concept of an international competitiveness of nations also could be used with respect to political efforts to strengthen the international competitiveness of domestic enterprises. Governments should not only try to attract new investors and other production factors, but they also should adjust their national politics in order to promote business activities and the competitiveness of domestic firms which are involved in foreign trade. Consequently, the international competitiveness of the nation could be viewed as the aggregated international competitiveness of its firms. The crucial point to be acknowledged in this respect is that although this interpretation of 'international competitiveness of nations' actually refers to the international competitiveness of domestic enterprises, not only companies themselves but also national governments and their politics decide about the international competitiveness of firms by setting the right institutional framework for private business activities and by avoiding arbitrary and direct interferences which rather harm the economic development. Whether it is adequate to call this 'international competitiveness of nations', comes down to a mere semantic issue.

To sum up, a differentiation between these two forms of competitiveness and an acknowledgement of the fact that governments can take influence on the competitiveness of firms – for example by means of competition policy – could help to reconcile the conflicting positions as regards the microeconomic and macroeconomic dimension of competitiveness. As already mentioned above, some economists, who support a purely micro-

[421] A similar differentiation can be found in Müller and Kornmeier (2000) p. 21.

economic approach, also accept the existence of a locational competition between nations.

4 National Competition Policy and International Competitiveness

The debate on an international harmonization and centralization of competition law and policy touches two crucial issues. Firstly, one has to analyze the necessity and the modalities of an international harmonization and centralization in antitrust. This issue focuses on the question whether international competition rules are inevitable to protect national and international competition. Chapter 2 has dealt with this question. Secondly, one has to take into account the positive and negative effects which could result from an international harmonization and centralization of competition law and policy. With regard to this task, this investigation focuses on negative effects on the international competitiveness of nations. Both aspects – i.e. the analysis of the necessity of international competition rules and the description of possible negative effects – have to be weighed against each other, so that even if there were some arguments in favour of international competition rules, the importance of *national* competition policy for the international competitiveness of a nation probably could be taken as a justification for keeping up *national* competition policy.

As regards the first question concerning the necessity and the modalities of international competition rules, the whole debate on international antitrust mainly concentrates on this issue. Furthermore, many authors do not even discuss the necessity and concentrate on the modalities. Consequently, the debate on international competition policy gets a bias towards the alleged necessity and advantages of international harmonization or centralization in antitrust. Nonetheless, Chap. 2 has led to the conclusion that a far-reaching harmonization of competition law or the establishment of an omnipotent global competition authority is not necessary.

As regards the second question concerning the negative economic consequences of the diverse models of international competition policy, these problems are often neglected. Especially the effects on the international competitiveness of nations generally are not taken into account. Correspondingly, compared to other factors of competitiveness, the role of *national* competition policy – as counterpart to *international* competition policy – has been neglected within the competitiveness debate although competition policy *in general* is known as an instrument to support industrial policy and other political activities. Consequently, the following investigation will take a critical point of view against harmonization claims; the negative effects on the international competitiveness of nations will be the focus of attention.

In accordance to the above definition of international competitiveness of nations (see Chap. 3.2.2.1), *national* competition policy has to be analyzed with regard to the question whether it is a useful and feasible instrument to enhance the attractiveness of an economy for foreign investors and skilled people and to promote the international competitiveness of domestic producers in order to increase national welfare, mainly indicated by a strong domestic currency, in the long run. This issue also includes the question whether *national* competition policy is a more effective method to promote international competitiveness than an *international* harmonization and centralization of competition policy. This aspect, i.e. the promotion of international competitiveness, cannot be reduced to the interim aim to protect national and international competition because the protection of competition is only one of many factors which can be used to foster international competitiveness by means of national competition policy. Though, the protection of competition always has to be guaranteed.

These questions will be taken into account within the following investigation, in which the positive effects of national competition policy on the international competitiveness of nations are to be emphasized. The investigation will start with the description of some introductory remarks in Chap. 4.1, including the fundamental assumptions and guiding principles of this investigation. In Chap. 4.2, we will highlight several general and rather indirect negative effects of an international harmonization and centralization of competition policy on the international competitiveness of nations. After this preliminary work, Chap. 4.3 will describe the central issues, i.e. the *direct* influence of *national* competition policy on promoting the international competitiveness of the nation. Here we will concentrate on two central questions. Chapter 4.3.2 underlines diverse positive effects of *national* competition policy which result from its ability to take into account the specific characteristics and interests of the national economy by maintaining a certain degree of flexibility in antitrust. Chapter 4.3.3 also refers to this issue of flexibility by describing the advantages and disadvantages of practicing a rather permissive, protectionist, or strict competition policy.

4.1 Fundamental Assumptions and Differentiations

The following investigation about the positive effects of national competition policy on the international competitiveness of a nation is based on some fundamental assumptions about national competition policy. National competition policy has to meet several standards and prerequisites in order to be a valid factor of international competitiveness.

4.1.1 The Existence of a Modern Competition Law and Policy

Firstly, this investigation presupposes the existence of a modern and comprehensive national competition law including the major substantive and procedural provisions against restrictive business practices. Furthermore, national competition policy has to be endowed with sufficient financial and human resources in order to enforce these laws.[422] For instance, the antitrust regimes of the European Union and the United States could be taken as a benchmark. This assumption is necessary because otherwise national competition policy would not be able to achieve better results in its antitrust enforcement compared to an international competition policy regime. This is not only important with regard to merger and concentration policy, which traditionally has been used as an instrument of industrial politics in order to promote international competitiveness. National competition authorities also have to be well equipped with regard to the fight against anticompetitive agreements because, as already mentioned above, international cartels and other modern forms of inter-firm cooperation have become the most severe challenge for the protection of global competition so that future harmonization claims could concentrate on this problem. Consequently, national competition policy increasingly has to focus on these issues in order to protect competition and competitiveness.

---

[422] For a short overview as regards (a) the major 'substantive conduct and structural provisions relating to business activity' and (b) 'additional procedural provisions on administration and enforcement' which determine the institutional arrangement, see Khemani (1998) pp. 148ff. Also cf. Anderson and Khosla (1995, pp. 21f.) who give an overview of the main institutional requirements for an effective competition policy.

4.1.2 National Competition Authorities

The *particular* organizational structure, division of labour, and institutional embedding of *national* competition policy can be seen as a factor of international competitiveness. Nonetheless, national competition policy should meet certain *standards* which should not be part of the international regulatory competition. A crucial issue is the degree of the national competition authority's political independence. In general, an *independent* competition authority and independent judges can be seen as a key factor for an effective protection of competition, whereas government antitrust officials 'have an interest in an excessively interventionist antitrust policy' that makes 'competition law depart from a consumer welfare ideal'[423]. Though, as regards the competitiveness debate, the question arises to what extent national governments should be allowed to take direct and discretionary influence on antitrust policy in order to promote the international competitiveness of the nation. This is a critical question because, in certain cases, there could be a trade-off between the protection of competition and the promotion of international competitiveness. The politicians could be willing to take decisions in strict opposition to the antitrust authority's and judges' point of view. This could result in governmental interventions that have adverse consequences for the country's trading position and its international competitiveness.

In order to avoid this problem, an independent national antitrust authority or antitrust court generally should be responsible for all cases of antitrust, even if these cases touch fundamental issues of international competitiveness. The protection of competition has to be the primary aim. Though, independent competition authorities and judges[424] also could use their scope of action to take into account additional considerations like the international competitiveness of domestic companies. As regards the role of national politicians, there remains a significant scope of action for them, for example by means of legislation and certain institutional functions. The

---

[423] McGinnis (2004) p. 128. The bureaucrats desire to maximize budgets, prestige, and employment opportunities also affects an independent competition authority, but an independent competition authority offers more institutional options to reduce or control this problem of rent-seeking and interventionism.

[424] Areeda (1992, pp. 32f.) has underlined the crucial and beneficial role of independent lawyers and judges in US antitrust enforcement: 'There is no other country in the world in which such important national economic decisions are made on such a decentralized, undebated, and largely nonexpert basis'. Areeda mainly refers to antitrust decisions that played a major role in US industrial policy. He doubts that governmental administrators and planners would do a better job than the courts.

government and the parliament still would be allowed to decide on fundamental issues like, for instance, the general exemption of industries and business practices from antitrust law. Furthermore, they could keep a discretionary scope of action by means of certain legal institutions, for example in merger control in order to guarantee the priority of superior national interests over mere antitrust considerations (cf. the so-called ministerial permission in German merger control).

4.1.3 Exclusion of State-Induced Protectionism

This analysis also has to consider the question to what extent national competition policy can be seen as an internationally acceptable way to improve international competitiveness or whether this would generally lead to protectionist and discriminatory strategies which promote the international competitiveness by harming global competition, applying beggar-thy-neighbour policies, and promoting international market concentration and monopolization.

Former approaches concerning the relation between competition policy and competitiveness also deal with the protectionist misuse of competition policy, especially by means of state-induced concentration politics in recent decades in order to create national champions and to prevent imports from foreign competitors.[425] Furthermore, export cartels are a prominent example.[426] In contrast to these cases of discriminatory and protectionist abuse of competition policy, the following investigation exclusively concentrates on non-protectionist and non-discriminatory possibilities to practice a national competition policy that strengthens the international com-

[425] Cf. Berg (1983) pp. 6ff. Berg describes the unsuccessful attempts of several European industrial countries since the fifties of the last century. These countries wanted to promote the competitiveness of their national computer industry by means of concentration policy.

[426] As regards export cartels, one has to differentiate between (a) export cartels that have been initiated by exporting enterprises and that are tolerated by the domestic antitrust authority and (b) export cartels that are enforced by the government of the importing country so that it works like a so-called voluntary export restraint. In the latter case, the export cartel is an instrument of trade policy and should be covered by the WTO (cf. Chap. 2.4.1.1). These voluntary export restraints are especially harmful for domestic consumers and sometimes even beneficial for foreign exporters. For an analysis of how export cartels can be used as a protectionist instrument by the importing country, see Stearns-Bläsing (2004) pp. 67ff., 78ff.

petitiveness. Though, the probability and the possible legitimacy of protectionist strategies in exceptional cases are considered in Chap. 4.3.3.2, too.

It is important to emphasize that making use of all legal instruments of national competition policy is only legitimate as long as it is not misused for discriminatory, protectionist or other unfair measures. In general, protectionist measures are neither ethically, nor economically acceptable and recommendable. Consequently, a plea for *national* competition policy has to make clear the scope of *excellent* national competition policy[427] – i.e. the promotion of international competitiveness through national competition policy without harming global competition and without discriminating and harming foreign enterprises and countries – and to highlight the resulting advantages compared to internationally harmonized competition policy. In this way, excellent national antitrust is allowed to pursue local interests, but on the basis of neutral national antitrust laws that do not discriminate among domestic and foreign companies: 'Advanced industrial democracies ... have developed formal rules and a legal culture that require decision makers to consider only those criteria that the law makes relevant. Thus, the judiciary, and to some extent the bureaucracy, will be constrained to take foreign interests into account'[428].

4.2 General Negative Effects of International Competition Rules

The introduction of international competition rules would touch some fundamental characteristics of present antitrust policy. The most fundamental effect would be the far-reaching abolition of *national* competition policy so that national antitrust authorities would – to a far extent – lose the possibility to *directly* use antitrust politics to strengthen the international competitiveness of the nation (cf. Chap. 4.3). Besides this, an international antitrust regime would cause some institutional changes that itself could be harmful for the international competitiveness of participating nations, though in a more indirect manner. The following subchapters describe these problems.

[427] Cf. Chap. 4.3.1.

[428] McGinnis (2004) p. 134.

4.2.1 Problems of Case and Competence Allocation

The establishment of an international competition authority would probably lead to a network of national and international institutions which have to cooperate and which have to organize the allocation of antitrust cases. The experience within the European Union shows that such a network – which probably would be characterized both by parallel competences and by a dominance of the international competition authority – has problems to allocate and to re-allocate cases and competences. The borderline between national and international cases can not be clarified thoroughly, the deficiencies of the formal case allocation system can not be removed entirely by new laws. Criteria like 'affecting the international market' or 'affecting at least two national markets' are just a theoretical starting point of case allocation, but they do not solve the problem of inefficient case allocation. Consequently, an international antitrust regime would not necessarily lead to an efficient case allocation. Furthermore, it could be subject to frequent competence allocation debates in order to reduce present deficiencies and to adjust to new developments.

Correspondingly, as regards a solution for this problem within the EU, the European Commission meanwhile tries to solve this problem by means of a rather *in*formal mechanism, the European Competition Network (ECN), established in May 2004[429]. The ECN is a forum for discussion and cooperation that shall help to improve the previous attempts of efficient cooperation between the national competition authorities and the European Commission. It underlines the aim to achieve a consistent application and enforcement of *European* competition law, especially with regard to the anti-cartel rules. Even if this system would prove to work within the European Union, it is doubtful whether such a system that is based on a combination of binding supranational competition law and a rather informal discussion forum would be acceptable and workable on the global level. A global system of decentralized and centralized responsibilities and competences, combined with supranational law and *in*formal mechanisms of cooperation and discussion, automatically causes non-transparency and a mixing, disordering, and blurring of liabilities. Furthermore, there would be more potential for conflicts on the global level because the informal mechanism could be misused by the more powerful countries to enforce their interests at the expense of other countries.

As regards the international competitiveness of nations, frequent changes within the international case allocation system and the resulting lack of transparency and long-term liability of antitrust could reduce the

429 Cf. European Commission (2004); cf. Chap. 2.3.2.2.

effectiveness, motivation, know-how, and sense of responsibility of national and international competition authorities. It would become difficult for national antitrust policy to pursue a long-term and balanced strategy to protect competition and to strengthen the international competitiveness of the nation. Furthermore, the fight for competencies between national and international institutions also could weaken the central aim to protect competition because – as a consequence of competence allocation conflicts – competition law and competence allocation probably would no more be determined by the insights of competition theory but by international negotiations.

4.2.2 Consequences of a Growing Workload

The issue of a growing workload is closely related to the above problem of efficient case allocation. The centralization of competition policy in the European Union had led to an enormous workload for the European Commission, which mainly derived from the authorization system within EC competition policy. Too many inter-firm agreements or concerted practices which were 'believed to fall within the scope of the prohibition of Article 81(1) of the EC Treaty had to be notified in order to be granted exemption (Article 81(3); Article 4(1) of Reg. 17).'[430] Consequently, the wide interpretation of Article 81(1) – admittedly promoted by the European Commission itself – had caused a vast number of notifications irrelevant of their actual or potential anti-competitive effects.

The European example shows that even within a centralized system, a supranational competition authority could be forced to make use of an exemption regime, especially 'block exemptions' and non-binding 'comfort letters'. Such an exemption regime has to be applied with a certain degree of flexibility and it causes heterogeneity, inconsistencies, and a lack of transparency. In some cases, a general exemption regime even leads to less flexibility for single cases. As regards the EU, this exemption regime was not completely founded on antitrust principles. The European Commission was overtaxed by the notification system so that the Commission's *workload* became a crucial factor, a criterion that normally should not play a significant role in antitrust considerations. Consequently, the European Commission had caused a significant loss of flexibility by increasing the

[430] Wißmann (2000) p. 128. Cf. Council Regulation 17/62/EEC of 6 February 1962, First Regulation Implementing Articles 85 and 86 of the Treaty. This regulation as been replaced by the new Council Regulation (EC) No. 1/2003 of 16 December 2002 on the Implementation of the Rules on Competition Laid down in Articles 81 and 82 of the Treaty.

number of block exemptions at the expense of individual exemptions, and the European Commission's tendency to close files by means of informal comfort letters had caused a lack of legal certainty and transparency because they are legally non-binding and they do not need to be published.[431]

Finally, as regards the EU, the growing workload and the vast increase of the exemption regime had led to a fundamental change of antitrust enforcement by substituting a new ex post-control (so-called 'Legalausnahme') for the former ex ante-control ('notification'). Presently, the enterprises have to examine themselves whether their agreements and concerted actions conform with Art. 81 III EC. In addition to this, they have to bear the burden of proving that the conditions of Art. 81 III EC are fulfilled. This also causes an increase of legal uncertainty, non-transparency, inconsistencies, and heterogeneity. Therefore, one could argue that it would be efficient to reallocate the competences to the national level whose flexibility could be used in favour of the international competitiveness of the nation and where arbitrary and not economically orientated criteria like the increased workload become irrelevant.[432] Such a development can be observed within the European Union, too. Certain competences have been reallocated back to the national competition authorities, following the principle of subsidiarity and enhancing the capacity of the European Commission so that 'the Commission will be able to focus its resources on the fight against the most serious infringements like cartels and abusive behaviour by dominant firms'.[433] The old notification system would have led to a paralysis of the European Commission's enforcement activities.

As regards the international competitiveness of nations, the growing workload of an international antitrust institution leads to similar problems as the deficiencies of competence allocation in an international antitrust regime, because a burdensome overload of work leads to questionable competence and case reallocations. Furthermore, it is obvious that an overtaxed international competition authority could become a danger for its

[431] Ibid. p. 130.

[432] The question arises whether such a reallocation of competences could be taken as an argument against or in favour of the internationalization and centralization of competition policy. On the one hand, the reallocation of competences shows that the former transfer of competences was unnecessary. The development of the European competence allocation system reveals that there was no straight line to deal with the delegation of competences. Non-transparency and inconsistencies resulted from this. On the other hand, a reallocation of competences indicates that even within a system of supranational competition policy, there remains a scope for flexibility and adjustments to new challenges.

[433] Monti (2003) p. 7.

central aim to protect competition. The experience within the European Community shows that pragmatic approaches in order to diminish the problem of a growing workload often are not guided by modern antitrust standards.

4.2.3 The Influence of Political Economics

An international harmonization and centralization of competition policy could be seen as an adequate solution in case that national competition authorities are not institutionally independent from the political parties and in case that national interest groups have too much influence on national competition authorities.[434] One may hope that the delegation of competences to an international institution which (a) hopefully is not subject to political pressures from national interest groups, (b) does not depend on democratic elections, and (c) does not allow for discretion in the interpretation and enforcement of competition law, could reduce the danger of lobbying activities, partisan political considerations, and other problems of political economics.

This hope is not well founded in logic and fact. To the contrary, both the legal passing of international competition rules and their implementation and enforcement would be influenced by the polit-economic sphere because international institutions are also object of lobbying activities. There are several reasons why an *international* competition policy regime would not generally be exposed less intensely to polit-economic activities than a national competition policy regime.

Firstly, there are still possibilities to improve the independence of national competition authorities and to minimize the influence of national politicians and interests groups. Before starting to transfer substantial competition policy competences from the national level to an alleged politically neutral international institution, the responsible governments could reduce their discretionary competences on competition policy, especially on merger control. In Germany, for instance, the Federal Minister of Economic Affairs has – according to Sec. 42 GWB (German Antitrust Act) – the right to overrule merger prohibition decisions made by the Federal Cartel Office. He can authorize mergers in case that the probable lessening of competition, caused by the merger, would probably be outweighed by overall economic advantages of the merger or in case that the merger can be justified by an outstanding public interest. The international competitiveness of the involved merger parties has to be taken into account (Sec.

[434] Vaubel (1992) p. 35.

42 I 2 GWB) so that this so-called ministerial permission ('Ministererlaubnis') can be viewed as a legal instrument to improve the international competitiveness of domestic enterprises. But there is a temptation to misuse this instrument for party political reasons or motivated by personal interests. Consequently, discretionary competences of national governments like the ministerial permission should be protected against political misuse, for example by means of additional restrictive criteria[435] or by giving a third party like the German Monopolies Commission the right to veto instead of just asking for its advice.

Secondly, every international competence allocation is interest-driven. When national governments agree to transfer competition policy competences from independent national anti-cartel offices to an international competition policy regime, then it is likely that they also do so because they expect to have more influence on a new international, non-transparent organization – created by themselves and less subject to democratic control[436] – than on an independent national competition authority which has a long national tradition and a good reputation because of its independence. In general, national politicians prefer to transfer those national competencies to an international institution which have been allocated at an independent national institution before.[437] The European Union can be taken as an example for this phenomenon, because both competition policy and monetary policy, which formerly had been under the control of politically independent national institutions, have been allocated at the European level and have become central pillars of the European competence allocation system. The political (discretionary) influence on the competition policy of the European Commission is institutionally embodied, and there are

---

435 Cf. Kinne (1997, 63ff.) who has analyzed several ministerial permissions in merger control with regard to the criteria or aims which have been relevant for a ministerial permission – i.e. the benefits of rationalization, the international competitiveness of domestic enterprises, safeguarding technological resources, safeguarding domestic employment, safeguarding supply on domestic markets, redeveloping domestic enterprises, overcoming a structural crisis, and reducing public subsidies. Kinne also describes the limits of these criteria in German merger control. The international competitiveness of domestic companies can be taken as an argument for a ministerial permission if the merger is necessary for the domestic companies to achieve long-term international competitiveness, but it is a problematic argument for a ministerial permission if the merger causes an international monopolization or if the merging companies already possess a strong position on global markets.

436 McGinnis (2004) p. 126.

437 Vaubel (1992) p. 46.

also political attempts to take influence on the European Central Bank.[438] Ultimately, an international harmonization and centralization of political competences could be regarded as a polit-economically induced attempt to cartelize, both as regards the private markets and the international regulatory competition. On the one hand, governments who want to create a supranational competition authority that is under their control could try to practice collusive behaviour as a substitute for private cartels and other forms of anticompetitive and protectionist conduct. Furthermore, an international harmonization could be compared with a cartel of governments that want to stop the international systems competition.[439] Both strategies could reduce international welfare.

Thirdly, even a rule-guided international competition policy could not stop the influence of political parties, interest groups, international bureaucrats, and powerful incumbent firms on an international antitrust institution. There still would remain a significant legal scope of action for politicians and bureaucrats who would have to negotiate and enforce the international competition rules. On the one hand, as regards the advantages of international harmonization, international negotiations could reduce the power of national pressure groups in one country, because these groups 'may be offset by opposing groups in another'[440]. It is more difficult to establish homogeneous pressure groups on the international level than on the national level.[441] Furthermore, depending on the exact institutional arrangements of an international antitrust authority, international bureaucrats could have 'considerably less rule-making authority than their domestic law counterparts, so they have a more limited ability to pursue their own interests in this way'[442]. On the other hand, in times of economic globalization, it is unlikely to establish absolutely neutral international antitrust rules that are not influenced by international interest groups. Firstly, 'more rents are available on the global scale'[443] so that interest groups have an additional incentive to capture the international antitrust regime and to enforce interventionist practices. Secondly, according to Stephan, 'interest groups enjoy an advantage in the international lawmaking process'[444]. Probably, their efforts would be more successful on the global level because international antitrust lawmakers 'do not face the same kind of poli-

[438] Kösters (2004) p. 19.
[439] Cf. Christl (2001) p. 79; cf. Berg (1983) p. 3.
[440] Guzman (2004) p. 366.
[441] Nagy (2002) p. 179.
[442] Guzman (2004) p. 366.
[443] McGinnis (2004) p. 129.
[444] Stephan (1999) pp. 35, 55.

tical discipline that national and local ones do'[445] and international antitrust bureaucrats would become a 'distinct class with a distinct interest – that of growing the international antitrust apparatus – that is not likely to mirror the interests of national governments, let alone citizens'[446]. Accordingly, a centralization of international antitrust could cause new principal-agent problems between national governments (principals) and international bureaucrats (agents). Furthermore, it is impossible to define absolutely neutral and reliable international criteria under which a national or international competition authority would be forced to pass decisions that would meet with overall approval from all concerned countries and interest groups. Therefore, issues of political economics would remain an important problem both in a system of centralized and decentralized application of international antitrust rules.[447]

Fourthly, the experience of the WTO regime shows that it is the industrialized nations that set the agenda on the international level and that especially the powerful industrialized countries and their interests groups often try to disregard the initially agreed international rules in order to achieve an advantage for their economy. Consequently, international competition rules would lose their initial function to abolish the right of the strong and to enforce the rule of law. Instead, especially small and less powerful countries, which anyway lack the resources to apply the effects doctrine, would even lose this instrument to defend themselves in case of need. Furthermore, they would no more be able to protect themselves against lobbying activities on the international political level. Both could weaken their international competitiveness.

In sum, it has to be underlined that politicians and bureaucrats would use their influence on the international competition authority not only in order to protect international competition and to increase the nation's international competitiveness, but also to pursue personal or party political interests. Consequently, the institutional arrangement of an international antitrust regime – both as regards the political decision about its initial institutional arrangement and the afterwards daily antitrust enforcement activities – would be influenced by polit-economic factors because it is impossible to establish an international antitrust regime that is totally independent from political influences. Therefore, the outcomes would be the result of unequal bargains, decisions at the expense of third countries, logrolling, package deals, and an international political horse-trading, influ-

---

445 Ibid. p. 35.

446 McGinnis (2004) p. 129; also confer Neugebauer (2004) pp. 135ff.; cf. Grimes (2003) pp. 257f.

447 Cf. Nagy (2002) pp. 179ff.

enced by a multitude of international interest groups. Compared to national competition policy, an internationally coordinated antitrust enforcement would even allow new forms of polit-economic activities and some countries, especially the small and weak ones, would no more be able to protect themselves against these activities which formerly took place on the national level and now would take place on the international stage. As an example for new forms of polit-economic activities, both in case of a decentralized and a centralized model of international competition policy, the possibility to get confidential business information from abroad could be an incentive for politicians and bureaucrats to file a case against a foreign enterprise.

Ultimately, competition policy does not only depend on institutional precautions which try to guarantee its political independence. The effectiveness of competition policy also depends on the competence, attitude, and political orientation of the enforcement authorities: 'In most leading jurisdictions, the meat of competition policy lies in judicial precedent and agency practice rather than in legislation'.[448] This is an open door for politicians and lobbyists to exert influence on the international level.[449] In contrast to this, a national competition authority like the German Federal Cartel Office has gained a high degree of independence in the course of time. This immunity of the Federal Cartel Office against interest groups would not be transferred automatically to an international competition authority that would partly depend on political decisions.[450]

4.2.4 Selective Effects of International Harmonization

It has to be emphasized that every kind of international harmonization has selective effects and leads to new distortions with respect to international competition and competitiveness. This problem of harmonization occurs in two different dimensions.

Firstly, a total harmonization of one specific political field like, for instance, antitrust policy would not lead to a totally fair international compe-

---

448 Bush (2005) pp. 5f.

449 Business associations partly also call for a further centralization of competition policy so that these interest groups automatically become an ally of an international competition authority, which also wants to maximize its mandates, competencies and budgets. The international competition authority would be tempted to allow significant influences of these interest groups on important decisions in return for the interest groups support for further centralization and harmonization.

450 Cf. Niederleithinger (1990) pp. 112f.

tition and a fair framework for fostering international competitiveness. To the contrary, the total harmonization of only one specific political field like competition policy could lead to new distortions. This is because international competition and the international competitiveness of nations are influenced by many political fields and by a multitude of additional factors[451], even by unchangeable conditions like climate, natural infrastructure (e.g. landlocked countries), and the population. It is impossible to harmonize all these factors that are relevant for international competitiveness and international regulatory competition. Hence a harmonization of only one political field would be advantageous for those countries that do not depend on this factor. Correspondingly, a harmonization would be disadvantageous for those countries whose competitiveness strongly depends on an individual use of this factor. For instance, relatively low social standards and a high degree of monopolization are important instruments in developing countries to strengthen their international competitiveness.

Secondly, it is almost impossible to establish a totally fair harmonization within one specific political field like antitrust. This applies to minimum standards and total harmonization, too.

1. As regards international *minimum* standards, they cannot cover all possible cases so that they lead to new asymmetries and distortions of competition. For instance, the introduction of international per se rules concerning certain forms of cartelization probably would not involve more innovative, subtle, and hidden forms of inter-firm collaboration. Consequently, countries whose domestic firms mostly practice these more innovative or hidden forms of anticompetitive practices could get an advantage over countries whose firms are rather involved in classic forms of cartelization which would be covered by the prohibition. Furthermore, minimum standards and other forms of selective harmonization give incentives for enterprises to use evasive manoeuvres so that certain forms of anticompetitive behaviour would be substituted by others with similar effects. Especially the dominant, more competitive enterprises would be able to adjust to these new conditions so that they would achieve a further competitive advantage over less competitive firms. Consequently, minimum standards could be advantageous especially for the more competitive, industrialized countries. In order to avoid this discriminatory and selective effect of harmonization, international minimum standards would have to cover the total range of anticompetitive behaviour, but this would be hard to realize. Furthermore, international minimum standards would have to

[451] Cf. Chap. 3.2.2.3.

be transformed into national law and to be enforced by national competition authorities.[452] Consequently, national competition authorities would keep a significant scope of action, which could be used to undermine the harmonized per se rules. This could lead to unfair distortions.[453] Every form of a decentralized application and enforcement of harmonized competition law leads to such system-inherent ambiguities. For instance, a usual way for taking influence on the enforcement of internationally harmonized competition rules would be to apply an own definition of the relevant product and geographic market in every single case; every nation state has different consumer preferences so that the necessity to define close substitutes and other relevant factors gives wide discretionary powers to the national competition authorities. Those countries trying to enforce the harmonized rules as correctly as possible could harm their international competitiveness. Consequently, Meessen suggests that minimum standards could be either ineffective or, in the long run, they could cause a constraint towards total harmonization.[454] In contrast to this, Fuchs[455] states that Meessens' pessimistic view with regard to minimum standards could be too extreme. He points out that minimum standards would at least prohibit certain kinds of anticompetitive behaviour (especially hard core cartels) and this would already be a significant gain for international competition. Furthermore, he contradicts the alleged coercion towards total harmonization. According to Fuchs, minimum standards are an absolutely necessary framework or prerequisite for international regulatory competition. But this is only the one side of the coin, because minimum standards would also limit the regulatory competition and prevent new approaches in competition policy (cf. Chap. 4.2.5.4). In summary, one can say that it is difficult to foresee the actual future effects of international minimum standards so that both views – Meessen and Fuchs – should be considered. Nevertheless, Meessens' critical point of view is a warning against international minimum standards because it is obvious that a selective harmonization (minimum standards) leads to new distortions. Furthermore, the growing dominance of the EU competition policy gives an

[452] Cf. Meessen (2000) pp. 8f.

[453] Cf. Rosenthal and Nicolaides (1997) pp. 366f. The authors underline the existence of nontrivial differences in antitrust enforcement in the United States although the courts, the FTC and the DoJ all apply the same federal antitrust law and the binding decisions of the US Supreme Court.

[454] Cf. Meessen (2000) pp. 8f.

[455] Cf. Fuchs (2000) pp. 367ff.

empirical example that minimum standards have a tendency to be the first step towards a total harmonization.[456]

2. As regards the aim of a *total* international harmonization of competition policy, it has to be underlined that it is impossible to harmonize all relevant factors in this field of international regulatory competition. Firstly, every country is already characterized by certain forms of market structure and business practices that could not be changed entirely by an internationalization of antitrust. Even a single global competition authority enforcing supranational competition law would not be able to change the present industrial organization and market structure within all member countries. Secondly, there is no realistic chance to enforce a completely fair international harmonization and it is not possible to create an absolutely fair international (regulatory) competition. The creation of a so-called level playing field is an 'illusion'[457]. A far-reaching harmonization in antitrust policy would produce winners and losers; some countries probably would have to accept a significant reduction of their international competitiveness and it would be difficult to grant a compensation for this disadvantage.

4.2.5 International Harmonization versus Competition of Competition Rules

The establishment of a workable global systems competition in antitrust is a main prerequisite for economies to strive for international competitiveness – by means of national competition policy – in a fair manner. In this respect, it is necessary to differentiate between different types or functions of regulatory competition.[458] Firstly, one has to underline the efficiency-enhancing, evolutionary, and innovative function of international regulatory competition as a fundamental argument against the establishment of inter-

---

456 Cf. Chap. 2.3.2.2.

457 Cf. Siebert (2000) p. 21.

458 For a more detailed description of different types of international regulatory competition, cf. Kerber and Budzinski (2003) pp. 413ff. and Kerber and Budzinski (2004) pp. 31ff. The authors differentiate between four types of international regulatory competition: regulatory competition via mutual learning (yardstick competition), via international trade (improving the international competitiveness of domestic firms), via interjurisdictional competition (competition for mobile production factors), and via free and direct choice of law (firms can choose directly between the laws of different nations without being forced to accept the whole bundle of national laws and without having to be located in this nation).

national competition rules and against every kind of international harmonization. Regulatory competition is an important instrument to reduce the general problem of limited knowledge. It supports institutional innovation within a competitive environment. This function of regulatory competition is not only important with regard to the development of competition theory and policy and the chance to learn from each other ('yardstick competition'), but also with regard to the international competitiveness of nations. Secondly, regulatory competition allows countries to practice a fine-tuned competition policy that can support the own international trade position. Thirdly, international regulatory competition reduces the incentives of national governments to practice a policy that is guided by personal interests and that is harmful for the majority of mobile production factors. Instead, governments are increasingly forced to provide for attractive locational conditions, i.e. they are deeply involved in locational competition (interjurisdictional competition). Especially the new political economics underline these beneficial effects of a global systems competition whereas static neoclassical equilibrium theory emphasizes the danger of a race to the bottom.[459]

The following chapters describe the consequences of a decreasing international regulatory competition for the international competitiveness of nations. Chapter 4.2.5.1 raises the question to what extent competition policy is a prerequisite or a *factor* of international regulatory competition. After having answered this initial question, Chap. 4.2.5.2 deals with the workability and the limits of regulatory competition in competition policy.[460] Finally, we have to consider the consequences of an international regulatory competition in competition policy. The question at hand is which fields of competition policy would fall out of the regulatory competition in case of an international harmonization or centralization of competition policy

[459] Cf. Stearns-Bläsing (2004) pp. 15ff.; cf. Müller (2000) pp. 32ff.

[460] The theory of federalism, the theory of international regulatory competition, the new institutional economics, and the new political economics offer a theoretical basis for such an analysis, though these theories can not be presented here. For detailed information about the theoretical basis of a concept of international regulatory competition, see Tiebout (1956) pp. 416ff; Müller (2000); Streit (1998) pp. 239ff.; Stearns-Bläsing (2004) pp. 7ff.; Streit and Wohlgemuth (1999); Cassel (1996); Wohlgemuth (1995) pp. 71ff. – For publications with a special focus on international regulatory competition in antitrust policy, see Kerber (1998) pp. 199ff.; Kerber and Budzinski (2003) pp. 411ff.; Kerber and Budzinski (2004) pp. 31ff.; Stearns-Bläsing (2004) pp. 32ff.; Sinn (2003) pp. 178ff. – For a sceptical view on the workability of an international competition of competition rules, see Sinn (1997) pp. 248ff.; Sinn (1999); Basedow (1998) p. 56.

(Chap. 4.2.5.3). Furthermore, the consequences for the international competitiveness of nations will be taken into account (Chap. 4.2.5.4).

4.2.5.1 Competition Policy: An Essential Part of the International Competition Framework or a National Factor of International Competitiveness?

In order to establish a workable global systems competition which allows the economies to strive for international competitiveness in a fair manner, it is necessary to distinguish (a) the parameters which constitute the global competition framework and which have to be set by an international agreement from (b) those parameters which have to be determined by each single state as an essential factor of international competitiveness. Consequently, it has to be analyzed whether antitrust policy is an indispensable prerequisite for regulatory competition and therefore an absolutely necessary element of a workable international framework for systems competition or whether antitrust policy belongs to the instruments each economy should be able to use individually in order to be successful in global systems competition and to enhance its international competitiveness.

According to Meessen[461], only those parameters belong to the international framework, which are absolutely necessary to keep up a 'fair' international systems competition. As already described in Chap. 2, international competition rules are not indispensable for practicing sound competition policy and for protecting international competition. The status quo of international antitrust generally works well and existing deficiencies could be eliminated without far-reaching harmonization efforts. In this way, from an empirical point of view, one could say that global systems competition does not depend on an international harmonization or centralization of competition policy. Consequently, *national* competition policy could be regarded as one of many factors of international competitiveness and should be preserved. Though, there is still one question that has to be answered. Theoretically, the workability of a global systems competition in antitrust could be endangered by a race to the bottom. The following chapter deals with this issue.

4.2.5.2 Prerequisites, Workability, and Limits of International Regulatory Competition in Antitrust

Economists who plead for international competition rules often refer to new international challenges in antitrust which result from economic globalization and which allegedly can not be dealt with on the national level.

[461] Cf. Meessen (2000) pp. 15.

Though, on the other hand, economic globalization also has helped to meet the prerequisite conditions for a workable international systems competition. Globalization has led to a further international integration of markets, it has increased the international mobility of scarce production factors[462], it has reduced international transaction costs, and it has led to an increase in the number of (heterogeneous) national competition laws. Furthermore, the existence of heterogeneous preferences as regards national competition rules can be assumed. Moreover, competition on private markets has become more intense in the course of further globalization. All these developments have improved the theoretical conditions for a workable international systems competition. Nevertheless, there is no consensus about the workability of an international regulatory competition with respect to antitrust policy.[463] Special concern – especially from a static neoclassical point of view – exists (a) with regard to the danger of a race to the bottom when nations try to improve the international competitiveness of domestic firms and the locational attractiveness of the national economy for mobile production factors by a strategic, protectionist, and discriminatory use of competition policy, and (b) with regard to negative effects of international regulatory competition on the intensity of inter-firm competition and the allocative efficiency on international markets for private goods.

As regards the actual workability of international regulatory competition in antitrust, it has to be conceded that the current regulatory competition, especially the locational (interjurisdictional) competition, is already restricted. The status quo of international antitrust enforcement, characterized by the effects doctrine and bilateral cooperation as described in Chap. 2, has two effects with regard to the workability of systems competition. On the one hand, the effects doctrine, bilateral cooperation and the unsystematic convergence of competition policy (bottom-up-harmonization) are causes of a slowing down of the systems competition. On the other hand, these instruments offer a framework for a workable international regulatory competition between competition rules. Consequently, there is an ambi-

[462] Though, for the sake of completeness, it has to be said that the international mobility of production factors is not as high as often believed. Only *financial* capital has such a high mobility that it possibly could exert a competitive pressure on governments, whereas physical capital and human resources are rather immobile. Furthermore, the so-called Feldstein-Horioka-Paradoxon describes the close relationship between national savings and investments, indicating an international immobility of financial capital, too (cf. Apolte (2000) pp. 91f.; Feldstein and Horioka (1980) pp. 314ff.).

[463] Cf. Kerber (1998) pp. 199ff.; cf. Fuchs (2000) pp. 367f.

valence between the effects doctrine and the bilateral agreements on the one hand and the regulatory competition on the other.

First of all, one can say that the effects doctrine helps to maintain the regulatory competition because the effects doctrine is the present antithesis to international harmonization. And as long as the effects doctrine produces satisfactory results, no international harmonization is needed. Nevertheless, international regulatory competition in antitrust is weakened by the effects doctrine. If a domestic enterprise is about to restrict international competition, it will be confronted both with domestic and with foreign competition law and policy. In general, there is no escape for the enterprise if it does not change its behaviour on the affected markets. This is why, for instance, a removal of the headquarter from one country to another does not fundamentally change the company´s situation; a different location or nationality of an enterprise does not change its legal situation as regards prosecution from domestic antitrust authorities.[464] The enterprise can not exit so that it can not put pressure on the domestic competition policy to become more pleasing.[465] In this respect, the systems competition does not work perfectly. Consequently, the application of the effects doctrine limits the locational competition between open economies in a considerable degree. But this effect does not mean that competition policy loses its role as a factor in international regulatory competition. Furthermore, international regulatory competition is more than just locational competition to attract foreign companies with the promise of a lax competition policy that does not prosecute particular anticompetitive business practices. Antitrust law affects a multitude of locational business conditions so that the international regulatory competition takes place in several additional fields of antitrust:

1. International firms do not only decide on the location of their headquarters or additional foreign direct investments, they also decide to take up business activities with foreign customers and suppliers in different countries so that the characteristics of national competition policy become a relevant factor, too.[466]

---

464 Cf. Fuchs (2000) p. 369.

465 McGinnis (2004) p. 131.

466 In contrast to this, some authors show a narrowed view on international regulatory competition in competition policy because they reduce it on the locational decision of firms to escape national antitrust standards. They conclude, that the benefits of an international regulatory competition do not exist in case of national competition policy because the nationally applied effects doctrine covers all enterprises regardless of whether they are located at home or abroad (cf. Fuchs (2000) p. 369; cf. Röder (2000) pp. 376f.).

2. Moreover, national competition policy has an influence on market structures, market behaviour and market performance so that regulatory competition can exert a significant influence on the international competitiveness of the nation that goes beyond its influence on foreign enterprises' behaviour within an international locational competition environment.
3. In addition to this, the application of the effects doctrine does not stop the development of good and innovative antitrust rules ('yardstick-competition'), which is a central function of regulatory competition.[467]

Secondly, bilateral agreements are an ambivalent component of the present regulatory competition as well. On the one hand, they are an instrument to avoid global harmonization and to maintain the primacy of *national* competition policy. On the other hand, bilateral agreements can be an intermediate stage on the way to multinational harmonization and centralization. The EU Group of Experts once recommended a 'twin-track' approach to international competition rules.[468] Firstly, the group of experts suggested extending and enhancing bilateral cooperation. Bilateral agreements could build a frame for closer international cooperation. The second step would be to transfer these agreements into a plurilateral or multilateral framework. In general, bilateral agreements could be regarded as a synthesis of bottom-up-convergence and top-down-implementation, so that regulatory competition is restricted, but not eliminated. It has to be conceded that a nation's interest to keep up its bilateral and multilateral cooperation in antitrust limits its possibility to pursue an antitrust policy that also promotes the international competitiveness of the own economy compared to foreign countries. Nevertheless, there still remains a wide scope for national excellence in antitrust to strengthen the international competitiveness.[469]

Finally, the effects of an unsystematic bottom-up convergence have to be considered. As already mentioned in Chap. 2.3.1.2.2, several economists (by applying static neoclassical equilibrium theory) fear that a so-called race to the bottom could be the result of an uncoordinated convergence. Similar to competition on private markets, regulatory competition could result in a ruinous competition and lose its static and dynamic functions to force governments to practice an efficient economic policy, to achieve an efficient (static) allocation of governmental resources, to produce innovative regulations, and to help to adjust to new developments on

[467] McGinnis (2004) p. 131.
[468] Cf. Chap. 2.3.2.1.
[469] Cf. Chap. 4.3.

dynamic markets. This deregulation race – which in practice probably would be a sequential process because several countries would follow with delay – could cause a cartelization of national markets, for example because firms that profit from permissive competition policy could attempt to achieve an international Stackelberg leadership role by means of national cartelization.[470]

According to a simple two-country model of game theory, discriminatory antitrust practices in a non-cooperative, non-zero-sum, one-shot-game with simultaneous moves would result in an inefficient outcome. Both countries would be trapped into a prisoners′ dilemma, characterized by a Pareto-inefficient Nash equilibrium where both countries receive a payoff of 2 (see Fig. 4.1), although – in case that both countries were practicing a non-discriminatory antitrust policy, for example because of international cooperation – they could achieve a payoff of 4. This inefficient equilibrium could be regarded as the end of the international regulatory competition in antitrust.

		Country 2	
		Non-Discriminatory Antitrust	**Discriminatory Antitrust**
Country 1	**Non-Discriminatory Antitrust**	4 / 4	1 / 5

[470] Sinn (1999) pp. 30f. In a theoretical model provided by Sinn, the international systems competition could cause a process of international antitrust deregulation and national cartelization. One country would start to allow national cartelization to achieve first-mover advantages. This cartelization of national markets could increase domestic firms′ profits (at the expense of foreign firms); eventually – at least in a short- and mid-term perspective – this cartelization could even be beneficial for domestic consumers because the cartelizing firms could attempt to achieve an international Stackelberg leadership position by credibly setting a high production capacity. This could increase aggregate supply and reduce prices. Then, a second country would also try to achieve a Stackelberg leadership position with respect to the remaining market shares and so on. Ultimately, this process would result in a deregulation race, but Sinn′s model depends on several assumptions, especially on the homogeneity of countries and firms and whether countries and firms are able and willing to achieve a Stackelberg leadership position (Ibid. pp. 10ff., 30ff.).

	Discriminatory Antitrust	5 / 1	2 / 2

Fig. 4.1: Payoff Matrix of a Prisoners' Dilemma of National Antitrust Authorities

Nevertheless, this theoretical argument against international regulatory competition is doubtful. It is unlikely that competition between (independent) national competition authorities leads to a self-destructive race to the bottom.[471] Some counter-arguments have to be mentioned:

1. The international regulatory competition is a multi-period game. Such games are characterized by the possibility of learning processes. For instance, if a national competition authority recognizes that foreign competition authorities practice a tit-for-tat strategy, then it probably would change its discriminatory or permissive strategy. This change of strategy also could be achieved or supported by some bilateral consultations; an international harmonization of competition law and policy would not be necessary.

2. National competition authorities have several additional incentives to practice a rather strict competition policy. Especially *independent* competition authorities, which generally do not have to consider protectionist aims, are not interested in permissive or even protectionist competition policy because this would reduce their reputation, authority, and independence. But also national governments have incentives to use a rather strict competition policy for certain political aims.[472] Hollis and Yuan even provide a model where countries even choose antitrust policies that are too strict 'in the sense that they will prefer to have more firms than is globally optimal'[473].

3. A race to the bottom is an unlikely scenario because of the effects doctrine and the different forms of international cooperation. In many (though not in all) cases, the effects doctrine results in the ineffectiveness of unilateral permissive and protectionist decisions, when foreign countries are affected by the anticompetitive behaviour of domestic firms. The foreign competition authorities would rather apply their present competition law against domestic enterprises than

[471] Cf. Meessen (2000) p. 11.
[472] See in detail Chap. 4.3.3.3; cf. Meessen (2000) p. 11.
[473] Hollis and Yuan (2004) pp. 179ff.

answer with likewise permissive decisions in favour of their domestic companies.

4. As regards the international locational competition in antitrust, a race to the bottom is unlikely because firms do not decide on their location only because of antitrust considerations. They have to take into account the entire bundle of national policies which affect their business. Furthermore, many companies rather prefer strict competition rules (cf. Chap. 4.3.3.3.2).

5. The present international regulatory competition does not give any empirical evidence of a race to the bottom or a downward convergence of competition policy. On the contrary, there is an unsystematic bottom-up convergence on a high level, though there are still significant differences between national antitrust enforcement.[474] The process of convergence is supported by the signing of bilateral agreements and by the cultivation of formal and informal cooperation between competition authorities (see e.g. the erection of the ICN).

To sum up, one can say that the present international regulatory competition works well. Economic globalization has improved the prerequisite conditions for a workable international systems competition. Furthermore, there are some legal institutions (effects doctrine, bilateral agreements, bottom-up convergence and international fora) that weaken this regulatory competition, but these institutions help to prevent protectionist practices and a race to the bottom. In conclusion, there is no significant risk that a race to the bottom will occur. The international systems competition is more about how to practice an excellent national antitrust policy than to implement unfair practices at the expense of foreign countries.

4.2.5.3 Fields of Competition Policy Falling out of the Regulatory Competition

International competition rules would weaken or even eliminate the international regulatory competition in antitrust because several main fields of competition policy would be harmonized. In addition to this, central competences could be transferred from the national to the international level. Chapter 2.3 has described the arguments of the proponents of international competition rules. According to these arguments, probably only those fields of competition policy would remain under national responsibility which do not affect *international* competition. In the course of further globalization, where antitrust cases increasingly have an international di-

[474] Cf. Chap. 2.4.4.

mension, the vast majority of antitrust cases, and especially the important cases, would be covered by *international* law and antitrust enforcement and nearly all important areas of competition policy would be subject to a harmonized competition law and would no more be part of the international regulatory competition.

Also in case of a *decentralized* enforcement of international antitrust law, the harmonization (and probably even supranationalization) of competition law would prevent both a regulatory competition and a far-reaching consideration of national interests and local diversity. The experience of supranational competition policy within the European Union has revealed the tendency of a supranational competition authority to maximize its power and to expand its competences even in case of decentralized antitrust enforcement (cf. Chap. 2.3.2). In order to avoid a heterogeneous decentralized law enforcement, the supranational institution would try to play the decisive role as regards the final interpretation of international competition law so that the national competition authorities have to adapt to the international interpretation and enforcement practices. In the long run, they will be demoted in influence and become a mere executive instance of the international competition authority.

In addition to this, the European Community can also serve as an example of how an internationally harmonized competition policy takes influence on antitrust cases which do not affect *international* competition. In the long run, both the international harmonization of competition policy with regard to international antitrust cases and the decentralized application of supranational antitrust law can be accompanied by an international harmonization of *national* antitrust law. Consequently, *national* competition law is going to be marginalized or 'internationalized' so that even antitrust cases which do not affect international competition become subject to internationally harmonized competition law. The 7th amendment of the GWB in 2005, which has resulted in a far-reaching 'Europeanization' of national competition law, can be taken as an example: 'The German legislator realized that, in principle, it had not been reasonable to uphold national rules which could be applied only to local or regional cases according to Art. 3 (2) Regulation No. 1. Instead, these cases should follow the same rules as cases within the scope of Art. 81 EC Treaty.'[475] Consequently, the international regulatory competition in antitrust would nearly completely be eliminated if an international competition policy regime results in similarly ambitious harmonization efforts as the European competition policy regime.

---

[475] Cf. Klees (2006) p. 401.

4.2.5.4 Consequences Resulting from an Abolition of the International Regulatory Competition

A significant reduction of the international systems competition would result in ambivalent effects on the international competitiveness of a nation because international harmonization is in a position to strengthen and to reduce international competitiveness.

On the one hand, national governments vote for harmonization because they want to be assured that international competition is fair and intensive so that domestic enterprises have free access to foreign markets. One could claim that international competition rules protect international competition more effectively than national competition policy so that the international competitiveness, sovereignty and welfare of a country would no longer be reduced by deficiencies of international antitrust, for example protectionist behaviour of foreign enterprises or foreign competition authorities. Considering this aspect, countries would be able to increase their welfare and international competitiveness by means of international harmonization.

On the other hand, as already described in Chap. 2, the merits of international harmonization and centralization compared to national competition policy and non-binding cooperation are questionable, possibly even nonexistent. Furthermore, both international competition and the international competitiveness of nations could suffer from an abolition of regulatory competition because of the following reasons.

The Lack of Innovation. Competition policy can develop itself only within a so-called 'competition of competition policies', which works like a Hayekian[476] process of experimentation, discovery, cultural evolution, and mutual persuasion.[477] Therefore, regulatory competition is especially important with regard to competition policy. Competition theory and policy will never achieve a status of complete knowledge on best antitrust practices and their optimal application in each individual case. On the contrary, competition policy is – in contrast to the instruments of foreign trade policy – an economic discipline determined by the complexity and the dynamics of its research object. This is because free market economies and private markets are characterized by evolutionary competitive processes.[478] Free market economies permanently produce new products and new market forms, innovative business strategies, and new kinds of anticompetitive behaviour so that antitrust problems and challenges change in the course of time. Furthermore, there are many uncertainties and theory pluralism as

---

[476] Cf. Hayek (1968) pp. 3ff.

[477] Cf. Meessen (2000) pp. 11, 15.

[478] Cf. Hayek (1968); cf. Schumpeter (1975) pp. 118- 121.

regards the antitrust analysis itself and the effects of competition policy on markets, competition, and international competitiveness. These dynamic and unforeseeable developments have to be identified and examined by each competition authority, and in many cases there are no clear answers about how to evaluate the anticompetitive effects of new business strategies and how to react efficiently in order to protect competition and international competitiveness. Because of these uncertainties, there is a permanent task to innovate and change antitrust theory and policy so that an international regulatory competition would be helpful to discover efficient competition policy practices as an adequate response to these new challenges. Even in case of new forms of *international* anticompetitive conduct and new *international* markets, it could be more effective to apply *different* national competition laws in order to set incentives to each nation to innovate and to develop an efficient antitrust policy that enhances national and international competition. In contrast to this, an abolition of the current systems competition would cause general inefficiencies of the public administration and a lack of theory innovations. The paradox of international harmonization is that the international antitrust rules, which would be needed to deal with all current and future forms of international business conduct, automatically would be the result of the previous international regulatory competition in antitrust, but this regulatory competition would be abolished or strictly reduced by international harmonization.

The Lack of Versatility. The complexity of antitrust problems and their change in the course of time does not only necessitate permanent innovations in antitrust theory and policy but also flexible changes in antitrust policy. An international harmonization and lawmaking regime would discourage beneficial change and lead to a lack of versatility as regards the once internationally agreed competition rules and standards (so-called lock-in problem).[479] Necessary adjustments to new economic developments or because of new knowledge about competitive theory (for example oligopoly theory, game theory, simulation models) and policy would depend on lengthy international and interstate negotiations. 'International institutions are hard to create and even harder to reform'[480]. For instance, it would have been harmful for international competition and the international competitiveness of nations 'if the rigid US merger guidelines that existed around 1970 had been written into an international agreement'[481]. These problems of inflexibility and a lack of regulatory innovation would arise

[479] McGinnis (2004) p. 126.
[480] Stephan (2004) p. 80; cf. Guzman (2004) p. 368.
[481] Tarullo (1999) p. 451.

both in systems based on unanimity decisions or majority decisions between the participating member countries. Therefore, a competition policy regime must remain open in order to permanently generate and allow new temporary assessments and policy changes.[482]

The question arises whether these negative effects of harmonization could be avoided by following a decentralized approach combined with international *minimum* standards instead of implementing totally harmonized competition rules. One could even hold that minimum standards are a *prerequisite* for international regulatory competition. But this is doubtful because there are ambivalent effects. Minimum standards would also limit the systems competition and they would cause new distortions instead of 'leveling the playing field'.[483] Moreover, international minimum standards could send the wrong signal to competition authorities about good competition policy; minimum standards could be an incentive to practice a more permissive national competition policy and to refrain from developing more innovative approaches. Furthermore, minimum standards would lead to a lack of versatility. A paradigm shift becomes rather impossible if minimum standards have to be obeyed; each absolutely new approach for protecting competition would have to be examined and accepted by all member countries. This effect would cause a restriction of the systems competition, too.

The Lack of Diversity. Diversity in antitrust has to be distinguished from innovativeness and versatility in antitrust. Innovativeness and versatility partly also would take place within a totally harmonized international competition policy regime, though highly restricted compared to international regulatory competition. In contrast to this, diversity of antitrust can only be maintained within a system of non-harmonization, implicating the maintenance of international regulatory competition.

Competition policy is one of the areas of economic policy where a scientific and a political consensus about optimal strategies and concepts is hard to achieve by a top down harmonization.[484] The diverging enforcement strategies in different countries and the existence of conflicting theoretical approaches like the Austrian Tradition (Ludwig von Mises, F. A. von Hayek, Israel Kirzner), the Harvard School (Workable Competition), the Chicago School of Antitrust Analysis, the concept of the optimal intensity of competition in a wide oligopoly (Kantzenbach[485]) and the Contestable Markets Theory illustrate this problem. Diversity in antitrust has sev-

[482] Cf. Budzinski (2003) p. 29.
[483] Cf. Chap. 4.2.4.
[484] Vaubel (1992) p. 34.
[485] Kantzenbach (1967) pp. 193-241.

eral reasons and it also affects the international competitiveness of nations. Besides differences in culture, social and economic goals, and preferences resulting from partisan politics and political interest group pressures, there are several specific features of antitrust which cause its existing international heterogeneity.

The first reason for diversity of competition policy is the controversial debate on competition itself, concerning its nature, benefits and limits. States are characterized by differences in information, know how, and experience as regards antitrust matters.[486] The scientific community has developed different concepts as regards the following fundamental questions: (1) What is the nature of competition? (2) What are the preconditions for competition? (3) What are the functions and goals of competition? (4) In what way can competition promote economic efficiency?[487]

Another reason for the heterogeneity of ideas, concepts, instruments and aims is the dynamics and complexity of private markets and international regulatory competition. Market conduct, market performance and market structures are part of a dynamic process and the final effect of this process on competition is hard to perceive. Furthermore, these dynamics are not foreseeable and they do not occur on all national markets at the same time and in the same manner. Some new market developments are regional, but very intense. Some are global, but rather weak. Markets frequently give way to absolutely new phenomena, which often have a regional coloring. Consequently, the scientific and political reaction on the evolution of (new) markets is a complex and difficult process, with different scientific and political perspectives and perceptions because of different local circumstances and preferences of the citizens.

A third reason for the lack of political and scientific consensus is the ambivalent effect of many antitrust-instruments on competition. There are conflicting antitrust-strategies and values that 'both supposedly promote competition'[488]. Consequently, antitrust authorities have different views on concepts like 'market power' and they act differently to find a proper balance between the pro- and anti-competitive effects of their instruments. For instance, there are ongoing problems, both on the national and international agenda, to evaluate …

1. 'the actual harm predatory pricing can cause in the marketplace'[489];

---

486 Guzman (2004) p. 364.

487 Cf. Martin (2004) pp. 16ff.; cf. Vickers (1995) pp. 1ff.

488 Rosenthal and Nicolaides (1997) p. 368.

489 Ibid. p. 368. The positive effects of restricted intra-brand competition on inter-brand restriction could legitimate certain forms of vertical integration (cf. Stearns-Bläsing (2004) p. 103).

2. 'whether and when restrictions on intrabrand competition cause more harm than the benefits of interbrand competition that such restrictions may facilitate'[490];
3. 'whether monopolists should have a unilateral right to refuse to deal with individuals or classes of customers'[491];
4. when a horizontal agreement between firms results in an anticompetitive cartel and when it may lead to market benefits[492];
5. when the anti-competitive effects of vertical restraints compensate their pro-competitive effects, for example less free-riding, quality control, incentives for new investments[493];
6. when and whether antitrust rules with regard to mergers and unilateral behaviour (abuses) 'create disincentives to investments and innovation by leading firms' and when these business activities would reduce the incentives of other market players[494];
7. when a rule-of-reason approach (high flexibility) or a per se rule (high predictability) is more likely to create incentives or disincentives for inter-firm cooperation that could result in more competition and innovativeness;
8. when or whether a far-reaching protection of property rights, for example by granting broad patents, increases the incentives to invent.[495]

As regards the debates on international antitrust harmonization and the international competitiveness of nations, one has to take into account that 'pluralism in competition theories and policy paradigms is neither a shortcoming of science nor a temporary selection problem'[496]. Consequently, an international harmonization of competition rules would hardly lead to a better competition policy and more competitiveness. Quite the reverse, it is important to underline that diversity and decentralism in competition policy and theory are a reflection of the high complexity and dynamics of competition, too. The diversity of anti-trust politics and law is an inevitable consequence and political reaction in order to cope with the multitude of permanently new challenges – caused by free and dynamic markets –

---

[490] Rosenthal and Nicolaides (1997) p. 368.
[491] Ibid. p. 368.
[492] McGinnis (2004) p. 145.
[493] Calkins (1998) p. 213.
[494] Monti (2004) p. 4.
[495] Merges and Nelson (1992) pp. 217f.
[496] Budzinski (2003) p. 29.

and to find an antitrust strategy that takes into account national specifics. Pluralism and decentralism (a) result from and (b) promote further theory and policy innovations which take into account both the aim to protect competition and to promote the international competitiveness of the nation. The systems competition produces institutional alternatives so that countries have the possibility to choose competition rules that fit best with their national market and its environment.

4.2.6 Conclusion

Both international competition and the international competitiveness of nations can be strengthened by a workable regulatory competition supporting the development of better competition law and policy. The effects doctrine and bilateral cooperation agreements build a framework that supports the workability of regulatory competition. Even in case of a bottom-up convergence, regulatory competition would still be workable and help to identify new international best antitrust practices and practices that fit best for certain countries. In contrast to this, an international top-down harmonization would limit the international regulatory competition and would produce several effects which reduce international competition and competitiveness: inefficient case allocation, distortions through selective harmonization, globalized lobbyism, false international compromises, weakened standards at the lowest common denominator[497], missing innovativeness, versatility and diversity, time-consuming international negotiations, and political horse-trading which also would involve other political areas.[498]

[497] In order to avoid a weakening of standards by international harmonization, Fuchs (2000, pp. 370f.) proposes to limit the number of countries which should be allowed to sign an international agreement on minimum standards. If the number of participating countries were limited to those that pursue a national competition policy and that are willing to enforce the principles of a market economy, then the minimum standards could be set high enough to mitigate the problem of false compromises and weakened standards. But there are at least two problems with this statement. Firstly, the mere existence of a national competition policy and the will to enforce a market economy does not mean that these countries want to contribute to relatively high minimum standards. Secondly, if the member countries would fulfil these prerequisites and if other countries are excluded from the agreement, then the question arises whether the agreed minimum standards are still absolutely necessary.

[498] These problematic aspects of international relations could be supplemented by additional problems of ex post opportunism which arise from international relational contracts between sovereign states. These dangers of opportunism could be analysed in more detail by political economics and institutional eco-

Furthermore, a top-down harmonization would probably only lead to an apparent international political consensus, producing a false contentment, governmental failure, and an accumulation of the negative effects of false harmonization.

4.3 The Direct Influence of National Competition Policy

As a consequence of an international harmonization and centralization of competition policy, nations would give up an important instrument to foster the international competitiveness of the domestic economy: for the most part of antitrust, they would no more be able to practice a sovereign, independent, adaptable, flexible, excellent and innovative national competition policy that *directly* could strengthen the international competitiveness.

The following sections describe the possibilities of *national* antitrust authorities to pursue this aim to increase a nation's international competitiveness by means of *national* competition policy. The benefits of *national* competition policy will be highlighted in comparison to an *international* competition policy regime which would be based on international harmonization. Chaps. 4.3.2 and 4.3.3 deal with these issues.

Despite this focus on the differentiation between national and international competition policy, one has be aware of the fact that the mere maintenance of the status quo – i.e. the dominance of *national* competition policy – instead of implementing *international* competition rules can not be regarded as a *sufficient* condition for international competitiveness. In the end, international competitiveness only exists in comparison with other countries, as an unforeseeable result of international regulatory competition and national excellence. Therefore, Chap. 4.3.1 starts with some introductory remarks on a nation's challenge to develop national excellence and international competitiveness within the framework of the international regulatory competition.

nomics (cf. Richter and Furubotn (2003) pp. 526ff.; cf. Melamed (1999) pp. 432f.). On the other hand, by putting aside all political economy issues, transaction costs would remain as one of the most significant impediments to achieve an agreement on optimal international antitrust rules (cf. Guzman (2004) pp. 363ff.).

4.3.1 National Excellence in a Positive-Sum Game

As regards the advantages of international regulatory competition for each economy, it is important to highlight at the beginning that it is the task and responsibility of the national governments and competition authorities to make use of the positive effects *national* competition policy can exert on the international competitiveness of the economy. International regulatory competition is a challenge that has to be taken up if one does not want to lose competitiveness and welfare.

This freedom of action to practice an autonomous and excellent national competition policy has to be distinguished from protectionist activities.[499] Similar to the competition between private firms, the regulatory competition allows innovative competitive behaviour and should involve only those activities that do not harm or eliminate competition. Furthermore, as already mentioned in Chap. 4.2.5.2, the status quo of international antitrust policy – i.e. the application of the effects doctrine and bilateral and multilateral cooperation – limits protectionist behaviour in antitrust. The existing forms of international cooperation make possible both (1) a common understanding on best practices and case-by-case antitrust remedies on the one hand and (2) an innovative and individual national reaction on new problems and challenges in antitrust on the other.

In this respect, the present international regulatory competition has the potential to be a positive-sum game because international competition is strengthened globally. Nevertheless, some nations will be more successful than others because it is unlikely that all nations develop the same abilities, capacities and excellence in national antitrust to strengthen their international competitiveness.

The scope for national excellence in antitrust can be highlighted by the following examples of antitrust policy which are not business as usual:

1. Unprecedented forms of market conduct and new markets are of special importance with regard to a nation′s possibility to perform better than other countries and to foster both competition and competitiveness. The antitrust authority′s excellence already starts with its ability to identify early new forms of anticompetitive behaviour and new markets. Relatively new market phenomena like two-sided markets, strategic alliances, and international horizontal mega-mergers were and are still controversial in economic literature as regards their effect on competition and how to deal with them in antitrust. For instance, two-sided markets were a challenge for antitrust policy because 'two-

[499] Cf. Chap. 4.1.3.

sided markets and firms in those markets behave in ways that seem surprising from the vantage point of traditional industries'[500]. The antitrust analysis of two-sided markets has to consider specific economic principles that determine price levels, price structures, and investment strategies in these industries: 'Prices do not and prices cannot follow marginal costs in each side of the market. Price levels, price structures and investment strategies must optimize output by harvesting the indirect network effects available on both sides. By doing so, businesses in two-sided industries get both sides on board and solve the chicken-and-egg problem.'[501] Consequently, because of such exceptional characteristics of new market phenomena like positive network effects, economic research and competition authorities do not automatically understand the economic and competitive principles of these new market forms so that there is both a need to learn by trial and error and to take into account regional or national specifics. This problem can be highlighted by the theory of oligopoly, too. Although there has been much research on this dominant market form, the analysis of the effects competition policy exerts on oligopolies is still incomplete[502], and probably the actual effects also depend on regional specifics. These uncertainties and regional implications open a wide scope for national antitrust experts to develop national excellence and innovativeness in antitrust and to strengthen the international competitiveness of the nation. In general, one can say that – according to the specifics of certain industries and enterprises – national competition policy profoundly can influence the development of new markets, industries, and corporate strategies which strengthen the international competitiveness.[503]

2. Many competition restraints are borderline cases, they generate ambivalent effects on competition and competitiveness. For instance, a merger could increase competition in one market but simultaneously reduce competition in another market.[504] Competition authorities need a lot of sensitivity for the relevant markets and both for national and

---

500 Evans (2002) p. 69.

501 Ibid. p. 70. The crucial issue is that, compared to traditional industries, price structures in two-sided markets mistakenly could be interpreted as an abuse of market power or as a price cartel, overlooking the fact that these price structures are necessary to get both sides on board and to generate positive network effects for all market participants.

502 Steckelbach (2002) p. 1f.

503 Cf. Becker (1999) p. 164.

504 Tarullo (1999) pp. 453f.

cross-border interrelations. In case of such ambivalent effects on competition and competitiveness, there is a wide scope to weigh the advantages and disadvantages of further concentration. Occasionally, such cases even require 'tradeoffs to be made concerning the economic effects'[505].

3. Many restraints of competition are unique, complex, and fact-intensive cases which require considerable investigations and a high degree of expertise of the responsible competition authority, taking into account the particular circumstances and regional features of this case. For instance, the competition authority has to identify, to quantify and to judge all relevant information as regards the actual and the expected market structure, market conduct, and market performance, i.e. there is a need to forecast the short-, medium- and long-term intensity of competition on the relevant markets. In order to fulfil this task, there is a need to collect a multitude of local, national and international data, for example to discover price trends, lacks of innovation, barriers for market entry and exit, and indications of collusion. Furthermore, in order to assess the evolution of competition in each industrial sector, antitrust authorities have to evaluate the rate of switching of suppliers by customers, and they have to observe trends of development in capacity. In merger control, for example, the responsible competition authority especially has to determine the relevant market, the long-term market concentration, potential scale economies, the contestability of the market, the role of alternative products, and the probability that the merged enterprises will abuse their increased market power on domestic (and foreign) markets. As a consequence of such an individual investigation, a national competition authority could give up its focus on the market structure as the basis of its antitrust decision in case that the authority has acquired detailed knowledge and experience about the management´s bias to apply or not to apply anticompetitive business practices.

This list of specific antitrust enforcement activities is just a small and selective survey of the multitude of activities that belong to the investigative and analytical practices and instruments of competition authorities. Nevertheless, these examples are sufficient …

1. … to show that international regulatory competition is not only about the *codification and readjustment of national antitrust laws*, but also

505 Shelton (1999) p. 60.

about *the challenge to be successful* in all these activities of daily antitrust enforcement, to take the right decisions in each individual case;

2. ... to underline that all these activities offer *a wide scope of action* for national authorities to develop national excellence and competitiveness compared to other countries; and
3. ... to point to several – often underestimated – *factors or parameters* which can and must be influenced by every nation in order to attain national excellence in antitrust. Some of these factors are, for instance, the institutional characteristics of national antitrust courts and competition authorities, the financial and human resources of national antitrust authorities, the political and social system. Other factors like chance and culture are also relevant, but they can not be influenced by governments.

To sum up this aspect to strive for national excellence in antitrust, one aspect has to be emphasized. *National* competition policy is a prerequisite for *every* country to make use of this scope of action, to achieve *its own degree of excellence* in dealing with antitrust problems, and to use these legal possibilities to strengthen the own international competitiveness. The more nations attempt to be successful in this regulatory competition, the more this regulatory competition generates innovative antitrust practices all countries can profit from in the long run, though some more than others.

4.3.2 Flexibility in Antitrust: Taking into Account Specific Characteristics of the National Economy

An international agreement on international competition rules would not only cause a loss of national competence and sovereignty in competition policy. Moreover, national competition authorities would have to give up their possibility to practice a flexible competition policy which takes into account local interests and special characteristics of the national economy, for example the size of the domestic economy, the economic stage of the economy, current technological developments on national and international markets, and the actual competitiveness of certain industries. Every economy is characterized by some of these individual and unique conditions, regional features, and interests that probably make it seem advisable to keep competition policy under the control and responsibility of national competition authorities.

These aspects – some of them will be described more precisely in the subsequent chapters – are one reason why national competition laws differ across countries 'in terms of coverage, content, enforcement procedure, legal system, and with regard to the social, political, cultural, and historical background'[506]. Consequently, it is unlikely that international competition rules automatically improve the economic performance and competitiveness of every country. To the contrary, an international harmonization could reduce the international competitiveness of an economy, because *national* competition policy has – on the basis of its specific and context-sensitive knowledge – a special focus on these national characteristics and can become a comparative advantage in international trade and within the international locational competition. Therefore, compared to an international antitrust authority, national competition authorities that are resident in the affected territory, are more appropriate to practice a specially tailored competition policy, to protect competition on domestic markets, and to increase the international competitiveness of the nation. This can be underlined by some additional remarks.

1. It can be assumed that national antitrust authorities are more conscientious to consider national specifics and to practice a specially tailored antitrust policy, because there is – resulting from geographical proximity – more responsibility and personal interest to protect competition on domestic markets. Especially an independent national competition authority has a genuine interest in the welfare and long-term competitiveness of the domestic economy.

2. The dynamics of private markets (changing technologies, products, marketing instruments, competitive strategies etc.) lead to significant dynamics of competition policy so that competition authorities often have to act pragmatically, hurrying on ahead of the presently existing theoretical insights of anti-trust theory.[507] In order to meet with these challenges, they can not rely on stylized facts and per se rules which could result from an international harmonization.

3. A national competition authority's geographic proximity to the relevant market provides for several further advantages. This is because good competition policy requires a permanent intensive observation of the national markets, and national competition authorities are more suitable to collect relevant information, to observe and forecast national market structures and market processes, to identify anticompetitive behaviour, and to decide on the most effective and efficient

[506] Lin (2002) p. 5.
[507] Berg (1983) p. 21.

remedies.[508] An international competition authority, antitrust court, or dispute settlement mechanism would not have the ability and incentive to observe and judge all domestic markets with the same intensity as the national competition authorities. Consequently, an international antitrust authority would have limited possibilities to protect competition on national markets and to take into account competitiveness considerations.

4. Competition authorities already possess a profound knowledge about the domestic markets and about regional or local peculiarities and preferences. This know-how is decentralized and it is unlikely that one could transfer this knowledge into an international organization – to say nothing of the necessity to keep this knowledge up to date. For instance, an internationalization of antitrust could reduce the informational basis of antitrust experts because domestic enterprises would be much more restrictive as regards the exchange of confidential business information with antitrust experts who could (be obliged to) transfer confidential information to foreign countries. Therefore, an international antitrust authority´s right to ask national antitrust authorities to provide information and expertise in case of need is limited, too. Furthermore, this approach is problematic with respect to the international competitiveness. The national competition authorities would have to obey the internationally harmonized rules and could degenerate into a mere supplier of information and expertise; the final decision would be up to the international competition authority.[509] This could even be the case in a more decentralized approach like the DIAC[510], which suggests an application of international minimum standards by the national competition authorities, combined with a final responsibility of an international antitrust agency (IAA) that has a right to initiate international antitrust cases (so called 'international procedural initiative'). It is doubtful whether the separation of expertise and decision-making, based on inflexible and harmonized rules and regulation, leads to more competition and more competitiveness. The question arises whether the international competition authority would be able and willing to take optimal and responsible decisions based on – probably distorted and contradictory – information that has been provided by several national competition authorities.

---

508 Cf. Vaubel (1992) p. 34.

509 The international bureaucrats who would have to enforce the international competition rules or their application would 'depend ultimately on the support of national governments' (McGinnis (2004) p. 130).

510 Fikentscher and Immenga (1995).

4.3.2.1 The Use of Abstract Terms and Concepts in National and International Competition Law

In general, competition law can not provide detailed regulations for antitrust cases because it needs a high adaptability with regard to future antitrust cases.[511] This is why present competition law mainly serves as a guideline in antitrust practice. For instance, the USA emphasize the benefits of a flexible national competition policy. The primary sources of US competition policy – the Sherman Act, the Clayton Act, the Robinson Patman Act, and the Celler-Kefauver Merger Act – 'are relatively concise and lacking in detail. In reality, most antitrust policy in the United States originates in court interpretation of the broad language of the statutes'[512]. Many details and even definitions – e.g. as regards the relevant market and the term 'market dominance' – are left to be determined within an evolutionary and dynamic process by national competition authorities and the courts of jurisdiction. Consequently, the US antitrust enforcement and especially the courts have the possibility to amend and improve their former scholarly and economic convictions as a reaction to new imbalances or developments in national and international competition.[513] Similarly, the competition provisions of the EC Treaty 'are all written in general terms, dependant upon appropriate application by experienced enforcers and judges in complicated and differing circumstances'[514].

In contrast to this, an international harmonization and centralization of competition rules would lead, on the one hand, to an inflexible antitrust policy and enforcement, but on the other hand to an increase of unsystematic interventions and over-hasty attempts of further harmonization. This sounds contradictory, but such a situation could occur when the participating countries do not find a consensus for a long-term framework reform of the established legal institutions. Short-term interventionism – i.e. the attempt to neutralize the negative effects of the status quo instead of solving the source of a problem – would be used as a substitute for long-term solutions. These two negative effects of international harmonization – i.e. the resulting inflexibility and the danger of increasing interventionism – could occur simultaneously, because interventionism often is a consequence of a structural reform jam.

This problem could be weakened but cannot be solved by the enactment of an international competition law that also provides a wide range of how to implement and enforce the rules. The most important problems of inter-

---

511 Immenga (2007) p. 10.

512 Fox and Pitofsky (1997) p. 240.

513 Drexl (1998) p. 16.

514 Tarullo (1999) p. 451.

national antitrust – especially international hardcore cartels – would have to be solved by a 'rule of law' approach so that a 'rule of reason' treatment and a 'more economic approach' could not be used to provide enough flexibility for excellent competition policy.[515] Though, an international competition law – like national competition laws – could be based on abstract concepts like 'market', 'market power', 'relevant market', 'dominance', and 'exclusion', and the international competition authority could apply 'advanced economic theories to *define* these terms and develop elaborate doctrines to *apply* them'[516]. Bush[517] underlines, that 'sound competition policy is a moving target' so that 'antitrust law keeps up with economic theory through reinterpretation of laws and revision of regulations – often without legislative action'. But even if the international competition regime would make use of this scope to reinterpret the international competition law in the light of current economics, four problems would still remain:

1. On the one hand, abstract concepts and terms only offer a limited scope, they are not a substitute for all necessary adjustments or fundamental reforms which have to be undertaken by an international competition authority in order to keep up with economic theory and market developments.
2. Furthermore, it is doubtful whether an international competition authority should have the right to reinterpret international laws without legislative action of the member countries. This could be seen both as a too strong limitation of national sovereignty and as a serious democratic deficit.
3. Thirdly, abstract concepts and terms on the international level, which are to be applied on the national level (decentralized approach), would lead to a heterogeneous application and enforcement of international competition law and could undermine the original intent to reduce international distortions and conflicts.
4. Fourthly, abstract concepts and terms could be an obstacle to achieve an international consensus while (re)negotiating and modernizing the

---

[515] Both the 'rule of reason' approach and the 'more economic approach' offer the flexibility to consider the specifics of each individual antitrust case. Both approaches require more antitrust resources than a 'rule of law' and a non-economic approach, but they generally lead to more appropriate antitrust decisions in each particular case (cf. Maahs (2005) p. 52).

[516] Cf. Bush (2005) p. 4.

[517] Ibid. p. 4.

international antitrust laws. In this way, abstract terms could increase the short-term flexibility of antitrust enforcement, but they would reduce the long-term flexibility to adjust international antitrust rules because abstract terms lead to international heterogeneity and could result from a lack of international consensus.

4.3.2.2 The Size of an Economy

An important question concerning international harmonization is whether small market economies – i.e. both developing and industrialized countries with little spending and purchasing power, a relatively small population or a high population dispersion[518] – have an advantage or disadvantage by voting for international antitrust standards and an international antitrust authority.

On the one hand, an international institution could support the interests of small countries to protect themselves against international mega-mergers and international cartels. Small countries generally possess the ability to apply the effects doctrine, but their political and economic power to enforce their interests against large countries is limited. Furthermore, small countries can profit from an adoption of competition law of large jurisdictions and from international harmonization because this would reduce transaction and compliance costs both for the small economy and for enterprises that want to do business in small countries. For instance, foreign investors probably are not willing to learn the competition laws of small economies if these laws diverge significantly from other jurisdictions.[519] On the other hand, there is a danger that small economies could be outvoted within an international framework. The experiences within the WTO show the ambivalent effects of harmonization and centralization with respect to the interests of developing countries. Something similar could happen to all small countries in case of international competition rules because it is rather unlikely that the large industrialized economies would not use their economic and political power to control the international institution.

A second question is whether small economies are characterized by certain features and natural conditions which – with regard to the international

[518] Gal mentions three main factors which influence the market size: 'population size, population dispersion, and the degree of openness to trade'. Furthermore, 'a combination of additional economic, geographical, technological, legal or political factors that create market boundaries and restrain entry of potential competitors' influence the size of a market (Gal (2003a) p. 3).

[519] Gal (2003) p. 259.

competitiveness of the nation – generally necessitate a special, strictly context-sensitive competition policy so that an international harmonization of competition policy could be harmful. According to Gal, small market economies – like, for instance, the Israeli economy and many developing and least developed countries – are characterized by 'highly concentrated markets protected by entry barriers'[520]. This is true not for all, but for many domestic markets in small economies so that there is a need for a special competition policy.

On the one hand, small markets necessitate a strict competition policy. Especially developing countries often only permit a small number of companies, leading to oligopolistic and monopolistic market structures.[521] Consequently, the marginal cases of large economies, i.e. oligopolistic and monopolistic markets with high market power of a domestic incumbent, often 'constitute ... the mainstream cases for small economies'[522]. In many domestic markets, small economies have limited or no possibilities to promote competition in case of need because the small economy and population only permit a small number of companies. Moreover, small markets are characterized by limited self-correcting powers[523], there is less probability of new market entries and potential competition from abroad. Even in case of an absolutely open economy, small economies are often not attractive enough for foreign companies, for example because of the impossibility to reach the minimum optimal scale (MOS)[524], because of a lack of skilled labour, or because of concentrated vertically linked markets.[525] Because of these market entry barriers, the elasticity of supply in small economies is relatively low and market power has a relatively high durability so that 'in small economies the typical market share which signifies market

---

520 Gal (2003) p. vii; cf. Gal (2003a) pp. 2ff.

521 For a critical point of view as regards the alleged necessity of monopolistic and oligopolistic market structures in developing countries, see Lachmann (1997) pp. 205f. Lachmann underlines that – although scale economies could be generated on monopolistic and oligopolistic markets – the size of an enterprise does not automatically indicate its international competitiveness. Consequently, small market economies do not necessarily imply oligopolistic and monopolistic markets.

522 Gal (2003a) p. 2.

523 Gal (2003) p. 253.

524 On the other hand, a small domestic market could make it easier for a foreign enterprise 'to redirect part of its supply to discipline any supercompetitive prices in that nation' (McGinnis (2004) p. 145). Though, it is doubtful whether foreign enterprises are always interested in disciplining local monopolies in small economies.

525 Gal (2003) pp.21ff.

dominance should be lower than in a large one'[526]. This recommendation to use smaller market shares as an indicator of market power can be supported by the probability that companies in small economies have a lower elasticity of supply 'owing to the prevalence of scale economies and oligopolistic interdependence'[527]. This all is why there is a general need for stricter competition policy compared to large economies. Small economies especially have to practice a stringent ex post control of abusive business practices with regard to dominant companies. Furthermore, merger control and anti-cartel policy have to be on the alert to prevent further concentration and collusion because small markets and a small number of suppliers intensify the oligopolistic interdependencies and make it easier to practice parallelism or to cartelize.[528] Especially vertical restraints 'are more harmful to buyers the smaller a national (or other) economy is'[529] because of high market entry barriers. With respect to the problem of market shares, Gal also refers to a special problem of applying a strict competition policy in small economies. In case that an antitrust authority enforces remedies against anticompetitive business practices so that a company decides or is forced to exit the market, the high market entry barriers that are characteristic for small economies could be increased and would prevent new market entries so that strict competition policy finally could cause a further concentration of the relevant market.[530]

On the other hand, small economies often deliberately choose a permissive competition policy and a high level of market concentration and monopolization. There are several reasons for this strategy:

1. Small economies have to deal with the risk to generate inefficient capacities if too many domestic enterprises – which are not successful exporters yet – supply the domestic market (cf. the 'excess capacity theorem'[531]).

2. Correspondingly, small countries frequently strive to reach the MOS of enterprises in order to produce efficiently for the domestic markets (so-called efficiency defense) and to have a chance to compete with foreign companies. In this way, economic efficiency becomes the primary objective of competition policy and dominates other political

[526] Gal (2003a) p. 9.
[527] Gal (2003) p. 255.
[528] Ibid. p. 254.
[529] Fikentscher (2003) p. 10.
[530] Gal (2003a) pp. 9f.
[531] See Chap. 4.3.2.3.

and economic aims in small countries.[532] Relatively small economies like Canada rather pursue a so-called 'total welfare approach' whereas large economies, like for example the USA with regard to their merger enforcement policy, generally favour a consumer surplus approach.[533] This is why antitrust policy – especially with regard to mergers and inter-firm cooperation – in small economies sometimes has to be more lenient compared to large economies like the USA, the European Union, and Japan.

3. Furthermore, small economies like Belgium, the Netherlands, and Switzerland often make use of the so-called 'vent-for-surplus' strategy, i.e. they have a relatively high export quota because their own market is too small to absorb domestic production. This is why a more permissive competition policy with respect to export industries could be necessary in order to reach the MOS and to become internationally competitive. On the other hand, small economies often also have a relatively high import quota so that consumers are vulnerable to foreign market power.[534] In this case, a strict competition policy against foreign exporters could be justified.
4. Moreover, small economies could be interested to practice a permissive competition policy in order to increase the contestability of domestic markets. For instance, in specific industries there could be 'a strong concern toward the concentration of ownership of its conglomerates' because these conglomerates are often 'the main challengers to incumbent monopolies, which are often controlled by other conglomerates'[535]. This statement is in line with the theory of contestable markets which underlines a multi-product firms′ ability to penetrate new markets and to become a potential competitor.

As regards the empirical evidence for developing countries, there is no clear answer which strategy is more apt to promote economic growth and to strengthen the international competitiveness. In some cases, a monopolization or cartelization of national industries – partly combined with governmental aid – can result in economic growth. In other cases, this strategy was not successful.[536] In order to balance this trade-off between productive

532 Gal (2003a) p. 6; cf. Anderson and Khosla (1995) pp. 12, 99.
533 This is also why 'the Canadian competition policy model is somewhat more flexible than its U.S. counterpart with respect to aspects of industrial restructuring' (Anderson and Khosla (1995) pp. 56, 94).
534 Cf. Norman (1998) p. 58.
535 Gal (2003) p. 253.
536 Lachmann (1997) pp. 215, 218f.

efficiency and allocative efficiency, small economies have to apply a rule of reason approach that allows to weigh the advantages and disadvantages of more or less market concentration and that offers enough flexibility to react on unprecedented developments, considering the actual competitive situation of the market and specific (superior) public interests without being bound to a theoretical antitrust concept. For instance, in small economies merger transactions and similar business conduct are more likely to affect substantial public and superior interests. According to Gal, in a small economy 'the interdependencies in the interests of various stakeholders are likely to be more significantly affected by a particular market transaction'[537].

With regard to the need to allow a higher market concentration in order to generate scale economies, the competition policy of a small economy could practice an efficiency and welfare approach. The primary aim to achieve technical and productive efficiency could be pursued by following some of the basic principles of the Chicago School of Antitrust Analysis. Though, on the other hand, with regard to the problem of high and durable market concentration and allocative inefficiency in small economies, the competition policy has to combine this rather lenient approach with specially tailored solutions for each market. For instance, besides the above mentioned necessity to practice a strict ex post merger control and to fight against an abuse of dominant market positions, the long-term market concentration could even require a regulation of dominant companies – for example in case that these dominant firms try to exert political pressure – or governmental (financial) support for potential new competitors, for example by lowering market entry barriers. In the long run, it would be an optimal solution for these concentrated domestic markets if all domestic enterprises became internationally competitive and if international trade and the global integration of national markets provided for more competition. Though, it is unlikely to realize this optimistic scenario for all sectors in all small economies.

As regards the debate about international competition rules, there are several aspects why international competition rules could be harmful for small economies. Firstly, it is likely that international competition rules would be based on the economic paradigms of large economies so that they would not apply to small economies. Secondly, international competition rules likely follow a rule of law approach and consist of 'fit-all' formulations[538] because otherwise there would be too much potential for international conflicts resulting from a heterogeneous application by the

[537] Gal (2003) p. 252.
[538] Gal (2003a) p. 2.

member countries. Consequently, international competition rules would not consider the need of small countries for more flexibility and to carefully balance competing considerations.[539] Thirdly, an internationally harmonized competition law that has to be applied and enforced by the *national* competition authorities would not deter foreign companies from anticompetitive conduct within small economies because these small economies do not have the political and economic power to enforce the harmonized rules. Furthermore, the small country possibly would harm its own economy by excluding the foreign companies from their domestic market. Therefore, even an international organization or dispute settlement mechanism probably would not help to avoid this problem because the foreign companies cannot be forced to go on doing (fair) business in the small country. In sum, small countries have to be very cautious with regard to international antitrust harmonization. Only in case that international competition rules offer enough flexibility to deal with the specific situation of small economies, harmonization might be welfare-enhancing for small economies.[540]

4.3.2.3 The Economic Stage of an Economy

The economic stage of an economy raises several questions with regard to the role of competition policy, too. Firstly, it is a controversial question whether and to which extent developing countries should implement competition rules and foster competition on domestic markets in order to support their development goals.[541] Secondly, as regards the debate about an international harmonization of antitrust enforcement, one has to consider to which degree developing countries or countries in transition should favour a different kind of competition policy compared to modern industrial countries. These two questions arise because of the fundamental economic differences between developing and industrialized countries. Developing countries are handicapped compared to industrialized countries and they have to take into account several national characteristics and needs which depend on specific development strategies and which refer to certain structures of markets and industries: for example small markets (cf. Chap. 4.3.2.2), infant industries, the role of natural resources, the high dependence on imports, and the importance of a specific sector for the whole economy. Developing countries and countries in transition do not necessarily focus on safeguarding competitive markets. Instead, they strive for

---

[539] Gal (2003) p. 255.
[540] Ibid. p. 260.
[541] Liang (2004) p. 110.

growth, they want to catch up with the industrial countries and therefore there could be a need for a special competition policy that is tailored to their stage of social, cultural, and economic development. Furthermore, governmental interventions like e.g. industrial policy, subsidies, and market foreclosure, could become a more important instrument than strict antitrust policies.

Consequently, especially developing countries are in an ambivalent situation as regards the effects of international competition rules. On the one hand, they could profit from an international antitrust enforcement mechanism. An international competition authority could take into account the interests of developing countries that are unable to protect themselves against international restrictive business practices. According to Levenstein et al., especially developing countries are negatively affected by international hardcore cartels[542], and they often do not have the economic and political power to protect themselves against hard core cartels and dumping laws of the industrialized countries.[543] Furthermore, international mergers, which have been approved by the industrialized countries, could cause a too high concentration on the markets of developing countries. In general, the industrialized countries do not take into account the interests of other countries when deciding on the remedies and conditions before allowing a merger.[544] Theoretically, the developing countries could forbid the merger by applying the effects doctrine, but in practice they often would have to accept the situation without being able to change the merger conditions significantly.[545]

Because of these problems, in 1973 several developing countries had initiated negotiations on the UN-RBP, which had been adopted in 1980 by the UNCTAD.[546] Furthermore, they had proposed an implementation of competition rules against private competition restraints in 1986 during the WTO Uruguay Round (1986-1994), but the industrialized countries re-

---

542 Levenstein et al. (2003) pp. 10ff.

543 Evenett (2003) pp. 29ff.; cf. Immenga (2004) p. 17; cf. Tarullo (1999) p. 452.

544 For instance, the merging companies could be obliged by the industrialized countries to grant licences or to cut certain long-term supply contracts which endanger competition within the industrialized countries. Other long-term contracts which harm developing countries probably would not be offended; to the contrary, the industrialized countries could be interested in maintaining these contracts and not to grant licences to licensees located in developing countries. On the other hand, developing countries also can profit from antitrust policy of industrialized countries and take a free-rider position (cf. Guzman (2004) p. 362).

545 Moeschel (2005a) p. 604.

546 Cf. Chap. 2.2.5.2.

fused to do so.[547] The developing countries feared the anti-competitive practices of transnational corporations. This is also why they insisted that the 1999 review of the Agreement on Trade-Related Investment Measures (TRIMs), which had to take place five years after this agreement was put into force in 1994, should include a reflection on the necessity of additional rules on investment and competition policy (Art. 9 TRIMs).[548]

On the other hand, many developing countries and the UNCTAD are reserved as regards an agreement on competition policy in the WTO and an international harmonization of competition law.[549] Such an agreement, which probably would include the WTO principles of non-discrimination (national treatment; most-favoured-nation treatment) and transparency, could be a threat to many domestic enterprises which are not able to compete on equal terms ('non-discrimination') with the enterprises of the industrialized countries. Furthermore, it is doubtful to what extent an international competition policy regime could take into account the interests of developing countries.

Because of this ambivalence, the UNCTAD underlines that 'in the context of developing countries, flexibility in applying competition law and policy may be particularly necessary in order not to impede efficiency, growth or development goals ... and coherence would need to be ensured between competition policy and other policies aimed at promoting development'[550]. Therefore, the UNCTAD favours a decentralized and subdued approach for international competition policy which makes it possible 'to strengthen information exchange among competition authorities ... this might promote convergence among competition policies and support national and international efforts to promote competition, efficiency and consumer welfare'[551]. As a first step to achieve this aim, the UNCTAD is promoting competition policy in developing countries in order to strengthen their international competitiveness and their growth and welfare.[552] Fuchs[553] holds that minimum standards could promote competition policy in developing countries and this could be considered a 'comparative advantage' compared to economies without national competition policy. But

547 Wins (2000) p. 157.

548 Meiklejohn (1999) p. 1247.

549 Cf. Meessen (2000) p. 9.

550 UNCTAD (1998) p. 3; Cernat (2004) pp. 2ff.; Brusick et al. (2004). Similarly, Adhikari and Knight-John (2004, pp. 1ff.) state that each developing country should have its own competition policy and law which fits to country-specific requirements.

551 UNCTAD (1998) p. 3.

552 Cf. UNCTAD (2002).

553 Cf. Fuchs (2000) p. 365.

with regard to an international harmonization, the UNCTAD itself is rather skeptical and seems to favour certain forms of cooperation like exchange of information and bottom-up convergence.

Apart from this, one could generally doubt the relevance of competition policy for developing countries because the success of economies such as Singapore, PR China, and South Korea gives evidence that (strict) competition policy is not the crucial factor for the economic growth of developing countries: 'In fact, competition policy played a negligible role in the era of rapid economic development in South Korea ... Without competition policy, Hong Kong and Singapore have realized high economic growth performance over decades ... the experience of post-war Japan could also be treated as a demonstration of the irrelevance of competition policy for rapid economic growth even in a large and relatively closed economy'[554]. Free trade, good governance, state-led development, and national flexibility with regard to the application of trade policy and industrial policy seem to be the decisive factors for the success of developing countries. Therefore, it has been claimed that modern competition policy becomes more relevant once that the economy has caught up with the industrialized economies. In the early stage of economic development in which developing countries try to catch up with the industrialized countries, they are rather characterized by the adoption of technology from the industrialized countries, i.e. by means of imitation (cf. PR China). This investment-based imitation strategy often depends on governmental interventions such as investment subsidies and limits on product market competition.[555] After having reached the technological frontier, the economy has to switch to an innovation-based strategy. During this late stage of catching up with the industrialized countries and generating a national competitive advantage, the government has to cut back its industrial policy

[554] Liang (2004) pp. 75ff.; also cf. Cernat (2004) pp. 2f.

[555] These limits to product market competition have been supported by various economic arguments whose evidence at present is more or less disputed. Firstly, one has to think of the classical infant industry argument. Secondly, according to the 'excess capacity theorem', it has been stated that promoting competition by establishing monopolistic competition could generate inefficient production structures so that the economy would benefit from a reduction in the number of monopolistic competitors because this would reduce the extent of unused capacities (Chamberlin (1933) pp. 104ff.; cf. Margolis (1985) pp. 265ff.). For a critical point of view towards the excess capacity argument, also see Lachmann (1997) pp. 205f., who holds that overcapacities must not be seen as a waste of resource. Instead, excess capacities could be regarded as a necessary feature of workable competition. Thirdly, there have been arguments on the danger of excessive and ruinous competition (cf. Liang (2004) p. 115).

and has to practice a rather strict competition policy because ultimately it is not governments who generate innovations; it is competitive markets that produce innovation and national champions.[556]

Lin doubts this 'first-industrial-policy-then-competition-policy' argument and states that nowadays increasing globalization could make it difficult for countries to grow 'without inflow of foreign capital and technology, without liberalizing its domestic industries and opening up trade with the rest of the world'[557]. The early adoption of a modern competition policy could help to attract foreign investment and to promote trade and competition.[558] Furthermore, the role of industrial policy is still ambivalent. Despite the success of Asian industrial policy in identifying strategically important industries and potential national champions, 'no systematic positive relationship has been found between firm size and profit, export activity, or R&D, and an equally large number of notorious failures of industrial policy can be cited'[559]. Similar to this argumentation, the OECD underlines the importance to build up a competition culture and states that there is 'persuasive evidence from all over the world confirming that rising levels of competition have been unambiguously associated with increased economic growth, productivity, investment and increased average living standards.'[560] This is because 'there are strong links between competition policy and numerous basic pillars of economic development, such as policies on governance, privatization, deregulation or regulatory reform, trade liberalization, the attraction of private risk capital, the creation of a strong entrepreneurial class of SMEs, agriculture, health, innovation, poverty alleviation and education.'[561]

In conclusion, the empirical and theoretical evidence shows an ambivalent role of competition policy and industrial policy as regards the economic growth and competitiveness of developing countries. On the one hand, even developing countries agree on the general importance of sound competition principles, especially to protect themselves against abusive business practices, international cartels, and anticompetitive mergers among multinational enterprises.[562] Nonetheless, national sovereignty and flexibility in practicing competition policy and industrial policy could be crucial factors for catching up and attaining international competitiveness

[556] Cf. Acemoglu et al. (2006) pp. 37ff.
[557] Lin (2002) p. 34.
[558] Ibid. p. 34.
[559] Cernat (2004) p. 3.
[560] OECD (2003) p. 8.
[561] Ibid. p. 8.
[562] Winslow (2001) p. 130.

because, 'in the light of the existing disadvantages of developing countries and the reality of existing trade barriers, free trade is insufficient to enhance competitiveness'[563]. Instead, 'governments need to be enabled to give short-term, degressive, limited waivers (second best solution) in order to help their industries become competitive on a national and international level.'[564] Consequently, an international harmonization of competition law and policy could be disadvantageous for catching up with the industrialized countries. Hence developing countries should adopt a pragmatic approach. This would also be beneficial for them in case that modern competition policy nowadays plays a more important role for generating economic growth and competitiveness. The governments of developing countries should be able to apply a national competition policy in a flexible manner which serves their developing goals and which can be adapted to their industrial policy and their stage of economic development, too.

4.3.2.4 The Relation Between Competition Policy and other Political Fields

A further example highlighting the importance of *national* decision-making power for the international competitiveness results from the close connection between competition policy and other political areas. Antitrust policy also can serve to achieve 'secondary objectives'. The effects of competition policy could affect (a) political areas like defence and public security, which have a rather *indirect* influence on the international competitiveness of the nation, and (b) political areas like research policy, education policy, media policy, tax policy, ecological policy, structural policy, and distribution policy, which have a rather *direct* influence on the international competitiveness. A sovereign and autonomous national competition policy is able to consider these economic, social, and political aims within an overall context and to find individual and flexible solutions by looking after the interests and the international competitiveness of the state. In extreme cases, a government could grant a general exemption of certain domestic industries from national competition law, especially with regard to superior national interests like defence, national and public security and so on which mostly have a rather indirect influence on the international competitiveness. This subject will be dealt with in Chap. 4.3.3.1.2.

The following examples give an idea of the close linkage between competition policy and other themes of economic policy, focusing on those ar-

---

[563] Cf. Lachmann (1999) p. 37; cf. Lachmann (1997) p. 218.
[564] Cf. Lachmann (1999) p. 37.

eas with a rather direct influence on the international competitiveness of the nation[565]:

National Competition Policy in Politically and Economically Sensitive Sectors. Mergers – but also other kinds of competition restraints – can affect substantial national interests such as press diversity[566], a safe and sound banking sector, and modern supply grids owned by domestic enterprises. For instance, the location of an indispensable industry could be at risk in the course of merger negotiations and merger control procedures. Strategically important know-how and jobs could be outsourced or cut back, for example in basic research and in certain high-tech industries. Consequently, the anti-trust considerations of an international competition authority are not a sufficient substitute for national policy. In such cases, the national competition authorities and the national governments have to keep their sovereignty and their supervisory power in the relevant politically and economically sensitive sectors.

For instance, a national competition authority should be able to decide autonomously on necessary conditions which have to be imposed on merging enterprises. Merger conditions can be imposed precisely in the interest of national competition and competitiveness, e.g. the condition to give up certain business activities, to sell particular equities or subsidiary companies, to cancel anti-competitive long-term supply contracts, to accept certain product-standards, to give licenses, or to reduce license fees etc. This can be of great importance for the international competitiveness of domestic enterprises and the national economy as a whole.

In contrast to this, national governments often fail to protect national interests by following personal or other political interests, but this cannot be taken as an argument in favour of international harmonization or centralization claims. Instead, it is important to find an efficient division of labour between the government and an independent national competition authority. Competences have to be transferred to an *independent* national competition authority as far as possible; only absolutely fundamental decisions, which are dominated by the political sphere, have to be taken by national government (or by an additional sector-specific supervisory commission) so that superior national interests can be taken into account. This problem can be further clarified by two examples.

565 Cf. Mitschke (2006) pp. 30f.
566 Cf. Hutter (2006) pp. 112ff.

1. On the one hand, a recent decision of the independent German Federal Cartel Office against a weakening of press cartel rules[567] and against media concentration[568] has shown that an independent national competition authority is necessary in order to avoid polit-economically motivated decisions by the government.
2. On the other hand, the hotly disputed 2005 decree[569] of the French government to protect certain sensitive industries – like defence, bugging equipment, computer security systems, cryptology equipment, private security activities, and dual civil-military technologies – against foreign one-third stakes or takeovers by demanding a governmental pre-authorization has to be classified as belonging to the political sphere.[570] In this respect, it is the government´s task to protect fundamental national interests like the public order, public security, or national defence without falling into unfair protectionist practices.

Consequently, as regards the internationalization debate, it is important that the nations keep their right to take action against a merger for other than antitrust reasons. The ECMR includes such a special regulation so that 'Member States may take appropriate measures to protect legitimate interests other than those taken into consideration by this Regulation and compatible with the general principles and other provisions of Community law. Public security, plurality of the media and prudential rules shall be regarded as legitimate interests within the meaning of the first subparagraph' (Article 21 IV ECMR).

Furthermore, for example as regards the media sector, competition law and other specific laws (for example media law) have to be distinguished. The mere antitrust authority could be located at an international institution, but the media concentration competence would have to stay under national

[567] In 2004, the Federal Government of Germany planned a relaxation of the rules on mergers in the press sector. The draft rules have been met with strong resistance. This example shows that even national governments are not willing to protect competition, when political and personal interests are predominant.

[568] In 2005/06, the German Federal Cartel Office ('Bundeskartellamt') and the German Media Board (KEK) rejected plans by the German media group Axel Springer AG to take over the private broadcaster ProSiebenSat.1. This antitrust decision is in line with a strict interpretation of the relevant market by the Federal Cartel Office, whereas politicians frequently demand for a more permissive definition of the relevant market and its geographic dimension (cf. Frankfurter Allgemeine Zeitung (2006) p. 17).

[569] Decret No. 2005-1739 of 30 December 2005.

[570] Cf. OECD (2006) p. 43.

authority, preferably under the responsibility of an independent institution. In other words, if the international antitrust authority would allow a merger, the national authority still would be able to stop the merger.[571] It goes without saying that such a useful separation of competences would necessitate intensive cooperation and could cause efficiency problems and international conflicts.

National Competition Policy and Political Programs. Political programs and supportive measures – for example organized as a public private partnership – which depend on the existence of certain domestic industries, could be jeopardized if international mergers or cartels get strong influence on the relevant industries. For instance, the national aim to establish a new ecological policy, possibly in conflict with the interests of foreign countries, could be jeopardized if foreign enterprises try to get influence on domestic enterprises that are engaged in the relevant industries, for example the environment technology sector or the chemical industry. Although competition policy only has limited possibilities to prevent mergers and acquisitions and other forms of inter-firm cooperation that do not conflict with the protection of competition, national competition policy often has a small scope of action to take into account the political and national interest to carry on these political programs. For instance, antitrust remedies offer a scope to consider certain political programs without reducing allocative efficiency.

National Competition Policy and Strategic Investments. Strategic investments by the government could become worthless as a result of changes in market structure, relocations of plants, and a new management policy which could be caused by mergers or by monopolizing and cartelization processes in certain industries. For instance, well-established strategic investments in infrastructure, industry clusters, technology centers, science parks, business incubators[572], and research capacities (e.g. addi-

---

[571] Cf. Niederleithinger (1990) p. 109.

[572] Governments often invest in intermediaries like business incubators or technology centers which have the task to provide services and locations for new and innovative firms and to support technological networks and knowledge spillovers. These intermediaries could be classified as market failure in the venture capital markets because private markets show deficiencies in providing supportive infrastructures and investments for technological innovation and business start-ups (cf. European Commission (2002); European Commission (2004a) p. 15). Though, one has to be careful with this argumentation because in several cases it is doubtful whether governmental activities to promote R&D can be justified with the existence of market failure (cf. Fritsch et al. (2005) pp. 309ff.).

tional teaching and research capacities built up in a domestic university environment), possibly with strong local linkages and a high social rate of return (e.g. because of positive external effects within the domestic innovation system), could be thrown into jeopardy if a planned merger causes the relocation of an enterprise which is a main beneficiary of these public investments or which is essential for the entire investment.[573] Moreover, national attempts to improve the international competitiveness of the relevant domestic industries compared to foreign countries would be in vain because foreign firms would also profit from these measures in case of a cross-border merger. Foreign governments could even try to receive a free-rider position by supporting their firms to merge with domestic firms that have been supported by their governments in fields like research or by other preferential treatments.

As regards joint public-private investments in R&D, both the private and the public share of these long-term investments also could get lost because of the following reason. Theoretically, there is a possibility that actual or threatened mergers and acquisitions could 'make the companies involved less innovative' because 'R&D performing firms are vulnerable to take-over bids by raiders who, having gained control, cut back on R&D, realizing a capital gain in the process'[574]. Some 'raiders' could follow a myopic strategy that undervalues the future gains of R&D investments so that they downsize or stop R&D processes of the target firm.[575] Consequently, public investments in R&D would be in vain. The empirical evidence does not generally indicate that changes of control (mergers and acquisitions) have a negative effect on the R&D intensity and innovativeness.[576] However, in certain cases, a downsizing of R&D investments resulting from mergers and acquisitions could weaken the international

---

[573] Cf. Meessen (2000) p. 10. Also see McFetridge (1993) pp. 208ff., who underlines the negative effects that could result from shifting innovative activities abroad. An innovative firm is integrated within a complex domestic innovation system and it has at least three linkages within this system which would be cut off in case that this innovative firm is relocated abroad: (1) Collaboration with domestic users and suppliers to improve products also depends on close geographic proximity; (2) Innovative firms generate high-tech experts who become future high-tech entrepreneurs; furthermore they provide an incentive for students to specialize in high-tech science; (3) An innovative firm confers so-called demonstration benefits to local rivals, i.e. geographic proximity and direct observation supports the ability of rivals to imitate or copy product and process innovations.

[574] Cf. McFetridge (1993) pp. 201ff.

[575] Cf. ibid. pp. 201ff.

[576] Cf. ibid. pp. 203ff.

competitiveness. A national competition policy could take this aspect into account, although modern national competition laws provide only limited scope to consider such aspects.

National Competition Policy Combined with other Political Processes. Certain national and international antitrust cases could necessitate a fine-tuning and coordination of competition policy with other national political instruments. For instance, the aim to protect the fundamental benefits of a market economy – i.e. free markets and efficiency enhancing competition – and to strengthen the international competitiveness of the economy could be achieved by promoting small and medium sized companies and to reduce their structural disadvantages compared to large companies.[577] In order to avoid one-sided and strict interventions like subsidies or a total exception from competition law, which could be introduced in favour of small and medium sized enterprises, the aim to remedy the structural disadvantages of small and medium sized companies and to strengthen their competitiveness also could be achieved by a complex *bundle* of political measures and a pragmatic policy mix.[578] Competition policy – for example the promotion of inter-firm cooperation between small and medium-sized forms – would be one of these measures, besides others like fiscal policy (e.g. lower corporate tax rates and higher subsidies), labour law, corporate law, and anti-corruption measures. The combination of such bundles of political measures necessitates a fine-tuning and coordination on the national level. Furthermore, there could be unforeseen interactions between the different measures so that the bundle would have to be readjusted by the national authorities. These tasks could not be managed by an international competition regime.

Another example where there is a need to apply a policy mix that necessitates a national fine-tuning of competition policy could be a national or sectoral economic crisis. An economic crisis could require both pro- and anti-competitive measures in antitrust that (a) probably would not be allowed under an international competition policy regime if the international antitrust regime does not include a waiver for such an economic crisis, but which (b) would play an important role in order to overcome the crisis. For instance, there could be a need for more direct and indirect governmental intervention, regulation, and state participation in order to stabilize markets, for example by means of a temporary cartelization of certain sectors. On the other hand, the policy mix also could necessitate fine-tuned measures like divestments in order to shape more competitive market structures.

---

577 Cf. Poeche (1982) p. 134.
578 Ibid. p. 134.

Conclusion. All these different cases underline the role of *national* competition policy in regard to the international competitiveness of a nation and its enterprises. It is apparent that an international competition authority would not be able or willing to protect all these national interests. Even a decentralized system of international competition policy, i.e. the implementation of internationally harmonized competition rules combined with a decentralized decision-making of the national competition authorities, would not be sufficient to protect these vital national interests in case of need.

On the other hand, it has to be conceded that *national* competition policy has a limited scope to take influence on mergers and acquisitions that do not harm competition. The national competition authority always has to follow its fundamental principles so that there is no room for interventionist and arbitrary decisions that deviate from national competition law. The basic principles presented in Chap. 4.1 have to be obeyed; national competition policy would be misguided if it primarily followed competitiveness aims instead of protecting competition. Though, the national interest in protecting its international competitiveness could be considered in antitrust decisions, for example with regard to balancing antitrust remedies in merger control, or by certain legal initiatives of the government, for example by granting an exemption from antitrust (cf. Chap. 4.3.3.1.2).

4.3.3 Strategies of Permissive, Protectionist and Strict Competition Policy

Chapters 4.3.1 and 4.3.2 have shown that *flexibility* is essential for strengthening the international competitiveness of the nation. A major advantage of *national* competition policy is that the required dose of competition policy can be determined more flexibly from case to case. The national competition authority or the government can choose between a rather permissive or strict competition policy. The possibility of *flexible* decision-making exists both in domestic and cross-border cases. The advantages and disadvantages of each of these strategies, i.e. the chances and limits of applying these strategies with regard to the international competitiveness, are shown in the following subchapters. The underlying premise in considering these strategies or options is to judge each 'case' individually on the basis of a reliable, non-interventionist, non-discriminatory and non-protectionist competition policy that involves both mergers and acquisitions, inter-firm cooperation and cartelization, monopolization, and abusive practices. Only in exceptional cases, a protectionist antitrust decision could be justified (cf. Chap. 4.3.3.2).

Consequently, it has to be underlined the role of national competition authorities to *individually* take into account the national specifics and interests to strengthen its international competitiveness without being attached to a one-sided and extreme position in antitrust enforcement, i.e. without blindly following only one of these strategies. Accordingly, the following sections are no plea for certain antitrust schools like, for instance, the Chicago School of Antitrust Analysis or the Theory of Contestable Markets who are skeptical about the benefits of governmental interference and who therefore generally prefer a relatively permissive approach to antitrust.

4.3.3.1 Strategies of Permissive Competition Policy

In the period prior to economic globalization, the rather strict competition policy of many industrial nations generally led to good economic results within these economies. In Germany, for instance, rather strict competition policy in the tradition of the so-called ordo-liberal school[579] and the concept of workable competition (Harvard School and Kantzenbach) was supposed to be an adequate instrument to protect competition and to increase international competitiveness.[580] Nowadays, in times of economic globalization, the question arises whether strict competition policy, without allowing any exception for a more lax or permissive antitrust decision, must be regarded as a competitive disadvantage because it could reduce the international competitiveness of domestic enterprises and the economy as a whole.[581] There could be a trade-off between protecting national competition in the short run and strengthening international competitiveness and competition in the long run. Globalization is a challenge for economic policy and it implies the necessity to reconsider the traditional competition policy.[582] A more permissive competition policy in particular cases – this also includes national exemptions from competition law, possibly com-

[579] As regards the main characteristics of ordo-liberal competition policy and its influence on Germany´s competition policy, see Knieps (2005) pp. 69f.; and Mantzavinos (1994) pp. 76ff.

[580] The ordo-liberals successfully implemented a relatively strict anti-cartel and anti-monopoly policy in the post war period, 'though not to the extent that many radical ordo-liberals would have hoped' (Plumpe (1999) p. 279). On the other hand, Ludwig Erhard generally preferred large-scale companies so that 'neither Erhard nor anti-cartel legislation prevented the wave of mergers in the 1960s and 1970s, which to some extent corrected the consequences of postwar dismantlement' (Ibid.).

[581] Cf. Seong (1989) pp. 1ff.; cf. Sinn (2003) pp. 178ff.

[582] Sinn (1999) p. 31.

bined with an additional regulation – could be advisable with regard to mergers, acquisitions, and inter-firm cooperation agreements, as long as this permissive strategy does not cause a rise in prices that reduces consumers′ rent and national welfare.

4.3.3.1.1 Creating National Champions and Global Players

The academic and political discussion about the relation between market concentration and international competitiveness is not new.[583] As regards economic literature, especially the traditional industrial organization theory of horizontal mergers deals with this issue, considering both the technological, allocative, and dynamic (innovatory) efficiency of a company′s size and diverse market structures. For instance, the Williamson trade-off describes the conflict between technological and allocative efficiency, which corresponds to the conflict between competitiveness and competition.[584]

Though, all these former approaches are characterized by some limitations. Some of them mainly aim at industrial policy without a special focus on competition policy. Others exclusively refer to the efficiency and (inter)national competitiveness of *enterprises* – i.e. the *macro*economic concept of international competitiveness, the locational attractiveness of nations is not considered – and they do not explicitly distinguish between national and international competition policy, i.e. the advantages of *national* competition policy are not compared with the consequences of *international* competition rules. Instead, one can even find relatively simple proposals to establish international competition rules and a supranational competition authority.[585]

Creating National Champions by Means of Industrial Policy. As regards the political dimension, there have been many attempts to apply industrial policies in order to promote competitiveness, especially with regard to oligopolistic international markets. For instance, in the 1960s, there was an international dominance of the US computer industry, namely the International Business Machines Corporation (IBM). In Europe, several countries like France and Great Britain tried to answer this so-called 'American Challenge' and 'Technology Gap' by means of a state-induced concentration policy. These countries thought that there was a need to

---

[583] Cf. Berg (1985) pp. 3ff.; cf. Kantzenbach and Kinne (1997) pp. 67-84; cf. Kinne (1997) pp. 9ff., 26ff; cf. Stennek and Verboven (2001) pp. 3ff.

[584] Williamson (1968) pp.18ff.

[585] Cf. Kantzenbach and Kinne (1997) p. 68.

catch up with the United States; especially mergers and a higher degree of market concentration were supposed to increase the innovatory potential of domestic enterprises, their efficiency, and their flexibility to adapt.[586] This strategy was unsuccessful, costly and probably even harmful.

As regards these early attempts of industrial policy to promote international competitiveness, Berg concludes – in accordance with von Hayek – that governments do not know which industries have to be supported by means of a higher degree of concentration.[587] Although politicians are able to take into account some fundamental stylized facts – for example the differentiation between (a) domestic *exporting* industries, where further concentration would primarily harm foreign buyers and could increase national welfare, and (b) *import competing* industries, where further concentration would primarily harm domestic buyers and lead to a domestic profit shifting – there is a general lack of more precise knowledge so that politicians cannot decide ex ante on the optimal size of exporting or import competing enterprises and industries in each individual case. Competition is a continual process of discovery; the relevant dispersed and fragmented tacit knowledge can only be discovered and mobilized by entrepreneurs competing in a market process based on private ownership.[588]

Creating National Champions by Means of Competition Policy. Berg underlines that this lack of knowledge does not only concern governmental initiatives to promote concentration (industrial policy). In general, this problem also concerns merger control because governments and competition authorities do not exactly know where they should practice a rather strict merger control in order to avoid further concentration within national markets.[589] Though, this conclusion has to be made more precise because there is a difference between a concentration policy that is primarily initiated and motivated by certain political aims – for example industrial policy – on the one hand and traditional merger control on the other. In the latter case, enterprises themselves initiate the merger and the competition authority mainly judges the planned merger with regard to antitrust issues, i.e. its prime concern is the protection of competition and to protect the consumer. The consideration of aspects like production efficiency and the international competitiveness are only of secondary importance for the competition authorities, though they are still relevant, for example by applying the so-called efficiency defence. Instead, it is mainly the firms themselves who have to evaluate their potential efficiency and competitiveness gains

[586] Cf. Berg (1985) pp. 3ff.

[587] Berg (1985) p. 19.

[588] Adaman and Devine (1996) p. 532.

[589] Berg (1985) pp. 19ff.

resulting from a merger. Consequently, market decisions dominate and political decisions are of secondary importance. However, antitrust policy still plays an important role because antitrust generally should try not to discourage efficiency-enhancing business strategies like horizontal or vertical integration, i.e. the competition authority should practice a balanced and well-communicated anti-merger control that

1. does not deter companies (i.e. the market) from seeking more efficient and competitive organizational structures;
2. still considers efficiency gains under certain restrictive conditions (for example by forcing the merging parties to transfer the efficiency gains to consumers);
3. does not force companies to switch over to inefficient strategies like, for instance, certain forms of diversification.[590]

A 'confidential' relation between national antitrust authorities and domestic enterprises that helps restructuring firms is more likely on the national level where the antitrust authorities and the government also consider the international competitiveness. The German competition law could be taken as an example. On the one hand, it limits competitiveness considerations to the second stage of merger control, i.e. the German cartel office itself is not allowed to follow competitiveness considerations. Instead, German competition law allows exemptions from merger control by means of a ministerial permission because such a ministerial permission can be justified with competitiveness considerations.[591]

In contrast to this, the European Commission has – by abandoning the above mentioned European attempts to catch up with the United States by means of state-induced concentration policy – adapted a more pro-competitive attitude in merger control, but with the aim to promote the international competitiveness of the European industry: 'The benefits of competition also demonstrate the danger in arguments about the creation of 'national champions'. There is nothing improper in companies growing into a sufficient scale to compete globally. However, this has to come about within a competitive environment and in full compliance with the

[590] Cf. Becker (1999) pp. 182f.

[591] Cf. Sec. 42 GWB. The competitiveness considerations mainly refer to the creation of so-called 'national champions' and 'global players' (cf. Monopolkommission (2005) pp. 75, 111ff.). The application of a ministerial permission is a disputed issue because it could be an incentive for national politicians to follow their own interests and to become receptive to lobbyism activities (cf. Chap. 4.2.3).

competition rules. Competition at home enhances a firm's ability to compete abroad.'[592] The aim to promote international competitiveness has remained an important issue, but it is seen as a result of strict competition policy and intense competition (at home). Therefore, in comparison to the German ministerial permission, the EU Commission does not practice an exemption regime that attaches more importance to competitiveness considerations than to antitrust considerations. Though, on the other hand, in 2004 the European Union has introduced efficiency and profitability criteria into its guidelines on the assessment of horizontal mergers.[593]

These international differences show that, up to now, the conflicting approaches to the relation between market concentration on the one hand and international competitiveness and efficiency on the other could not be reconciled. Only in case that the merging enterprises are mainly export-oriented so that a horizontal merger would not threaten competition on national markets, both points of view – the productive and the allocative efficiency – could be reconciled, assumed that international competition would not be endangered as well. Though, the internationalization of markets and the need to achieve a strong position on global markets could be taken as an argument to allow domestic enterprises to strive for higher *national* market shares and, in exceptional cases, to attain a temporary *domestic* market position that is dominant or even monopolistic. A more permissive merger control would help to increase national welfare and international competitiveness without harming foreign countries.

In practice, the industrial nations have already widened their concept of the relevant market regarding its geographic dimension.[594] In many industrial sectors, a global market has been established and this global market is often seen as the geographically relevant market. This leads to a broader approach in competition policy and there is more latitude for judging market power.[595] Interestingly, compared to the time before globalization when too much state control (regulation and industrial policy) led to the creation of national monopolies, a more permissive competition policy nowadays, in times of economic globalization, could cause similar results of national

[592] European Commission (2004a) p. 4.

[593] European Commission (2004b).

[594] Cf. Beninca (2005) pp. 43ff.

[595] On the other hand, a widened concept of the geographically relevant market also could lead to a stricter competition policy in case that a merger leads to an increased market share only on the international market while the domestic market share does not change. Consequently, the domestic competition authority could prohibit the merger, taking into account potential feedbacks from the increasing international market power on the national market (cf. ibid.).

market concentration. But there are some differences between the old market concentration strategies and the new scope for practicing a more permissive competition policy. The following applications give some examples for this new approach.

Application 1: Generating First-Mover Advantages. In contrast to the old market concentration strategies, the new approaches for a more permissive competition policy are characterized by a different motivation, which is not a protectionist one. National governments want to allow companies to become so-called national champions and global players who occupy a powerful strategic position in global competition. For instance, according to Consideration No. 4 of the ECMR[596], corporate reorganizations, particularly in form of concentrations, 'are to be welcomed to the extent that they are in line with the requirements of dynamic competition and capable of increasing the competitiveness of European industry, improving the conditions of growth and raising the standard of living in the Community.' While this consideration of the European Union still demands to fulfill the 'requirements of dynamic competition', other national competition authorities could go one step further and give – at least temporarily – the aim of competitiveness priority over the aims of traditional competition policy because, to achieve the aim of competitiveness, it could be essential to be the first or one of the first competition authorities adopting a more permissive and innovative competition policy. In other words, competition policy partly has to free itself from static concerns, it needs to be 'couched in a forward-looking context'[597] and to become sensitive to the organizational needs of companies in order not to hinder technological and organizational progress that could support both the creation of competitiveness and welfare and the stimulation of future competition.[598] For instance, if the do-

---

[596] European Council (2004).

[597] Jorde and Teece (1997) p. 290.

[598] Interestingly, there are two opposing positions in antitrust theory which both claim to hold a *dynamic* and competitiveness enhancing position in antitrust. On the one hand, economists who strictly look at the present market structure and a high intensity of competition today, underline the *dynamic* effects of intensive competition, i.e. the generation of technological progress and adjustments to permanently changing market data. On the other hand, there are economists who define this as a static approach that, in the long run, could harm intertemporal efficiency. Therefore, they plead for a different kind of *dynamic* and forward-looking approach. They agree to restrict competition and to allow temporary market power today in order to support innovations that could foster competition and competitiveness tomorrow. For instance, Jorde and Teece have explored socially beneficial forms of cooperation – especially horizontal and lateral cooperation – and they refer to the success of cooperative R&D and

mestic producers are the first ones who are allowed to implement new (international) organizational structures that help to open foreign markets and to support innovativeness – e.g. strategic alliances, horizontal and lateral inter-firm co-operations[599], and strategies of diversification in order to get control over complementary products, to share costs, or to practice cross-subsidization – then they could achieve a long-term competitive advantage over foreign competitors by building up economies of scale and scope, global supply chains, research networks, industrial clusters or joint manufacturing structures.[600] In global competition, time is one of the most important factors of competitiveness. This could lead to so-called first-mover advantages, which often result in long-term dominant market positions and high profits.[601] The theory on first-mover firms analyzes economic advantages and disadvantages which result from pioneering investments. One of the central advantages of first movers is the possibility to capture market

---

R&D and related activities in the Western German machine tool industry (Jorde and Teece (1990) pp. 75f.).

[599] In a traditional view, innovation processes have been seen as a linear or serial model including successive steps like R&D, design, production, marketing, and services. Consequently, innovation processes often have been modelled as a vertical process. This partly resulted in a permissive competition policy toward vertical cooperation, but modern innovation processes could necessitate other forms of antitrust policy which allow more complex contractual arrangements, especially with respect to horizontal and lateral cooperation (cf. Jorde and Teece (1990) pp. 77, 81; cf. Schmalensee (1992) pp. 98ff.; cf. Baumol and Ordover (1992) pp. 89, 94f.). As regards the differences between nations how to deal with inter-firm cooperation, especially competitor cooperation, see Ullrich (2003) pp. 159ff.

[600] Cf. Porter (2004) pp. 317ff.; cf. Jorde and Teece (1997) p. 292; cf. Jorde and Teece (1990) pp. 75ff. On the other hand, it has to be conceded that the structure of markets seems to have little influence on the innovativeness of companies. Especially radical successful innovations often emerge outside the incumbent firms and established industries. Jorde and Teece conclude, that competition policy 'may not be central to the innovation process', but 'it would be wrong to assume that it is unimportant' (1997, p. 292).

[601] It is likely that new forms of beneficial cooperation and organizational structure that presently might restrict competition could lead to first mover advantages, especially because 'success in research and development does not automatically translate into a financial success ...; to succeed financially, innovative firms must quickly position themselves advantageously in the appropriate complementary assets and technologies', for example by 'bilateral and multilateral cooperative agreements' which also can be viewed as an alternative to mergers and acquisitions (Jorde and Teece (1990) p. 94; cf. Sinn (2003) pp. 178ff.).

shares without high competitive pressure from rivals. This advantage arises from several sources: the possibility to determine product standards, the achievement of technological leadership, the possession of patents, the pre-emption of scarce assets, customers brand loyalty, and buyer switching costs. The potential disadvantages of first movers are the costs of pioneering investments and the risk to fail. Moreover, former pioneers who already have established themselves as a successful first mover, are in danger to become subject to 'incumbent inertia', i.e. the formerly successful pioneer sometimes fails to adapt to new challenges and to transform himself, e.g. by means of a business reengineering process. New competitors or late movers can take advantages from these first-mover problems. They can avoid the pioneer's mistakes, they can profit from inter-firm diffusion of technology (e.g. by compulsory licensing), and they can try to revolutionize existing industries.

With regard to the debate on international competitiveness, it has to be conceded that the first-mover theory does not focus on governmental strategies as a source of first-mover advantages. As a management concept, it focuses on superior entrepreneurship as the most important factor, besides luck as the second significant factor. Pioneering opportunities are considered to arise endogenously.[602] Nevertheless, it is likely that economic policy and especially competition policy influence a firm's opportunities to become a first mover; pioneering business strategies in globalized markets can become relevant for competition policy. Consequently, a permissive and innovative strategy of antitrust is not a strategy of monopolization or protectionism, it is an attempt to act before it is too late to react. For instance, the dynamics of global oligopolization put pressure on domestic enterprises and national competition authorities to participate in this worldwide process of external growth of firms and to allow temporary monopolistic positions. Otherwise, they could lose their international competitiveness or become a candidate for a (hostile) takeover. The efficiency gains and cost savings resulting from a more permissive strategy could be passed-on to consumers in the form of lower prices, better products, better service etc.[603] These positive effects on welfare and competitiveness could compensate the potential dangers of a temporary dominant market position.

In order to achieve these positive effects, it is necessary to maintain a system of sovereign national competition policy. The national competition authority would have to give up its previously strict merger control and would have to practice a rule-of-reason approach and a strict post-merger

[602] Lieberman and Montgomery (1987) pp. 2ff., 10ff.

[603] Cf. Stennek and Verboven (2001) pp. 3ff.

control against a welfare-reducing abuse of the newly created dominant market position. Especially in case that the national industry is characterized by only few domestic enterprises but many domestic consumers, mergers and the resulting market power must be considered a danger to national welfare and international competitiveness.[604] In this case, a rise of prices resulting from an abuse of market power could reduce the competitive forces and the international competitiveness both of the merged firms and other domestic enterprises.

Application 2: Competition Policy in Markets of Rapid Technological Change. There are several reasons why it could be both recommendable for a nation and acceptable for the international community to practice a relatively permissive national competition policy in markets of rapid technological change. According to Jorde and Teece, 'market power can be ephemeral in industries – like computers, biotechnology, telecommunications equipment – characterized by rapid technological change'[605]. Theoretically, dominating enterprises may have more financial and intellectual resources so that they could be significantly faster in generating innovative products and thereby maintaining their dominant position and possibly abusing it. Though, on the other hand, there are several other reasons why a national competition authority could be allowed to be more permissive in industries of rapid technological change.

1. Firstly, certain forms of permissive competition policy – like concentration and horizontal or lateral inter-firm cooperation – could support future innovativeness and thereby improve the international competitiveness, especially in high-tech industries and industries with rapid technological change.[606] As already mentioned above in application 1, modern innovation processes in quickly changing industries often necessitate horizontal and lateral forms of cooperation and more complex contractual arrangements so that antitrust has to adapt to these developments in order not to impede innovativeness.[607] Furthermore, the resulting product innovations can help to reduce market power on other markets. National competition policy could use this effect in order to create both more competition and more competitiveness.

[604] Cf. Kerber and Budzinski (2003) pp. 413f.

[605] Jorde and Teece (1997) p. 293.

[606] Cf. Ordover and Willig (1985) pp. 311ff.

[607] Cf. Jorde and Teece (1990) pp. 77, 81; cf. Schmalensee (1992) pp. 98ff.

2. A permissive antitrust policy with respect to inter-firm cooperation, combined with an ex post control of abusive business practices[608], could be necessary in industries experiencing fast technological progress and change because time-consuming antitrust investigations and litigations could be far longer than the product life cycle so that those countries who are able to give 'quick and binding answers to tough questions, will take the baton'[609], especially if they apply a relatively permissive antitrust approach. Consequently, the permissive approach would have to balance between clarity and flexibility, i.e. between the application of simple rules and time-consuming rule-of-reason investigations.

3. In industries with rapid technological progress, a dominant market position can be challenged more easily by a newcomer and cartelization is relatively difficult if industries change quickly because of permanent innovation processes. Furthermore, there is empirical evidence that innovations – especially radical innovations – frequently occur outside the established companies and industries.[610] This could be especially relevant for industries with rapid technological change.

4. A relatively permissive competition policy that allows domestic companies to merge and to achieve a higher capital market value helps to prevent hostile takeovers. This is an additional instrument to foster innovativeness and competitiveness because 'hostile takeovers and the threat thereof' could be harmful to innovativeness and competitiveness.[611] On the one hand, as a result of the 'acquisition of medium sized domestic high-tech firms by foreigners', innovative activities could be shifted abroad and reduce the international competitiveness of the domestic economy.[612] Furthermore, the threat of a hostile takeover could reduce a company´s incentive to invest in R&D activi-

---

608 An ex post control is necessary in order to avoid patent pools and similar forms of know how monopolization which could block further technological progress. Especially industries of rapid technological change and cumulative technologies depend on a widely unrestricted access of firms to patents and know how. Cf. Merges and Nelson (1992, p. 216) who describe the innovation blocking function of broad patents on components in industries that are characterized by cumulative technology and multicomponent systems.

609 Easterbrook (1992) p. 132.

610 Ibid. p. 292.

611 McFetridge (1993) p. 214.

612 Ibid. p. 206.

ties.[613] This could be fatal in industries that are characterized by a fast pace of technological change.

5. Competition analysis in innovative markets 'is complicated by the fact that the products which might compete ... do not exist yet. Nor do the substitutes for them.'[614] Consequently, a relatively strict competition policy that refers to a static and rule of law approach on antitrust could lead to false decisions, neglecting the dynamics on the market and the future potential for product innovations and pro-competitive developments. Dynamic markets with rapid technological progress can be considered as a natural protection against long-term dominating market positions; though, dominant market positions still could be maintained over a long time, but they would be more fragile.[615]

As regards the debate on international competition rules, it has to be highlighted that countries would lose their present scope to consider the innovativeness and other special characteristics of markets and to practice a relatively permissive competition policy in quickly changing industries. This could be harmful for the international competitiveness of the nation. For instance, according to Jorde and Teece, 'innovators may sometimes need to constrain severely their business conduct in order to avoid violating competition laws'[616]. Consequently, there is a realistic danger that innovative enterprises will act too carefully and stop further innovation strategies and cooperation agreements if they fear to be prosecuted for attempts to monopolize markets. This problem is likely to become increasingly important in case that an international – and therefore rather anonymous – competition authority would apply relatively strict and schematic antitrust rules or if the national competition authorities would be forced to apply international competition rules by means of a rule of law approach. In contrast to this, a sovereign national antitrust authority is less likely to 'assign market power incorrectly to an innovating firm'[617]. It has more scope to practice a rule of reason approach and a more economic ap-

---

[613] Some authors also assume that hostile takeovers are partly planned by the acquiring company in order to stop costly R&D activities of the acquired company and to realize a capital gain (cf. Chap. 4.3.2.4.3). Though, this is a doubtful theoretical position because empirical evidence rather seems to show that 'acquisitions themselves are not causal factors' for R&D downsizing (cf. McFetridge (1993) pp. 201ff., 206).

[614] Ibid. p. 214.

[615] Jorde and Teece (1997) p. 297.

[616] Ibid. p. 293.

[617] Ibid.

proach, i.e. to define product markets and markets for know how[618], to take into account the special characteristics of the market, and to distinguish between desirable and undesirable forms of (horizontal) cooperation case by case. This is especially relevant in case that one nation is dominating a certain innovative market so that the national competition authority has more experience to deal with the special dynamics and features of the market. The US computer industry in the 1970s could be taken as an example.[619]

Conclusion. As regards the debate about the establishment of an international competition policy regime, one could say that an international competition authority would also use a wide concept of the geographically relevant market so that its decisions concerning merger control could be similar to the relatively permissive decisions of a national competition authority. But there is a fundamental difference between a permissive *national* competition policy and an international antitrust regime.

Firstly, an international competition authority probably would generally use a wide concept of the geographically relevant market, normally the global market, whereas a national competition authority can decide more flexibly which concept to use so that it can take account of specific national interests and problems. This is important because the creation of national monopolies or international oligopolies does not always have the same effects on national competition; many effects are not evident in the present or they are not relevant from the point of view of an international competition regime. The structural lack of knowledge which generally adheres to both a national and an international competition authority seems to be less serious when a national competition authority analyzes the effects of further concentration on its domestic markets. Furthermore, in case of unforeseen negative consequences for national competition, national competition authorities are more likely to revise their decisions in order to shield the national economy from anticompetitive behaviour and from decreasing competition, innovation, competitiveness, and freedom.

Secondly, international antitrust rules – either applied by an international antitrust authority or by national antitrust authorities – probably would be mainly characterized by a rule of law approach which, in many cases, could lead to a too static, schematic and thereby too strict antitrust

---

[618] According to Jorde and Teece, in industries that are characterized by a fast pace of technological change and a diversity of sources of new technologies, the market definition 'should be tailored to the context of innovation and should focus primarily on the market for know-how; specific product markets become relevant only when commercialization is included within the scope of the cooperative agreement' (1990, p. 89).

[619] Cf. Chap. 4.3.3.3.3.

decision. There could be too little scope for a more permissive rule of reason approach which allows certain mergers and inter-firm cooperation agreements after having taken into account specific features of the relevant market, e.g. the speed of technological progress on the market.[620]

4.3.3.1.2 Exemptions from Competition Policy

With regard to restrictions of competition, one has to distinguish between illegal private restraints of competition like cartels and the abuse of market power on the one hand and state-induced and state-tolerated competition restraints on the other. State-induced restraints of competition can result from a protectionist foreign trade policy, which is subject to the WTO regime, or from the economic *regulation* of specific business activities and industrial sectors. Consequently, there is an 'uneasy coexistence' between antitrust laws and regulation regimes because governmental regulation generally displaces competition.[621] Functional and sectoral exemptions from competition are – besides their codification in detailed regulation rules – often also codified in competition laws so that these exemptions are an element of national competition policy.

As regards the international competitiveness debate, these exemptions from antitrust presently can be used in order to practice a rather permissive competition policy and to promote international competitiveness.[622] Though, considering the theoretical legitimacy of exemptions from competition policy, there is no international consensus 'on a methodology or procedure for deciding which anti-competitive restrictions should be exempt from antitrust enforcement and which should not'[623]. Moreover, there is no international consensus on the method how to regulate industries that are exempted from competition. This is also because exemptions from antitrust often have ambivalent effects on competition and efficiency. Therefore, in the course of an international harmonization of antitrust, several

---

620 Cf. Jorde and Teece (1990) pp. 86f.

621 Cf. Easterbrook (2004) p. 189.

622 On the other hand, exemptions from antitrust and the resulting regulation of industries can have the effect of strict competition policy. Regulation can force the affected companies to fulfill certain standards, terms and conditions of supply that have been set by the government. The incentives and efforts to meet these standards and conditions could strengthen the international competitiveness of these enterprises. In this case, governmental regulation could exert a pressure on domestic companies that is higher than the competitive pressure on private markets.

623 Rosenthal and Nicolaides (1997) p. 374. As regards bank regulation, cf. Fischer and Pfeil (2003) p. 4.

functional and sectoral exemptions from competition could be forbidden, others could be allowed. Consequently, nations could lose a legal and non-protectionist instrument to strengthen their international competitiveness because regulations concerning exemptions for officially authorized conduct and for governmentally regulated industries could be justified by positive effects both for competition and for the international competitiveness of the affected firms and industries.

Functional Exemptions from Competition Policy. Governments and competition authorities can apply *functional* exemptions from competition policy so that certain forms of anti-competitive market conduct are allowed in order to promote competition and international competitiveness in the long run. An example is the European Commission Regulation No. 2659/2000 on the application of Art. 81 III of the Treaty to categories of R&D agreements.[624] While Art. 81 I of the EC Treaty prohibits all agreements between undertakings, decisions by associations of undertakings, and concerted practices which may affect trade between member states and which have as their object or effect the prevention, restriction, or distortion of competition within the common market, Art. 1 of the European Commission Regulation No. 2659/2000 declares that Art. 81 I of the EC Treaty 'shall not apply to agreements entered into between two or more undertakings (...) which relate to the conditions under which those undertakings pursue: (a) joint research and development of products or processes and joint exploitation of the results of that research and development; (b) joint exploitation of the results of research and development of products or processes jointly carried out pursuant to a prior agreement between the same parties; or (c) joint research and development of products or processes excluding joint exploitation of the results.' Consequently, the European Commission has to balance two different objectives: (a) ensuring effective protection of competition – for example by defining so-called 'black clauses' which represent agreements that are not covered by the exemption (cf. Art. 5 of Regulation No. 2659/2000) – and (b) providing an adequate legal framework which has positive effects on R&D within the European Union and which supports the European Unions′ Lisbon aims to become the most competitive and dynamic knowledge-based economy in the world.

Besides the aim to promote cooperative R&D, functional exemptions from competition law also exist for diverse other kinds of business activities, for example to protect exclusive rights explicitly granted by patent

624 European Commission (2000).

law[625], or to promote certain forms of cartels and inter-firm cooperation, for example in order to support small and medium sized enterprises, to form multinational enterprises, to defend against foreign market power[626], and to promote vertical and horizontal integration as a means of facilitating the access to intellectual property and supporting a more efficient way to organize supply chains. All these permissive practices, implemented by a national rule of reason approach, could be legitimated in certain cases, especially if they intensify competition in the long run and if they strengthen the international competitiveness without harming international competition.

Sectoral Exemptions from Competition Policy. Governments can introduce *sectoral* regulations which define branches of industry where certain fields of competition law are not applicable. According to their exact arrangement, sectoral regulations have different effects on the firms. On the one hand, domestic firms could obtain exclusive rights, for example a public licence or concession or the right to make horizontal agreements. On the other hand, the regulation of an industry can limit the scope of action of the concerned firms. A sectoral regulation empowers the government to set prices, to determine output, and to specify detailed conditions of supply.[627] For instance, the government could negotiate with the pharmaceutical enterprises about maximum prices and about a list of medicine that is not approved for the public health care. Though, in some industries, the sectoral regulation even leads to the erection of a legal monopoly.

The Justification of Exemptions and Their Effect on the International Competitiveness. As already mentioned above, there is no international consensus about the justification of exemptions from antitrust policy. Though, there are some common basic ideas and international developments as regards exemptions from antitrust that result from superior national interests or market failure.

Over the last three decades, regulation policy and exemptions from competition have undergone an ambivalent development. On the one hand, there has been a fundamental change towards more liberalization, privati-

---

625 Cf. OECD Secretariat (2001) p. 125.

626 For instance, domestic export cartels could be allowed in case of a foreign monopsony or in order to support the export activities of small enterprises (cf. Stearns-Bläsing (2004) pp. 75f., 96). Furthermore, *foreign* export cartels could be allowed in order to protect domestic infant industries or to prevent dumping prices, which harm domestic producers and consumers in the long run, too. In this case, the competition authority has to weigh the short-term disadvantages for domestic demand against long-term advantages.

627 Rosenthal and Nicolaides (1997) p. 364.

zation, and internationalization in many countries. The United States and the European Union were the main actors who abolished several exemptions from competition policy and led the way in deregulating and opening markets. Economic schools like the Austrian School of Economics (F.A. von Hayek) and the Chicago School of Antitrust Analysis pleaded for the elimination of public monopolies and other market entry barriers like, for instance, the exemption of whole industries and services from national and international competition, for example telecommunication and health services. On the other hand, as regards cross-border business activities like international mergers and acquisitions, many countries still try to prevent foreign enterprises′ plans for a takeover of domestic enterprises, especially in so-called sensitive industries which are closely related to superior national interests.

1. **Superior National Interests.** National exceptions to general antitrust policy could be justified by significant economic and non-economic goals which could contribute to the international competitiveness of the nation, for example if inter-firm collaboration in sensitive industries is important to competitiveness and to ensure that the products match characteristics defined by the government.[628] Indeed, many former and existing exemptions have been justified with superior national interests, i.e. with 'the legitimacy of values expressed in restricted competition'[629]. These forms of regulation often result from historical and cultural developments which are not necessarily motivated by economic objectives, especially not by protectionist goals.[630] The legitimacy of non-economic goals in competition policy is a controversial issue. In general, the 'public interest' is no adequate justification for private restraints on markets that are bad for consumers. Furthermore, incorporating certain public interests like, for instance, social policy in competition law could 'undermine the objectivity, justiciability and market orientation of the law'[631]. Therefore, economists call for more economics in competition policy (so-called more economic approach), i.e. they demand that economic theory and the efficiency doctrine should be the major basis of competition policy, not superior national interests.[632] Examples for such superior interests are the national security, economic stability, health issues, and cul-

628 Cf. Fox and Pitofsky (1997) p. 255.

629 Rosenthal and Nicolaides (1997) p. 375.

630 As regards the implications of national culture on antitrust policy, cf. Fikentscher (2003) p. 10; cf. Eguchi (2003) pp. 3ff.

631 Anderson and Khosla (1995) p. 52.

632 Cf. Budzinski (2003) p. 1; cf. Maahs (2005) pp. 49ff.

tural aspects. Some of the main economic sectors where such special regulations exist or existed are the financial sector, the media sector, agriculture and fishing, utilities (energy, water, postal services, public transport systems, telecommunications), natural resources, sports marketing, health service, and the liberal professions. In these cases, the government primarily pursues superior public interests by ensuring a high quality and sustainability of supply of certain goods, combined with stable and low prices. Consequently, the regulation also could serve to strengthen the international competitiveness. Though, in these cases where superior national or political interests are the crucial argument against free competition, the criterion of international competitiveness does not play an important role as an additional argument for the exemptions. Nevertheless, these cases are apt to highlight many of the *ambivalent effects* that exemptions from competition policy exert on the international competitiveness of the affected firms and the whole economy:

- On the one hand, many exemptions from competition policy have the effect of a market entry barrier that favours the already existing domestic firms, i.e. the incumbents. The exemptions often have a similar effect like (export) subsidies, state aids, or infant industry protection so that the protected sectors could become competitive by a preferential regulation which results in a comparative advantage over foreign competitors which do not profit from an exclusive right that increases their international competitiveness. Though, in many cases, a preferential treatment because of superior national interests was not justified, for example in case of formerly exempted national monopolies in the German telecommunication and postal services sector. In other sectors, an exemption from antitrust still could be justified and could help to achieve a high degree of know how, expertise, and competitiveness. An international harmonization of competition law could eliminate or reduce these advantages. For instance, the antitrust exemption for public water supply can be justified with superior national interests although it is theoretically possible to organize the water supply by private enterprises on competitive markets. On the pre-condition that the government practices a strict competition policy and an adequate regulation, a balanced contract with the private sector could be efficient. Especially countries that are characterized by corruption and political instability could profit from a privatization and from a competitive environment if the governments have proven to be unable to manage public utilities. In this case, privatization, competition, and a reliable production capacity would be a factor for improving the locational attractiveness and the international competitiveness of domestic enterprises that depend on a reliable and reasonable water supply. Nevertheless, non-economic factors could justify a total exemption from competition and allow monopolization. This is also valid for economic sectors which play an important role for the national culture, for example education and health services, so that a cultural protection could be justified.

- On the other hand, exemptions from competition policy can cause negative effects on the international competitiveness of domestic firms. Exempted industries are generally subject to the danger that they do not learn competition so that they cannot become competitive on international markets. For instance, an exemption for certain forms of R&D cooperation could restrict competition between the parties and consequently reduce their international competitiveness. Though one also has to take into account that R&D cooperation also can help to avoid that only one firm obtains the control over an innovation. This effect could promote competition and competitiveness.

Most of the above mentioned examples primarily refer to the regulation of domestic companies and the effects on their international competitiveness. Though, one also has to consider the ambivalent effects of sectoral and functional exemptions from antitrust laws on the *locational attractiveness* of the economy, especially in case of exemptions that are justified by superior national interests.[633] For instance, a legal preferential treatment of certain industries could serve to attract foreign investors who also want to profit from these advantages (see below application 2). On the other hand, in case that functional or sectoral exemptions cause a market foreclosure, for example by establishing a national cartel or monopoly, foreign investors could be excluded from the domestic market so that the economy could lose foreign direct investments which could have increased the international competitiveness of the nation.

---

[633] Exemptions that are based on superior national interests could create an industrial organization that is unique for this country so that foreign direct investments could be attracted. In case of exemptions based on competition and market failure (see the following section), it is likely that many countries practice a regulation so that there are no significant incentives for foreign companies to invest in this country.

2. **Competition Failure and Market Failure.** Another approach to justify economic regulations and exemptions from competition is the existence of an alleged competition failure or a so-called market failure. This approach is subject of the public interest theory according to which 'regulation is supplied in response to the demand of the public for the correction of inefficient or inequitable market practices'[634]. – As regards competition failure, the existence of high barriers to exit the market (for example because of high sunk costs) and structural overcapacities could lead to a ruinous competition and a sectoral crisis, characterized by a large-scale slide of prices and adverse selection on the supply-side, i.e. even competitive and respectable firms could be ruined.[635] Such a sectoral crisis could harm both the national welfare and the international competitiveness of the industry. Therefore, an exemption from competition policy, for example by permitting a temporary cartel in order to reduce overcapacities and to deal with the structural crisis, could be an adequate political reaction in order to protect the industry and its international competitiveness. But before implementing such strict political measures that restrict competition, the politicians should try to find a solution that deals with the actual causes of the competition failure. For instance, they could try to reduce the barriers to exit the market so that the more uncompetitive enterprises are motivated to leave the market. In the long run, such measures would improve competition and competitiveness and they also could attract foreign investors, for example if sunk costs have been reduced so that they are lower than in foreign countries. – As regards market failure, especially the existence of so-called natural monopolies has led to state-induced exemptions from competition.[636] The basic model of a natural monopoly describes an industry where the production of the demanded output is characterized by a subadditive cost function. In other words, *one* enterprise can generate such a high degree of scale economies that it can manufacture the total market output at lower (social) costs than two ore more enterprises.[637]

634 Cf. Posner (1974) pp. 1ff.; cf. Knieps (2005) pp. 80f.; cf. Vietor (1999) p. 213.

635 Cf. Lachmann (2004) pp 110f.

636 Cf. Finsinger (1991) pp. 79ff.; cf. Fritsch et al. (2005) pp. 87ff. In case of network utilities like the public infrastructure, natural monopolies even display multiple market failures. The price mechanism does not work because of monopolistic power, environmental externalities, and the public goods problem (cf. Helm (2001) pp. 301ff.).

637 Cf. Posner (1999) p. 1; cf. Knieps (2005) pp. 21ff.; cf. Weimann (2006) pp. 331ff.

Hence, economic policy should try to realize these efficiency advantages in order to obtain low prices for consumers and to increase the international competitiveness.[638] Consequently, the industry has to be regulated and a monopoly to be established.[639] – The approaches and methods to regulate natural monopolies vary both between countries and even within one and the same country in the course of time. Within the European Union and especially within Germany, there has been a fundamental change as regards the regulation of natural monopolies, but many deficiencies still prevail.[640] In the past, the regulation of natural monopolies in Germany traditionally determined that only one firm, in most cases a public enterprise, was allowed to produce. This has been the case in several utilities sectors (gas, water, electricity, postal services, telecommunication) where the construction of a supply grid causes enormous sunk costs while the marginal costs of production are low so that the cost function is characterized by subadditivity, i.e. the marginal costs are lower than the average per unit costs. Therefore an erection of a multitude of national supply networks could not be justified; the advantages of more competition would not have led to lower prices and more international competitiveness because of the high additional sunk costs. These sunk costs also are a reason why it is unlikely that a new private competitor risks a market entry. Consequently, a natural monopoly often automatically leads to a monopolistic situation without having the prospect of potential newcomers and contestability. This monopolistic situation necessitates an additional regulation. The government has to avoid a monopolistic pricing of the natural monopoly by choosing one of the different forms of regulation which try to find a second best solution, for example cost plus- or mark-up-regulation, rate of return-regulation, price cap-regulation, or a competitive bidding for the natural monopoly (so-called franchise bidding or Demsetz competition).[641] – In contrast to these traditional and permissive forms of ex ante regulation which prevent competition, create monopolies, and

---

[638] Cf. Weimann (2006) pp. 317, 330ff.

[639] Cf. Knieps (2005) pp. 28, 79.

[640] Helm (2001) p. 297ff.

[641] Cf. Klump (2006) p. 78; cf. Knieps (2005) pp. 29, 79ff.; cf. Demsetz (1968) p. 58; cf. Wolfram (2004) pp. 3ff.; cf. Finsinger (1991) pp. 107ff. Economic science had to develop these approaches to determine an optimal price because the equation P = MC ('price equals marginal costs') cannot be applied in case of a natural monopoly. The marginal costs are permanently below the average costs so that the industry would make losses in case of P = MC.

which cause several inefficiencies and false incentives[642], nowadays sector-specific (re-)regulation of natural monopolies in Germany intends to create competition. The government pursues a liberalization and opening of markets in order to make competitive market entries and efficient solutions possible. It is important to acknowledge that the creation of more competition in connection with natural monopolies does not mean that regulation can be completely replaced by competition policy. The liberalization efforts must not be confused with a massive deregulation because the liberalization often 'implies the *imposition* of procompetitive *ex ante* regulation, rather than the elimination of regulation'[643]. Therefore, as regards the utilities sectors, modern regulation enforces an unbundling, where possible, and sets an ex ante framework which allows a fair market entry for newcomers so that both the old monopolistic supplier and the new competitors are allowed to use the existing supply grid on equal terms. According to the division of functions between the national competition authority and the sector-specific regulatory authority, the regulator generally concentrates on the monopolistic bottleneck, i.e. on the infrastructure or supply grid (so-called disaggregated regulation), so that the access to the grid has to be regulated, but not the production of the network output.[644] – These changes of national regulation towards liberalization have been promoted by the European Union and implemented by the national governments, leading to ambivalent effects on international competitiveness. Application 1 gives an example for these ambivalent effects. It highlights the problematic influence of international institutions – which stop national exemptions from competition law and officially intend to practice a stricter competition policy by means of liberalization and harmonization – on the international competitiveness of nations. Application 2 and 3 will give two further examples for the advantages of rather permissive national competition policy.

Application 1: Liberalizing Natural Monopolies – An Example for the Deficiencies of International Antitrust. On the one hand, the above mentioned modern form of regulation, i.e. the liberalization, has several advantages with regard to international competitiveness. Firstly, the new

---

642 As regards the inefficiencies and negative incentives resulting from asymmetric information, principal-agent-problems etc., cf. Knieps (2005) pp. 81ff.

643 Haucap and Marcus (2005) pp. 14f.

644 Cf. Knieps (2005) pp. 95ff.; Knieps (2001) pp. 12ff. For further information about the theory of monopolistic bottlenecks and the possibilities to deregulate natural monopolies, see Weimann (2006) pp. 369ff.; Knieps (2004) pp. 2ff.

regulation still includes an exemption from competition for the supply grid itself so that the efficiency advantages of the natural monopoly still exist. Secondly, the new regulation has the potential to promote competition within the formerly monopolized market so that further efficiency gains could increase the international competitiveness. The formerly protected domestic enterprises have to learn competition and they are forced to become internationally competitive. Thirdly, the liberalization has opened the national market, also enhancing the national position within the international locational competition so that foreign investors could be attracted. Consequently, an efficient sector-specific liberalization and regulation that promotes competition as intended by the EU can increase the international competitiveness and – in case that foreign countries practice either no or an *in*efficient regulation – result in a comparative advantage. It is a central governmental task to regulate the national supply grids in an efficient way so that they attract new competitors and promote competition and competitiveness, especially by enforcing fair grid access fees.

Despite these positive developments, the success of regulation and liberalization has been limited up to now in several network industries.[645] The history of regulation of natural monopolies shows that governments often practice an inefficient form of regulation, either because of a lack of knowledge about efficient ways of sector-specific regulation or because of polit-economic factors. In these cases it would be more apt to speak of a government failure than of a market failure. This brings us to another possibility to explain but not to justify exemptions from competition. The limited success of recent liberalization efforts actually gives *double evidence* that polit-economic factors played and still play an important role for the establishment of antitrust exemptions[646]:

1. Firstly, the liberalization and new regulation of industries during the last three decades, both nationally and internationally, has shown that many former exemptions and public monopolies were economically unjustified because the private market sector has proven its ability to produce efficient results and competitive prices, for example in the telecommunications sector. These sector-specific exemptions from competition were primarily established and maintained under the influence of interest groups or because of protectionist aims and personal interests of politicians and bureaucrats. This problem is subject of the politic-economic theory, especially the capture theory of regula-

[645] Cf. Pelkmans (2001) pp. 453ff.
[646] Cf. Weimann (2006) pp. 372f.

tion[647] and alternative, more differentiated approaches which explain the behaviour of bureaucrats and politicians from a microeconomic perspective.[648]

2. Secondly, the limited success of recent liberalization indicates that polit-economic factors *still* exist and that these anti-competitive forces are strong enough to prevent an efficient liberalization on the national level.[649] For instance, the liberalization of the German electricity market has led to an abolition of antitrust exemptions for the power sector, but the liberalization also has resulted in the establishment of an oligopoly of four suppliers who control the energy market like a cartel so that, as a final outcome, the former natural monopolies presently enjoy a permissive antitrust policy – like under the former regulation regime that protected the natural monopolies, but the consumers have to pay relatively high prices. The German government had the competence to protect competition on domestic energy markets and to reverse the monopolization on the energy market, but it justified this market concentration with the alleged necessity to create so-called national champions and to promote international competitiveness. Finally the German competition policy and the sector-regulation have failed both to protect competition and to practice an effective ex-ante regulation or ex-post control of market power abuse. Therefore, the German electricity market is characterized by a lack of competition and by relatively high prices. Foreign competitors even cannot enter the market sufficiently because of a lack of cross-border power lines.[650]

These deficiencies can be explained by polit-economic factors both on the national and on the international level. As regards political economics on the international level and the relation between the international competitiveness of nations and an international harmonization of competition policy, the role of the European Commission has to be highlighted. There are two aspects to be underlined:

1. On the one hand, an international harmonization of competition policy could enhance the pressure on national governments to liberalize

---

647 Cf. Posner (1974) pp. 1ff.; cf. Stigler (1971) pp. 21ff.

648 Cf. Berry (1984) pp. 524ff.

649 Cf. Helm (2001) p. 301.

650 Cf. Kumkar (2002) p. 17. The capacity constraints for interconnectors still exist because there are no incentives for investments. The existing interconnectors have been built for security of supply in the European Union, but not for free trade in a common market (Pelkmans (2001) p. 453).

markets where this would improve the international competitiveness. The example of the European Union shows that it was also a political decision on the supranational level to enforce the liberalization of natural monopolies and the opening of national markets for new competitors; 'in part this was prompted by early national initiatives and regulatory emulation by a few EU member states'[651]. Though it should be taken into consideration that the aims of the European Union are not identical with the agenda of an international competition authority. The European Union intends to promote the European integration and to erect a common market. The liberalization of national markets is a central feature of this process of integration. Furthermore, the European Union explicitly aims at strengthening the international competitiveness of the common market by means of opening the member countries′ national markets (so-called Lisbon Agenda). In contrast to this, an international competition authority enforcing a global agenda would hardly pursue the aim to create a common market in order to increase the international competitiveness of a certain region. Its incentives to promote competitiveness would be less distinctive than within the European Union, and even the European Union has already shown several deficiencies and limits in promoting competitiveness.

2. This aspect leads us directly to the limits of international harmonization and its alleged aim to develop a stricter competition policy and to create more competition. The European competition policy gives an example that an international harmonization of antitrust, combined with the intention to eliminate national exemptions from antitrust, could even result in a reduction of competition and cause harm to the international competitiveness of nations. For instance, with regard to the liberalization of the formerly nationally regulated energy market, the EU eliminated the national exemptions from antitrust, but the European Commission has failed to enforce an intensive competition and to create a common market for energy although it possesses the competences and power to do so.[652] Consequently, the European networks are still inefficient, 'and this conclusion has a significant, though difficult to quantify, effect on the productivity and competitiveness of the European economy'[653]. The liberalization had a nega-

[651] Ibid. p. 454.

[652] This conclusion is only valid for the status quo because it is likely that the European Commission will enforce more competition and market integration in the future (cf. Kumkar (2002) p. 12).

[653] Helm (2001) p. 310.

tive effect on the international competitiveness because of higher energy costs for many European companies, especially in Germany.[654] Finally, both the European Commission and the national governments have to be blamed for this loss of international competitiveness because they both failed to protect competition after having liberalized the regulated markets. But this example especially shows the dangers of an international competition regime. An international or supranational competition authority that is organized similarly to the European Competition regime could demand a selective change of national competition policy (for example the liberalization of a national market), but it probably would not make sure that the implementation of this policy includes the application of strict competition policy. This could happen even if the international institution possessed both the competences and the power to enforce an efficient implementation. – One of the central reasons why this has happened within the European Union is that the international competition authority – i.e. the European Commission – did not identify itself sufficiently with the national customers who suffer from relatively high energy prices and lose their international competitiveness. An international institution is generally characterized by a remaining degree of at least temporary distance, ignorance, and indifference with regard to the actual negative effects of its decisions on certain countries. Furthermore, political economics could be a decisive factor for the lack of competition in the German and European energy sector. The present development on the European energy market which is characterized by several cross-border merger activities and a further market concentration on the European level also seems to be influenced by personal interests of national and European politicians and bureaucrats. On the one hand, the European Commission criticizes that the former national energy monopolies have maintained their market power and that they even increase their dominance. On the other hand, the Commission has approved the acquisition of the Spanish Endesa SA by the German E.ON AG without imposing any conditions: 'After examining the operation, the Commission concluded that the proposed transaction would not significantly impede effective competition in the European Economic Area (EEA) or any substantial part of it and has therefore approved the concentration. The Commission will continue to keep the development in the German and Span-

654 Krakowski (2002) pp. 296ff.

ish gas and electricity markets and the other markets concerned under review'[655]. This is, in a way, a contradictory position because ...

- ... the Commission has not yet provided for effective competition on the national energy markets so that an announcement of further reviews of the national markets are no credible statement anymore;
- ... the high profits which result from the dominant market position are the reason why the E.ON AG can afford further acquisitions on the European energy market. If the Commission had provided for effective competition on the national markets, the E.ON AG probably would not be able to buy the Endesa SA. Instead, the Commission approves further concentration so that the market power even increases and the chances to increase competition and to reduce prices on the national markets decrease.
- ... the Commission allows the takeover because the markets are 'still predominantly national in scope, *inter alia* due to varying degrees of liberalization, regulatory barriers and lack of interconnection capacity' and because 'the parties have limited overlapping activities in the electricity markets'[656]. This is a problematic point of view. Firstly, because it refers to the status quo and therefore it is based on a rather static and myopic argumentation. Secondly, because the Commission legitimates a new restriction of competition (further concentration by the E.ON/Endesa transaction) with an already existing restriction of competition (national market foreclosure and lack of competition on the national markets).

Consequently, political economics seem to be relevant to explain the European Commission´s antitrust policy with regard to the energy sector. Instead of promoting vigorous competition on the European energy market – as promised before liberalization – the Commission allows further concentration. Therefore, the present European competition policy on the energy market is similarly permissive as the former national exemption from antitrust, but the effect on the international competitiveness could be even worse.

Furthermore, the integration of the European Union shows that an international harmonization of competition policy generally reduces the national

[655] European Commission (2006a) p. 1; European Commission (2006b) p. 1.
[656] European Commission (2006a) p. 1.

scope of action. This problem also concerns a country's political options to pursue regional development goals by means of a permissive competition policy like exemptions from antitrust.[657] This problem must not necessarily reduce the competitiveness of the whole nation, but it would reduce the competitiveness of certain regions of the nation. For instance, a liberalization and deregulation of a natural monopoly like the postal services or the railway infrastructure could lead to a so-called cherry-picking of the most lucrative parts of the national market. This could happen if the former monopolist was obliged to practice a cross-subsidization of the more cost-intensive or unprofitable services in sparsely populated or remote regions. In case that the international competition authority does not consider such aspects concerning regional development politics and distributional issues, the liberalization could produce ambivalent effects on the international competitiveness of the nation. The former monopoly could possibly reduce its costs and increase its international competitiveness[658]; new competitors would probably support this effect. Simultaneously, the locational attractiveness of the negatively affected regions and their competitiveness could decrease when they are disconnected from the infrastructure or if they have to pay higher prices for its use.[659] As regards the role of the national government, there are at least two theoretical possibilities to react.

1. On the one hand, the national government could be interested to establish a new regulation, i.e. a new exemption from competition, for example in order to avoid a price-discrimination between urban and rural regions and to maintain the infrastructure in less developed or remote regions. In certain cases, the government would not be allowed to do so because of a transfer of competences to the international institution.

2. On the other hand, the government could be unwilling to implement a new regulation that re-establishes subsidies for certain regions because these subsidies would have to be financed by higher taxes or they would increase public debt.

---

657 Cf. Bundeskartellamt (2003) p. 42; cf. Monopolkommission (2004) p. 2.

658 The overall effect of liberalization on the international competitiveness of the former monopoly is hard to predict. On the one hand, the former monopoly loses privileges, for example the possibility to profit from relatively high prices on domestic markets. On the other hand, the former monopolist would no longer be obliged to cross-subsidize certain regional markets or to fulfil other public or political interests.

659 Cf. Weimann (2006) pp. 366ff.

In both cases, countries with many underdeveloped or remote regions could be at a disadvantage compared to countries where the vast majority of the people lives in big cities.

Application 2: Attracting New Competitors in Order to Promote Domestic Competition and Competitiveness. As regards to the role of competition policy to increase the locational attractiveness of the domestic economy, i.e. to attract new investors or to prevent a relocation of domestic enterprises, there are different positions in economic research. In 1996, the German Monopoly Commission attached little importance to the role of competition policy for a firm's choice of location because other factors like tax policy and the height of wages were dominant.[660] Though, further globalization, the international integration of markets, and the growing importance of high-tech industries with rapid technological change could increase the importance of competition policy for the locational attractiveness of nations.[661] National competition policy could be tempted to practice a permissive competition policy in order to attract foreign direct investments.

There is a range of cases where a more permissive approach could both attract foreign direct investments, strengthen national competition, and enhance the international competitiveness of the nation. In this case, a flexible national competition policy could try to meet the interests of new investors and competitors and strengthen competition simultaneously. As already mentioned above, new forms of inter-firm cooperation could create first-mover advantages, and it is likely that also foreign firms could be attracted to join these inter-firm cooperation. Furthermore, for instance, a national competition authority could decide to offer attractive conditions concerning certain forms of vertical competition restraints in order to attract foreign enterprises so that the market entry of the foreign enterprise results in an increase in the number of competitors on local or national markets. Though, the positive effects, which result for competition in a certain industry, have to be weighed against possible disadvantages that could result for other industries, especially on upstream and downstream markets.

The European regulation of the car industry partly could be taken as an example. There is a block exemption in European competition law as regards vertical agreements and concerted practices in the motor vehicle sector.[662] It is still in dispute whether this block exemption protects competition and consumers or whether it is just a result of lobbyism of the Euro-

---

660 Monopolkommission (1996) Sec. 924.
661 Cf. Stearns-Bläsing (2004) pp. 44ff.; cf. Koopmann (2000) p. 9.
662 European Commission (2002a).

pean motor vehicle industry. Theoretically, such a block exemption has ambivalent effects on competition and new market entries. On the one hand, the exemption could make it difficult for a new competitor (i.e. a foreign car manufacturer) to enter the market because most car dealers are closely tied to domestic car manufacturers. On the other hand, one could assume that the block exemption offers relatively attractive conditions for successful and competitive non-European car manufacturers to establish an own network of car dealers so that, as a final result, the intensity of competition between car manufacturers increases to the advantage of European consumers. Furthermore, the reinforced competition could strengthen the international competitiveness, too.

Such ambivalent or complex effects do not occur automatically in parallel cases, they often depend on the unique situation of competition in the national markets so that a national (or regional) competition authority is the right institution to deal with these cases to find an optimal solution for competition on national markets. A responsible weighing of the risks and benefits, which would on the one hand reduce, but on the other hand strengthen competition, is a task that has to be done by an independent national competition authority. This would not only lead to an optimal decision with regard to the intensity of national competition, but also with regard to the international competitiveness of the nation.

Application 3: Competition Policy and Technology Transfer Agreements. A nation's ability to pursue a permissive competition policy also can be illustrated by different restrictions and conditions for technology transfer agreements, for example with regard to patent licences. The old and deeply explored area of conflict between free competition and open markets on the one hand and granting a temporary patent monopoly for innovative enterprises on the other hand has to be balanced by the competition authority.[663] It is to balance consumers' interests with the protection of intellectual property rights.[664] This is a difficult task because the interface between antitrust policy and patent law is, especially in the short run, complicated – although both policies finally, i.e. in the long run, aim at increasing innovativeness, competition, and consumers' benefits. Consequently, the attitude of scholars and courts varies in the course of time and between nations. Although free and intensive competition is one of the most important instruments to generate technological progress, temporary patent monopolies are – from the point of view of many, but not all eco-

---

[663] The early debates about the patent system have been summarized in a critical article by Machlup and Penrose (1950).

[664] Gilbert and Shapiro (1998) p. 65.

nomists[665] – likewise an important legal institution to give both incentives for R&D efforts and incentives for the disclosure of new inventions. These incentives are essential tools to foster competition, innovations, and international competitiveness in the long run.[666] Competition and innovation participate in a self-reinforcing interaction, while patent rights are in a position both to foster and to reduce competition. Therefore, patent law, licence law, and competition law are challenged to solve this conflict by providing certain restrictions as regards the pursuance of patent rights in order to avoid antitrust difficulties.

While national patent law has to some extent already been internationally harmonized by means of several international agreements concerning the harmonization of substantive law[667] and the creation of common supranational procedures[668], competition law is still under national competence without any international top-down harmonization, so that every country can decide autonomously whether it wants to take a rather short run view of competition, emphasizing the necessity to protect competition in the short run and neglecting the protection of intellectual property rights, or whether it wants to adopt a dynamic view, underlining the long-term role of intellectual property rights in the competitive process.[669] Besides this fundamental decision, there is a lot of scope for national ex ante and ex post fine-tuning in order to achieve a welfare and competitiveness enhancing balance between the protection of competition and the protection of intellectual property rights. For instance, the optimal patent breadth and licence agreement also depend on the actual market position of the intellectual property rights holder and the licensee and on the licence agreement's potential to create a cartel – for example by means of a patent pool and cross-licensing – or to achieve efficiency benefits on the relevant market. Up to now, every country can define itself by means of a rule of reason approach how to weigh the *horizontal effects* – which are rather anti-

---

[665] The controversy indicates that many economists oppose to patent and copyright. The liberal economist Friedrich August von Hayek belongs to the most prominent economists who came out against patent-induced monopolies (cf. Kinsella (2001) p. 11; cf. Mantzavinos (1994) p. 128).

[666] Cf. Greif (2002) p. 181; cf. Busche (2001) pp. 345ff.; cf. Merges and Nelson (1992) pp. 185ff.

[667] International agreements on substantive harmonization are: Paris Convention on Patents 1883; World Intellectual Property Rights Organization (WIPO) 1967; International Patent Classification (IPC) 1971; Trade Related Aspects of Intellectual Property Rights (TRIPS) 1994; Patent Law Treaty (PLT) 2000.

[668] This has been achieved by the Patent Cooperation Treaty (PCT) 1970 and the European Patent Agreement (EPA) 1973 (cf. Greif (2002) p. 194).

[669] Cf. OECD Secretariat (2001) pp. 123ff.

competitive because they work like a horizontal cartel – against its *vertical effects* – which are rather pro-competitive because the licensee could become a new competitor – of a licence agreement. Furthermore, every nation can decide autonomously which licensing practices are generally allowed, i.e. which restrictions a licenser is allowed to impose on the licensee – for example grantbacks[670] – and which restrictions go beyond the subject and the limitations of the granted patent right. In the latter case, the restrictions are supposed to lead to unfair competition restraints and to restrict further innovation. Therefore, these restrictions can be prohibited by national antitrust laws. Examples for such hardcore restrictions in technology transfer agreements are the allocation of markets or customers (exclusive territories), price arrangements, output limitations and restrictions as regards further R&D.[671] These forbidden arrangements have to be defined and put in concrete terms by the national competition authority. Consequently, different national competition policy standards concerning the regulation of patent licenses and other technology transfer agreements have significant effects on license agreements because both the licensee and the licenser want to avoid unintended antitrust difficulties. Nevertheless, they both intend to profit from a license agreement so that hard bargaining is necessary to achieve an appropriate balance. The legislature needs to be sensitive to make such a balance possible, and it has sufficient latitude to set legal rules in competition law that are appropriate for the domestic enterprises and acceptable for the foreign enterprises. Two cases can be distinguished[672]:

1. Assuming that the domestic enterprises are rather licensers than licensees, it could be advantageous for the country and its enterprises to practice a relatively permissive competition policy, that is to say that the national competition laws allow its licensers to impose relatively many additional terms on the (foreign) licensees.
2. In case that the domestic producers are rather licensees, the competition authority could practice a more strict competition policy as regards license agreements. In this way, the authority could protect its domestic enterprises against too restrictive license agreements which

[670] A grantback provision in favour of the licenser obliges the licensee to license back to the licenser its own further innovations concerning the licensed technology. Such a grantback provision has the potential both to improve competition and to create a patent pool, depending on the individual case.

[671] Cf. Art. 4 TT-BER (Technology Transfer Block Exemption Regulation) in European Commission (2004c).

[672] Cf. Gottwald (1992) pp. 321ff.,344ff., 350ff., 437.

could reduce their international competitiveness. Even in case that the patent license agreement has been made by application of the licenser´s foreign patent and contract law and under taking into account the foreign antitrust requirements on patent licenses[673], the competition authority in the licensee´s country can offend the patent license agreement by making use of the effects doctrine, applying its strict antitrust law with respect to patent licenses which have been made abroad under foreign law. A competition authority can apply its antitrust law on all license agreements concerning its market, so it is irrelevant whether the license agreement is based on national or foreign license and contract law. For instance, the European Commission is allowed to apply the effects doctrine if a foreign license agreement that is based on US-American license and contract law appears to create a vertical or horizontal cartel which prevents competition within the Common Market. Then the agreement would be disapproved by the European Commission.[674] – On the other hand, a more permissive evaluation of the license agreement could support the dissemination of foreign know how to national enterprises. In this way, in May 2004 the European Commission has installed a new block exemption regulation for technology transfer agreements (No. 772/ 2004), which includes a more permissive handling of license agreements in order to improve the European enterprises´ access to new technology, to minimize administrative expenses and to enhance transparency and the legal security for firms (so-called 'safe harbour').[675] In contrast to the former block exemption regulation No. 240/96, the new one has reduced the former criteria (so-called white, grey and black clauses) to a new list of black clauses ('hardcore restrictions') which is narrower in scope than the previous regulation.[676] If a license agreement does not offend against one of these black clauses and if the involved companies´ combined market share does not exceed the legal thresholds, then the license agreement is exempted from the cartel ban in Art. 81 I EC according to Art. 81 III

---

673 In most cases, license agreements apply the national license and contract law of the licenser, but there are also many cases where a foreign inventor applies for a patent in other countries (for example by means of a PCT-registration) and wants to earn money by placing licenses in these countries so that the license and contract law of these countries becomes relevant. Finally, the contracting party with more negotiating power is able to determine which law is to be applied.

674 Cf. ibid. pp. 321ff.

675 Cf. European Commission (2004a) p. 11.

676 Ibid.

EC. This more permissive approach, which also applies to license agreements between enterprises located within the Common Market, can strengthen the technology transfer and thereupon the international competitiveness of the European Union.

To sum up, both the relatively permissive and the rather strict strategy of competition policy with regard to technology transfer agreements have the potential to increase the international competitiveness of domestic enterprises. However, in practice, there are several limits in using this scope of action. In both cases the antitrust legislature has to act cautiously in this field of competition policy because an unbalanced competition law with regard to technology transfer and patent licence agreements could harm domestic licensees or licensers, too. Especially industrialized countries and high tech industries are characterized by a high degree of technology transfer in *both* directions and these licence agreements are characterized by a high degree of international standardization, too. In many cases, technological advance by domestic enterprises depends on parallel and cumulative technological developments by other enterprises and industries, often located in foreign countries.[677] An unbalanced antitrust law, especially a too strict antitrust policy with regard to firms′ patent licensing practices, would impede the access to new or relevant technologies and could be discriminatory and deter foreign licensees and licensers from signing license agreements with domestic companies. Consequently, taking into account competitiveness considerations in the regulation of technology transfer agreements like patent licenses, requires a lot of sensitivity and fine-tuning while maintaining legal transparency and being in accordance with international standards and practices.

As regards the role of an international competition authority with regard to the international regulation of technology transfer agreements, it is doubtful whether it would show enough consideration and flexibility in this respect. The workload of an international competition authority and the need for international transparency could lead to a too simple and too permissive competition policy, which could be disadvantageous for licensees and, correspondingly, for the international competitiveness of certain countries, especially developing countries.

Conclusion. As regards the relation between the international competitiveness of nations and an international harmonization of competition policy, there are some aspects which have to be finally emphasized with regard to permissive competition policy.

---

677 Cf. Merges and Nelson (1992) pp. 185ff.

Firstly, there is still a lot of uncertainty about the legitimacy of exemptions, about efficient forms of regulation, and about the final effect on the international competitiveness. It is unlikely that an international competition regime would serve to reduce these uncertainties and to improve the theoretical knowledge and practical know-how about these issues. An international harmonization would not stop economic research on these issues and national competition and regulation authorities possibly would still be allowed to decide on certain exemptions from competition[678], but the current international regulatory competition seems to be more apt to produce new insights into these questions.

Secondly, exemptions from competition policy and other forms of permissive competition policy often produce ambivalent effects on the international competitiveness. Therefore, it is the task of the competition authority and the government to weigh the positive and the negative effects of regulation, to search for efficient forms of regulation, to observe the effects of functional or sectoral exemptions from competition law[679], and to use the legal scope of action to promote the international competitiveness of the affected domestic enterprises and the nation as a whole. This all has to be done without falling into protectionist, inefficient, and discriminatory practices. As regards protectionist practices, the liberalization efforts of the past decades have shown that many exemptions and regulations were unjustified.[680] Other exemptions have to be regarded as borderline cases

[678] According to Council Regulation (EC) No. 1/2003, the competition authorities of the EU member states are allowed to grant individual exemptions from Article 81 I EC Treaty, provided that these restraints of competition do not harm the integration of the common market. Furthermore, the members of an international antitrust agreement could be endowed with a right of veto in order to preserve essential or superior national interests. Though, especially with regard to superior national interests, there is a lot of potential for international conflicts within an international antitrust regime. The conflict between the European Commission and the Spanish government as regards the conditions for a takeover of the Spanish energy company Endesa SA by the German energy company E.ON AG can be taken as an example for this. While the Commission has approved the acquisition, the Spanish government intended to impose harsh conditions on a takeover. The Spanish government underlined the strategic public interests of Spain while the European Commission accused Spain of protectionism (cf. Härtel (2006) p. 59).

[679] For instance, it would be advisable to establish a legislative review of regulations or a temporary restriction of exemptions from competition (so-called sunset legislation). Several forms of exemptions from competition even necessitate a regular governmental control or temporal restriction, for example structural crisis cartels, recession cartels, and rationalization cartels.

[680] Bundeskartellamt (2003) pp. 41f.; cf. Monopolkommission (2004) pp. 66f.

which could be justified although they restrict competition, for example because of superior national interests. Partly, they could help to improve the international competitiveness. Some still existing exemptions from competition are economically legitimate, so that a good regulation helps to enhance efficiency and competitiveness, whereas a deficient regulation reduces competition and competitiveness.

Thirdly, the history of market liberalization within the European Union highlights the benefits, the limits, and the dangers of supranational decision-making and antitrust-enforcement with regard to exemptions from competition law and their effect on the international competitiveness.

4.3.3.2 Strategies of Protectionist Competition Policy

Permissive competition policy must not be confused with protectionist competition policy. The latter is a kind of national competition policy that in most cases has the spirit and the effects of classic beggar-thy-neighbour policies. It is the attempt to increase a nation′s welfare and international competitiveness by means of *private* competition restraints that are nationally legalized. Normally, these gains of welfare are generated at the expense of other countries′ welfare, for example by means of market foreclosing cartels and monopolization.

4.3.3.2.1 Illegitimate Protectionism

Illegitimate protectionist *competition* policy has to be distinguished from traditional instruments of foreign trade protectionism like high customs tariffs, import restrictions, export subsidies, local content clauses, voluntary export restrictions, and anti-dumping.

One important example of protectionist competition policy is the exemption of *export cartels* from national competition law. In many industrial and also developing countries, export cartels are shielded from antitrust action. A reason for this problem of current antitrust might be that ‘a country which allows cartels to be set up by its own firms while all other countries continue to carry out ordo liberal economic policies can place itself in an absolutely better position. It paves the way for credible quantity agreements in cartel contracts, which the firms can exploit as Stackelberg leaders. The result is a shift of profits from foreign to domestic firms which does not hurt the national consumers.’[681] As a consequence of such protectionist antitrust policies, according to Sinn, ‘it is more likely that there will be a deregulation race in which each country tries to create the

[681] Sinn (1999) p. 31.

best possible starting position for its firms'[682]. The likelihood of a deregulation race is one of the most important concerns with regard to protectionist activities. Theoretically, this could happen, and the fact that many countries allow export cartels could be interpreted as the result of such a deregulation race. On the other, the permission of export cartels rather seems to be a historic shortcoming of national antitrust, an exceptional case that could be eliminated without far-reaching additional measures of international harmonization.

A second example of how national competition authorities can act in a protectionist manner can be found in the abuse of dominant market power. They have an incentive not to punish a domestic enterprise if its abuse of market power primarily harms foreign enterprises and consumers. Similarly, national competition authorities could neglect their policy on vertical and horizontal competition restraints if domestic producers are not negatively affected. Such forms of *private* competition restraints can be considered a substitute for former *public* protectionism in foreign trade.

All these kinds of protectionist and discriminatory non-application of competition law are generally rejected by the majority of economists and jurists. Therefore, the question of how national competition policy can be regarded as an instrument to increase a nation′s international competitiveness is not: 'Do we need protectionism?' Nevertheless, it has to be examined whether protectionism is a realistic scenario in case that competition policy remains a competence of national authorities.

4.3.3.2.2 The Probability of Illegitimate Protectionist Competition Policy

The above chapter has described how countries could try to increase their international competitiveness at the expense of fair and intensive competition. One could state that there is a fundamental conflict of aims between 'international competition' on the one hand and 'international competitiveness' on the other. Consequently, a protectionist abuse of competition policy could become a ubiquitous problem in a globalized economy. But some arguments can be put forward against this pessimistic scenario (cf. Chap. 4.2.5.2).

Firstly, it is doubtful whether countries and companies really apply such protectionist strategies like export cartels in a large scale. This kind of protectionism could fail as a sustainable long-term strategy because a deregulation race would lead to an increased supply, falling prices and falling profits when the cartelizing firms get into a race for Stackelberg leadership

682 Ibid.

position (i.e. a race for starting positions).[683] In this way, a protectionist abuse of national competition policy probably would end in a prisoners′ dilemma. This is not attractive, neither for the affected companies nor for their governments.

Secondly, the application of the effects doctrine reduces the possibilities to cartelize and to start a race to the bottom. The effects doctrine does not prohibit protectionism, but foreign countries, which also apply the effects doctrine, have the possibility to defend themselves against beggar-thy-neighbour policies. As already mentioned in Chap. 4.2.5.2, a race to the bottom is a rather unlikely scenario for modern world trade and there is no evidence of a downward convergence of competition policy. Both the national governments and their competition authorities appear to be interested in promoting effective competition policy, not in protectionism and downward convergence. Nevertheless, one must admit that, from case to case, national decision-making can be like a tightrope-walk. The competition authorities have to develop much sensitivity, also for other countries′ interests, so that permissive decisions do not descend into protectionist tendencies.

4.3.3.2.3 Legitimate Protectionist Competition Policy

Although protectionist practices are generally to be condemned, it is worth discussing special cases where a protectionist use of competition policy could be legitimate. A brief consideration of the economic development of industrial countries reveals that many of them have achieved economic growth and international competitiveness by means of protectionist behaviour that is now forbidden under the WTO regime. In view of these empirical facts, the question arises whether today′s developing, transitional and new industrializing countries have the same right to attain higher growth rates by using protectionist instruments (cf. Chap. 4.3.2.3). For instance, Japanese car manufacturers have received public subsidies over decades and they have been protected against foreign competition on domestic markets. Accordingly, it could be legitimate for a new industrializing country to protect itself in the same way against car imports from Japan – for example by means of voluntary export restraints – and to support domestic enterprises to become competitive. It is likely that the demand for international competition rules and harmonization is a strategy of the industrial countries to protect themselves against new competitors. In general, many demands for harmonization are egoistically motivated, espe-

683 Cf. Chap. 4.2.5.2.

cially the widespread demand for an international harmonization of environmental and labour standards has a protectionist background.

4.3.3.2.4 Conclusion

In sum, protectionist competition policy is neither an acceptable nor a likely approach to strengthen the international competitiveness. Though, an exemption could be made in favour of developing countries. Similar to the preferential treatment of developing countries in the world trading system, there could be a legitimate scope for temporary protectionist practices applied by developing countries. Chapter 4.3.2.3 has described that developing countries especially need the sovereignty to practice a flexible competition policy. In exceptional cases, protectionist measures could be an element of flexible competition policy.

4.3.3.3 Strategies of Strict Competition Policy

The least controversial, though not totally uncontroversial method to increase a nation's international competitiveness by means of competition policy is to practice a *strict* competition policy, especially to provide for competitive domestic markets and an increase in the number of domestic enterprises. Strict competition policy is less controversial – both on the national and especially on the international agenda – because it is generally accepted as a pro-competitive, non-protectionist, and non-discriminatory antitrust strategy. The positive relation between strict competition policy and the intensity of competition and between vigorous competition and economic efficiency (both the short-term allocative and long-term dynamic efficiency), innovativeness, and a country's GDP growth are widely undisputed.[684] Furthermore, even in case of international competition rules, every nation still could be allowed to implement and enforce stricter antitrust rules so that there would not be wide scope for international conflicts.

Though, strict competition policy also could become subject to international conflicts. For instance, a national antitrust authority that closely adheres to the more liberal paradigm of the Chicago School of Antitrust Analysis could come into conflict with a foreign antitrust authority that

[684] Although competition theory has developed several different, partly contradictory academic schools how to establish and maintain competitive and efficient markets, the positive relation between competition policy (especially effective antitrust legislation and the protection of intellectual property), competition, efficiency, innovativeness, and GDP growth is generally undisputed and is supported by empirical evidence (cf. Fontenot and Wilhelm (2005) pp. 235ff.).

rather adheres to the strict antitrust concept of workable competition (Harvard School). Therefore, international minimum standards and close cooperation in international merger control would not automatically solve all interjurisdictional conflicts.

The following sections give some examples why strict competition policy – no matter in which field of antitrust – could be favourable for the international competitiveness of the nation. Furthermore, they underline that there is a wide scope for *national* competition authorities to provide for a relatively high intensity of competition – compared to foreign markets – in order to make domestic enterprises internationally competitive and to attract foreign investors by increasing the locational attractiveness. The instruments applied by the national governments and competition authorities in order to provide for intensive competition are partly distinctive features of the *domestic* market. Therefore, as regards the debate on an internationalization of competition policy, the question arises what difference it would make for the intensity of domestic competition and for the international competitiveness of the nation if the national competition authority would no more be allowed to maintain these distinctive features and to guarantee highly competitive markets.

4.3.3.3.1 National Enterprises and the Intensity of National Competition

A nation's decision to practice a strict competition policy has the general effect that domestic enterprises learn competition on their domestic markets so that their ability to compete on international markets will be strengthened. For instance, a national competition authority's strategy to refer mainly to the *national* market as the geographically relevant market could be interpreted as a strategy to strengthen the competitive forces of domestic enterprises.[685] As a positive side-effect of promoting competition on the

[685] As regards the national level, one might complain about a too strict merger control, for instance in case of the German competition authority's former practice to take, as a rule, the national market as the geographically relevant market during the first stage of its market analysis. This practice was based on a 1995 decision of the German BGH that, according to Sec. 130 (2) GWB, the geographically relevant market could not exceed the national market (BGHZ 131, 107 and KVR 17/94, WuW E BGH 3026ff. – Backofenmarkt). As regards cross-border competition, only exports and imports have been considered (Kinne (1997) p. 44). In its decision from 5 October 2004 (KVR 14/03, WuW DE-R 1355 – Staubsaugerbeutelmarkt), the BGH explicitly has given up this practice so that only the actual economic facts decide on the geographically relevant market. Consequently, the relevant market can exceed the national borders so that, for instance, also potential competition from abroad and for-

national market in most cases international competition and the international regulatory competition will be strengthened, too.[686]

An empirical and theoretical analysis of international competitiveness shows that, in the long run, the most competitive enterprises are those which were innovative enough to survive competition on their domestic markets.[687] There are several reasons explaining this phenomenon:

1. Firstly, intensive competition on domestic markets forces the enterprises to improve their organization, management, strategy, technology, and product portfolio continually. In this way, they develop a comparative or even an absolute advantage.

2. Furthermore, economies whose domestic markets are characterized by intensive competition, act as an incentive for domestic enterprises to develop or to discover new markets. For instance, during the recent two decades, many enterprises have been successful in developing sustainable solutions for ecological problems and to gain technological leadership in these industries. Many of these new products, for example ecological food and hybrid cars, are substitutes for products which did not take into consideration ecological aspects and which have been offered on markets characterized by intensive competition. On the other hand, one has to take into account that a monopolization and cartelization of markets by the incumbents can prompt innovations, too. The foreclosure of established markets can force newcomers to innovate so that new markets emerge. This factor might have been relevant, for instance, for the market for modern solar cells and

---

eign market power can be considered (cf. Beninca (2005) pp. 43ff.). The former practice was an instrument to strengthen the competitive forces on domestic markets, though, according to Kantzenbach and Kinne (see Kantzenbach and Kinne (1997) pp. 77ff.; Kinne (1997) pp. 45ff.), the 'observed' concentration and competitive environment of the market could cause some misconceptions about the real situation on the relevant (international) market. These misconceptions could have reduced the international competitiveness of domestic companies.

686 On the other hand, in several cases a more permissive competition policy that supports further industrial concentration on domestic markets could be more appropriate to strengthen international competition. Especially the strategy to allow mergers to generate national champions and global players that are able to compete on global markets would strengthen international competition.

687 Cf. Porter (1990) p. 68, pp. 117ff.

for internet telephone software (Voice over Internet Protocol – VoIP).[688]

3. According to Porter[689], there is an interaction between intensive competition on the one hand and demanding and sophisticated consumers on the other. Intensive competition is an incentive for consumers to demand high standards in service, quality, and innovation. The possibility to choose between different suppliers is the predominant motive for this behaviour. This consumer mentality forces the enterprises to meet or even to surpass the consumers′ expectations. As a consequence, they will be able to meet the expectations of foreign consumers, too.
4. Economies whose domestic markets are characterized by intensive competition, act as an incentive for the domestic enterprises to increase their export. There are two reasons for this effect. Firstly, the enterprises are able to export because of the high quality of their products. Secondly, they are willing to export because they also look for markets that are not as demanding as the domestic markets.
5. Intensive competition on a national market could work as an incentive for a multinational enterprise to transfer technology into this market in order to strengthen its competitiveness in this market. Consequently, intensive competition could ensure the permanent inflow of the best technologies. This technology transfer could result in a general technological upgrading that strengthens the international competitiveness of the whole economy.[690]

These aspects show that strict competition policy is an important strategy for becoming competitive. In the long run, domestic enterprises have to be independent from national shelter for being successful on global markets. In most cases, there is no risk that enterprises expend too many resources if they are confronted with both an intensive *domestic* competition and an increasing *global* competition at the same time. Instead, it can be said that necessary and costly investments in domestic markets are good invest-

---

688 In fact, for example with regard to the European Union, several ecological innovations also have been prompted by governmental regulations which demand higher ecological or safety standards, partly enforced by the European Commission. Consequently, in practice, there is often a multitude of factors which promote innovations. These factors can be determined both by competition policy or industrial or ecological policy.

689 Porter (1990).

690 Cf. Anderson and Khosla (1995) p. 11.

ments in the international competitiveness, too. In contrast to this, protected enterprises will likely run the risk of underperforming international benchmarks. When foreign enterprises penetrate the domestic market, the protected domestic enterprises might not be prepared to compete with them and operate on a global market. As a result, they would need further governmental help, especially if they are 'too big to fail'. This could lead to moral hazard and cause further negative influences on the international competitiveness of the nation.

Despite these fundamental insights about the positive impact of *strict* competition policy on the international competitiveness of nations, there have to be made some additional remarks. Firstly, one has to take into account that, in times of economic globalization, domestic enterprises often are already internationalized and many new enterprises directly try to be successful on foreign markets, too. Consequently, in many cases, there are no long periods to learn competition on domestic markets before entering foreign markets. Nevertheless, the competitive pressure on domestic markets can still be helpful to become and to stay internationally competitive, although this competitive pressure also forces foreign market entrants to become competitive.

Secondly, one has to take into account that every national and international market has to be analyzed intensively in order to be able to make balanced and reliable decisions about the necessary national market structure and degree of competition policy that helps to increase the international competitiveness. As already described above, permissive and protectionist strategies might be more adequate in certain (exceptional) cases in order to promote both international competition and international competitiveness in the long run. Finally, the degree of competition on domestic markets often results in ambivalent effects both on international competition and on the international competitiveness of the nation. Accordingly, the following examples qualify the role of *strict* domestic competition policy. They underline the ambivalent effects of strict competition policy and demonstrate the scope for national competition authorities to weigh the advantages and disadvantages of strict competition policy.

Application 1: The Ambivalence of the Number of Domestic Producers with Respect to Their International Competitiveness. The advantages of strict competition policy can be shown by means of the relation between the number of domestic producers and their international competitiveness. The point at issue is whether it is possible to increase the international competitiveness – especially the exports – by increasing or reducing the number of domestic companies within an industry.[691] Two strategies have to be distinguished.

Firstly, in case of falling marginal costs, national competition policy could allow more market concentration in order to increase domestic enterprises shares of the domestic and international market and to maximize economic productivity. For example, national cartels, vertical market integration (market foreclosure) and mergers could be an instrument to achieve this aim without a rise in prices.[692] Nevertheless, there is no guarantee that such an industrial concentration policy would be successful in increasing the long-term international competitiveness of domestic producers. Although some short-term economies of scale could be realized, the negative long-term effects of market-foreclosure and concentration – especially allocative inefficiency – could be more important in certain cases. Furthermore, mergers and other kinds of market concentration do not automatically increase the productive efficiency and the international competitiveness. There is significant empirical evidence that horizontal mergers frequently fail or that they do not generate significant cost savings.[693] In addition to that, many mergers are not only motivated by goals of efficiency and improved performance, but also by personal interests of the top management. For instance, successful companies can lose their good reputation and their MOS due to a merger or takeover. This would reduce their international competitiveness and, as a consequence of this, also the intensity of international competition.

The second strategy is to increase the number of enterprises in domestic industries, and this not only in case of constant marginal costs. If the domestic markets are characterized by a multitude of competing domestic enterprises, then the national economy often is too small to absorb all their production capacity. Therefore, the companies would try to increase their export sales, for example according to the so-called 'vent for surplus' theory. Bliss, who focuses on a one good cross-hauling model[694] with a production function with constant marginal costs[695], states that 'an increase in the number of identical producers in one country increases their sales in all

[691] Bliss (1996) pp. 322f.

[692] Confer the instruments of permissive competition policy in Chap. 4.3.3.1.

[693] Cf. Kleinert and Klodt (2002) pp. 17ff.; cf. Seong (1989) p. 115.

[694] A cross-hauling model describes an international competitive environment where a country imports and exports the same good in the same period, i.e. this model 'allows for trade in identical goods in both directions' (Bliss (1996) p. 321).

[695] Constant marginal costs exclude the generation of scale economies so that a further market concentration would not improve the productivity of domestic companies.

markets in which that type of producer is selling and lowers the price in all those markets. Lower prices must lower the profitability of each producer, and it is possible that they will do so to such an extent that some producers will not generate enough profit to cover overheads, when exit will result.'[696] In other words, it can be assumed that – in case of constant marginal costs – an increase in the number of domestic producers finally leads to an increase of the total share of the global market. The reduced profitability and the exit of some domestic producers do not hinder this final outcome.

In addition to this case of *constant* marginal costs, an increase in the number of domestic producers also could be beneficial in case of *falling* marginal costs. Both the increasing competitive pressure on the domestic markets and the growing need to become successful on foreign markets would force domestic producers to become increasingly productive and innovative, to generate further economies of scale and to reach the MOS. As a result of this competitive pressure, it is possible that the domestic companies will gain a greater share of the global market.

In conclusion, as regards the relation between the international competitiveness of a nation and an international harmonization of antitrust, it is likely that a *national* competition authority has more scope to enforce a strict competition policy in case of need. This could result in a more balanced competition policy by taking into account the ambivalence of certain cases and by considering the actual cost function and international competitiveness of domestic enterprises, especially with regard to so-called borderline cases where it is hard to decide whether an efficiency defense would be appropriate. In contrast to this, an international competition authority probably would generally use a wide concept of the relevant market, normally the global market, so that there is no broad scope both to balance ambivalent effects and to maintain a relatively high number of domestic producers.

Application 2: The Ambivalent Effect of Intensive Competition and Low Profits on the International Competitiveness. The German banking sector is characterized by a *relatively* high degree of competition and *relatively* low profits compared to other countries.[697] This is because the

[696] Bliss (1996) p. 324.

[697] Cf. Fischer and Pfeil (2003) pp. 48, 50; cf. Hewitt (2000) p. 54f.; cf. Pieper (2007) pp. 452ff.. The high competitive pressure in the German banking sector also results from the international liberalization of financial markets. Before this liberalization, the competitive pressure in the German banking system was relatively high, but still limited because of a high degree of bank regulation, which was restricting competition and sheltered the domestic banks from com-

German banking sector consists of three pillars of universal banks which are strictly separated from each other and compete against each other: the private commercial banks, the credit unions (cooperative banks), and the state owned Landesbanks and municipal savings banks, which are in public ownership.[698] This fragmented structure and competitive pressure on the German banking market is the result of both historical developments and political decisions and it results in *ambivalent effects* on the international competitiveness of German banks and other domestic firms:

1. On the one hand, the competitive pressure on the German banking market leads to high efficiency and many innovations.[699] The loan and deposit customers profit from relatively good banking conditions. Especially commercial borrowers profit from less concentrated markets because of lower interest rates and a growth of loans.[700] Furthermore, especially the municipal savings banks, which are strictly tied to local markets, promote competition both on the retail banking market and on other domestic markets because they have the legal duty to grant loans to small and medium sized enterprises.

2. On the other hand, the intensive competition in the German banking sector could have negative effects on the international competitiveness, too, so that competition authorities and regulators face a trade-off.[701] Firstly, a lack of consolidation in the banking sector could be responsible for inefficient overcapacities that cause high costs; this could reduce social welfare and international competitiveness.[702] Furthermore, it is possible that the competitive pressure between banks leads to credit rationing, especially for new or risky borrowers.[703] This

petition from abroad and from non-bank suppliers of financial services (cf. Fischer and Pfeil (2003) pp. 1f., 48). After the liberalization, the competitive pressure has increased because of several market entries, especially by foreign commercial banks.

698 Cf. Fischer and Pfeil (2003) p. 47.

699 Cf. Pieper (2007) p. 459.

700 Cf. Fischer and Pfeil (2003) pp. 21f.; cf. Cetorelli and Gambera (2001) pp. 617ff. Also cf. Karceski et al. (2005, pp. 2043ff.) who focus on the influence of a bank merger on the welfare of bank customers.

701 Cf. Cetorelli (2001) p. 46.

702 Cf. Angelini and Cetorelli (2000, pp. 9, 37), who underline that a consolidation in the banking sector (market concentration) might have ambivalent effects on the power of banks and on social welfare and industry structure.

703 Petersen and Rajan (1995) pp. 407ff., 422ff.; cf. Fischer and Pfeil (2003) pp. 42ff.; cf. Cetorelli and Gambera (2001) pp. 30f. Also cf. Nehls and Schmidt (2004, pp. 479ff.) who found empirical evidence of a supply side restriction of

restricted credit availability has ambivalent effects on the international competitiveness of the nation: innovative investments could be stopped too early; simultaneously, risky projects, which lead to an inefficient allocation, could be prevented. Thirdly, as a consequence of their *relatively* low profitability, German commercial banks lack behind foreign commercial banks as regards the possibility to carry out strategic and costly investments and to attract private investors. Instead, the commercial banks in Germany have a relatively low market value and could become a likely target of hostile takeovers.[704] Fourthly, the competitive pressure could have a negative effect on the locational attractiveness of the German financial markets for foreign banks.[705]

This ambivalent situation could be taken as an argument that the decision about the intensity of competition on the domestic banking sector should be made by the nation itself in order to take into account both aspects. Correspondingly, the former German government had put pressure on the big German commercial banks to carry out mergers; simultaneously, the German government also wants to maintain the three-pillar-system and the pro-competitive role of the savings banks.

4.3.3.3.2 Foreign Enterprises and the Intensity of National Competition

Similar to domestic enterprises, foreign enterprises generally can profit from the same benefits that result from intensive competition on the domestic markets. Though, in comparison to domestic incumbents, there are some additional aspects to be considered. The following examples highlight the benefits of strict competition policy for the international locational attractiveness of a nation and for the protection of competition on the national markets.

Application 1: Foreign Investors and the Intensity of National Competition. Firstly, it is likely that foreign investors may have little interest

loans on the German credit market, mainly determined by the drop in earnings in the banking sector. Though, on the other hand, high competitive pressure theoretically also could lead to a credit expansion if the banks try to attract new customers. In an extreme scenario, when the banks' conditions do not cover the true costs, this would be harmful for the international competitiveness.

704 Eggert (2004) p. 6.

705 As regards the influence of national bank regulation on the locational attractiveness of a national financial center, cf. Huang (1992) p. 272.

to invest in a location where they would be confronted with a dominant position of the main competitor on the relevant market. For instance, high market entry barriers, low customer switching rates, the threat of predatory pricing by the incumbent, and the probability of overcapacities – that may have been built up by a market dominating company that earns monopoly rents – could deter foreign investors from a market entry. Consequently, it is up to the national competition policy to weigh the negative effects that dominant incumbents exert on the locational attractiveness of the national economy against the positive effects of the high international competitiveness of these dominating incumbents. The economic benefits of a market-dominating incumbent who – as a national champion and global player – is 'only' subjected to a control of abuse of market power, could be overcompensated by the potential benefits that would result from an increased capital inflow (FDI). In contrast to an international competition authority, a national competition policy can use its legal scope to weigh these aspects and practice a competition policy that maximizes the international competitiveness without making compromises with respect to the primary aim, the protection of competition.

Furthermore, foreign investors would likely prefer a location that stands out due to intensive competition both between the potential suppliers and between the potential customers of the foreign investor. This aim has to be regarded as at least as important as striving for a permissive competition policy for the own business activities. National competition policy can try to meet the interests of potential investors by guaranteeing intensive competition both on the relevant market and on upstream and downstream markets.

With reference to the above example of the German banking sector, several foreign banks have entered the German banking sector and were confronted with more competitive pressure than on foreign markets. They adapted mostly successfully to the German market conditions, offering similar products like German banks and being content with a partly smaller profit rate compared to their foreign markets. Probably they will be able to compensate these lower profits by learning competition and becoming even more competitive and profitable on foreign markets.

Finally, foreign investors especially could be attracted by a competitive economy that is characterized by a dynamic, competitive, and innovative business environment and skilled labour force. The geographical proximity to competitors, suppliers, and customers that are highly demanding could be the decisive factor for staying or becoming competitive, too. Especially in high-tech industries, the direct confrontation with intensive competition in a certain region like the Silicon Valley could be more important than any other form of industrial policy, subsidies etc.

Application 2: Strict Competition Policy in Favour of Net Importers on Imperfectly Competitive Markets. Guzman, a proponent of an increased international cooperation including substantive antitrust rules, underlines the tendency of national competition authorities to discriminate against foreign interests: 'Agencies will be tempted to be lenient towards locals and tough on foreigners ... even if no such double standard is called for in the relevant legislation'[706]. Export cartels offer an empirical evidence for a discriminatory antitrust policy that is embodied in national antitrust legislation[707]; other antitrust decisions with a strong national bias are possible even without pre-determined discriminatory antitrust standards.

For instance, in case of a country that 'exports virtually all of its production in imperfectly competitive industries', domestic firms have an incentive to engage in anticompetitive business practices where 'the great majority of harm is felt by foreigners'.[708] Consequently, domestic antitrust policy could be tempted to practice a lax competition policy that favours the interests of domestic producers (exporters) over those of (foreign) consumers. Conversely, a country that imports virtually all of its (consumers) goods from imperfectly competitive industries could apply a strict competition policy that favours the interests of domestic consumers over those of foreign producers. According to Guzman, both strategies of national antitrust would be discriminatory and distorting trade, causing externalities which have to be internalized by international antitrust regulation or cooperation.[709]

As regards the debates on international competitiveness and international competition rules, it is necessary to refrain from such extreme scenarios which are based on simplified trade patterns and a one-sided focus on discriminatory and protectionist practices. In general, trade patterns are more complex and national antitrust laws and their enforcement should not and do not include a double standard that differentiates between domestic

[706] Guzman (2004) p. 356. Also cf. Head and Ries (1997, pp. 1105-1121) who focus on rather discriminatory antitrust decisions which aim at national efficiency gains for the merging firms′ home countries at the expense of global welfare, i.e. welfare effects of an international merger are not fully internalized. Consequently, decentralized merger regulation is not always efficient. On the other hand, 'there are plausible conditions under which national authorities, maximizing their own interests, would prohibit mergers that reduce world welfare', especially in case that domestic consumers account for a sufficiently high share of world consumer surplus.

[707] Guzman (2004) p. 356. Also cf. Evenett et al. (2001) pp. 1222ff.

[708] Guzman (2004) p. 357.

[709] Ibid. pp. 358, 364.

and foreign enterprises.[710] Discriminatory antitrust rules like exemptions for export cartels should be eliminated. An international consensus on this issue to establish neutral national antitrust laws should be possible and such a consensus would not necessitate any further steps of antitrust harmonization. This is because – besides these extreme scenarios – national competition policy mainly offers a non-protectionist and non-discriminatory scope for fine-tuned and specially tailored antitrust decisions that do not 'depart from an economically optimal regime'[711]. National antitrust can take into account the role of the national economy as *net exporter* or *net importer*, implying a rather permissive or a rather strict competition policy that is neither protectionist nor discriminatory.

1. On the one hand, national competition authorities can practice a non-protectionist and non-discriminating antitrust policy that nevertheless retains the possibility to consider the economy's role as a *net exporter*. For instance, according to Chap. 4.3.3.1, R&D cooperations could be treated more leniently by the national antitrust authority if the nation's industries are primarily engaged on competitive markets with rapid technological progress and if national industries possess a significant net exporting position in international trade. This would imply a national bias towards a rather permissive antitrust policy, i.e. national antitrust laws would be less strong than they would be in a closed economy.[712] Though, this would not necessarily include discriminatory practices. Severe anticompetitive business practices like export cartels often harm domestic markets and consumers' interests, too, so that, in general, also domestic antitrust authorities have a particular interest to stop cartelization and further market concentration.

2. On the other hand, a parochial bias towards a *stricter* competition policy could be recommendable in case that the state is a *net importer* of certain goods. This strategy – which is based on an extraterritorial application of national antitrust laws – also does not necessarily include discriminatory, protectionist or market foreclosing practices. Instead, strict competition policy primarily results from a relatively high sensitivity to protect domestic consumers and enterprises, for example with respect to further concentration processes on international markets. There are several reasons why a discriminatory or protectionist competition policy is rather unlikely. Firstly, the same anti-

[710] McGinnis (2004) pp. 134f.

[711] Ibid. p. 135.

[712] Ibid. p. 133. Also cf. Chaps. 4.3.3.1.1 and 4.3.3.1.2, giving the example of a permissive antitrust policy with respect to technology transfer agreements.

trust rules would have to be applied on domestic enterprises, too, so that the scope for discriminatory antitrust decisions – by applying national antitrust laws extraterritorially – is limited. As regards empirical evidence, 'there are relatively few examples of laws that are biased on their face against producers'[713]. Secondly, foreign companies are often multinational corporations so that domestic shareholders and stakeholders would be negatively affected by a too strict antitrust enforcement against these foreign corporations.[714] Thirdly, antitrust authorities know that they could become subject to retaliatory measures in case of discriminatory antitrust decisions. Fourthly, a rather strict competition policy against foreign exporting companies is an acceptable issue as long as it serves the protection of consumers' interests, especially on imperfectly competitive markets. In general, the application of *strict* competition policy against foreign exporters on imperfectly competitive markets is a less problematic issue than the application of a *lax* competition policy with regard to domestic exporters.

To sum up, it is likely that international competition rules and the establishment of an international competition authority would reduce the possibility to take into account the national economy's trading structure. Though, in case of international minimum standards or a decentralized application of international antitrust rules, there would remain some scope for national antitrust authorities to practice a relatively strict competition policy in order to consider the interests of net importing industries.

Application 3: The Role of Strict Competition Policy while Applying the Effects Doctrine. According to the effects doctrine, national competition law also has to be applied against anticompetitive business conduct from abroad that affects the domestic market. Consequently, a country that often has to apply the effects doctrine in order to protect itself against anticompetitive business practices from abroad could be well-advised to implement and enforce a rather strict competition law. This combination of strict national competition law and an intensive application of the effects doctrine can be found in US antitrust. In this case, strict antitrust rules are necessary because the national competition authorities have to apply the same national competition rules both on domestic and on foreign enterprises, i.e. they are not allowed to practice a discriminatory antitrust policy that favours domestic enterprises and discriminates against foreign companies by applying a separate, tough competition control. Though, in case of

[713] McGinnis (2004) p. 135.
[714] Cf. ibid. p. 134.

domestic enterprises, these rather strict competition rules could be interpreted more leniently in case of need – within the legal scope of their interpretation.

4.3.3.3.3 International Harmonization as an Obstacle to Strict Competition Policy

International competition rules are considered to generally provide for a stricter antitrust policy. The following sections show that, in opposition to this general supposition, an international harmonization of antitrust rules – especially in combination with a centralization of antitrust enforcement – could prevent strict competition policy, even in case of international minimum standards.

The Problem of Minimum Standards. Economists who plead for an international harmonization of competition policy partly demand international minimum standards.[715] Minimum standards that are not too strict would allow countries to practice – in case of need – a stricter competition policy in order to strengthen their international competitiveness. For instance, as regards international antitrust enforcement against unilateral behaviour (abuses), the former European commissioner for competition, Monti, said that there is less need for international convergence. He referred to minimum standards in European competition law under which the member countries were allowed to apply *stricter* standards under their national laws, according to their national preferences and needs: 'My last reflection relates to enforcement with regards to unilateral behaviour (abuses). I think that we should continue to build a common understanding across jurisdictions. However, I believe that in the short term there is less need for convergence in this area than in the others I've mentioned before, as long as the principle of non-discrimination on the basis of nationality is respected. ... Even within the EU there is not full convergence in the area of unilateral behaviour. Our member States are allowed to enforce stricter standards under their national laws and, therefore, it appears difficult to achieve uniformity at a wider level.'[716] Monti's statement can be understood as a plea for international minimum standards. This demand for harmonization is a rather reserved and cautious position compared to many far-reaching demands for international harmonization and centralization.

---

[715] Confer, for instance, Stearns-Bläsing (2004) pp. 325ff.

[716] Monti (2004) p. 4.

Nevertheless, it is doubtful whether minimum standards are recommendable.[717]

Besides the fact that minimum standards would prohibit more permissive antitrust strategies that might be reasonable in certain cases, minimum standards would also reduce a country's flexibility to practice a strict competition policy and, in case of need, to correct this strict policy by a more permissive antitrust decision in another case. The national competition authority needs, in every single case, much scope to decide on the appropriate degree of competition policy. International minimum standards could prevent such compensatory or correcting permissive antitrust measures. For instance, in case that a national antitrust authority generally follows the strategy to practice a rather strict merger control when in doubt about the future market developments, this antitrust authority could change its assessment of the market in the course of time. As a sovereign antitrust authority, it could try to change and correct its former strict decision by deciding more permissively in a later antitrust case that concerns the same market. For instance, it could intend to allow certain forms of inter-firm cooperation, possibly affecting the same enterprises. Though, in case of international minimum standards that prohibit certain forms of cooperation, the antitrust authority would lose its scope to correct its former strict anti-merger decision. Consequently, national antitrust authorities could be encouraged from the start to refrain from strict antitrust decisions in borderline cases. In particular, the government and the competition authority have to prevent that domestic enterprises leave the national economy because of a too strict competition policy which results from such a cumulative effect of international minimum standards and national standards applied together on the same enterprise in different cases. Such evasive actions would harm the international competitiveness of the economy.

The Problem of National Monopolies and Concentration. A further argument why an international harmonization of competition rules has to be seen as an obstacle to practicing strict competition policy is the danger of national or regional monopolies. This problem especially affects merger control, but also antitrust-policy as a whole. National monopolies are more likely when an international institution decides on a planned merger.

Firstly, in many cases, an international competition authority would likely use a wider concept of the geographically relevant market, normally the global market. Secondly, although an international competition author-

[717] In economic literature, minimum standards often refer to the classic hardcore cartels. Though, as regards the prohibition of hardcore cartels, there exists already an international consensus.

ity would be obliged to consider the effects of a merger on single national markets, it is in the nature of things that a *national* competition authority would be more sensitive to prevent further concentration and monopolization on national markets. Consequently, a domestic competition authority is likely to 'ban mergers that a global authority would allow', for instance 'if the share of domestic demand exceeds the domestic supply'[718].

In case of an internationalized merger control, a national competition authority would hardly have any possibility to practice a stricter competition policy and to create competition on the domestic market. A merger that has already been allowed by an international institution and that – possibly in the long run – leads to national monopolies can not be compensated by strict national competition policy because national competition policy is unable to produce new market entrants or a stronger market penetration of small competitors. This is of special importance for small and developing countries.

The Problem of High Market Power of Foreign and Domestic Enterprises. The abuse of market power – both by foreign and domestic enterprises – can lead to severe and long-term restrictions to competition which reduce national welfare and the international competitiveness. The status quo of antitrust, characterized by national competition policy, the application of the effects doctrine, and bilateral agreements, generally enables national competition authorities to react flexibly and rapidly with regard to abusive business practices like discrimination and exploitation, e.g. tying and bundling, exclusive dealing, refusals to supply, rebates, loyalty discounts, predatory pricing, selective price cuts, and excessive pricing. An international harmonization of competition policy, especially its centralization, could lead to the following problem.

In case of a *foreign* enterprise which abuses its market power – take for example the allegations of tying against the Microsoft Corporation which tries to sell its widespread software products (especially the Windows operating system) bundled with diverse additional features on the European market[719] – the national competition authority has the possibility to protect domestic markets by applying the effects doctrine. In this way, for instance, the European Commission has a legal handle against the Microsoft Corporation so that European consumers can not be exploited and European enterprises get a chance to compete against Microsoft Corporation with regard to certain software products. Another example is the antitrust debate about forcing Apple Inc. – who holds a dominant market position

718 Haucap et al. (2004) p. 18. Also confer Barros and Cabral (1994) p. 1049.
719 Cf. Crandall (2006) pp. 10ff.

both for portable digital music players (iPod) and for digital online music (iTunes) – to make the digital content bought at the iTunes online store to be playable on competitors′ hardware, too. An antitrust authority′s decision on this case especially depends on its assessment about the future market development, i.e. the danger that Apple Inc. could become a (vertical) monopoly for digital entertainment and hard disk mp3 players, similar to the Microsoft monopoly in operating systems for personal computers. These are difficult decisions because future market developments can hardly be predicted, but there could be a 'too late' to prevent a new monopoly. Consequently, a rather strict national competition policy that does not run the risk of a new monopoly and that allows domestic competitors to stay in the market could be an adequate decision that promotes both competition and international competitiveness.

It is doubtful whether the European market or national markets would be shielded from such (potentially) abusive business practices as effectively in case of an international harmonization and centralization of competition policy. In recent years, the European Commission took more legal action against the Microsoft Corporation than US competition authorities. The latter have been rather lenient on Microsoft Corporation, especially as regards fines.[720] Consequently, the influence of the USA on an international competition authority could lead to a more permissive assessment of the Microsoft Corporation′s market conduct within the European Union. Furthermore, if we assume that the enterprises that compete with the Microsoft Corporation are equally located in the USA and in the European Union, then the USA could have an additional incentive to use its influence in favour of a permissive judgement. In case that nearly all competitors are residents of the European Union, the USA would have an even stronger incentive to fight for a permissive antitrust policy. In both cases, also US-American competitors would lose competitiveness, but the European economy is likely to bear the main load.

In case of a *domestic* enterprise abusing its market power on both domestic and foreign markets, the domestic competition authority could have an incentive to stop this restrictive business practice in order to support the competitiveness of domestic competitors. For instance, in 1969 the US competition authorities had forced its domestic computer manufacturer IBM to cut short its bundling-strategy, i.e. the combination of several products (hardware, software, service etc.) had been forbidden in order to promote the market entry of competitors.[721] With regard to the Microsoft Corporation, the US government (DoJ) once even suggested a divestment,

---

[720] Cf. Jennings (2006) pp. 71ff.; cf. Renda (2004) pp. 1ff.

[721] Cf. Berg (1983) p. 16; cf. Anchordoguy (2000) p. 395.

i.e. a break-up of the Corporation into two separate units, one for the development of application software and the other for the production of the operating system.[722] In both cases, the US competition authorities wanted to promote competition within a domestic industry where a US-American enterprise was dominating both the national and the international market. They intended to support the international competitiveness of the US computer and software industry by means of competition instead of protecting the dominating firm.

The question arises whether an international harmonization or centralization of competition policy could hinder such a national initiative to promote competition and competitiveness. At first glance, it seems to be obvious that foreign countries generally would support such pro-competitive unbundling strategies because this could promote the international competitiveness of foreign competitors, too. Nevertheless, on closer examination, the foreign governments or the international competition authority could have reasons to refuse the initial plan presented by a national competition authority.

1. Firstly, far-reaching antitrust measures like divestments could be considered to be too extreme and it is doubtful whether international negotiations on international antitrust rules would include divestments as a remedy against dominant market positions and their abuse. Furthermore, instead of strict measures which solve the problem, international antitrust bureaucrats could vote for a stricter ex post control of abusive business practices because in this way they could achieve more long-term influence on foreign enterprises.

2. Secondly, the initial plan presented by the national competition authority could be considered to be one-sidedly advantageous for this nation, even if this plan would not include any protectionist intention. For instance, the planned measures to open the domestic market could be rather advantageous for domestic newcomers but not for foreign (potential) competitors, especially if there are no potential foreign competitors but several potential domestic competitors. The actual motive of the nation to open the domestic market could be to safeguard the international dominance of the national industry. As regards the above mentioned IBM case of the US computer industry, the US government primarily intended to support the US computer and software industry in order to maintain a long-term dominant position of US computer companies on global markets.

[722] Cf. Gray (2001) p. 42.

4.3.3.3.4 Conclusion

To sum up, strict competition policy to provide for competitive domestic markets can be considered in many cases to be a more useful method to increase international competitiveness than a market concentration policy. This is an important argument for the maintenance of national competition policy, because an international competition authority often would not be able or willing to pursue a strategy to increase the number of competitors in certain countries. On the contrary, international competition policy probably would rather lead to an increase in the number of national monopolies and market-dominating positions of international companies. While a strict national competition policy generally leads to intensive competition on both the national and the global market, an *inter*national competition policy could cause market-dominating positions in certain geographical regions, for example because the criterion of small global market shares can – in certain cases – lead to extremely high market power in a region where most international competitors have not yet developed competitive business activities.[723] In extreme cases, merging companies could receive the position of a monopoly in some countries or regions, partly just in the long run. Therefore, in case of an international competition regime, it would be important to vest the member countries with a right of veto in order to preserve essential national interests in competition. But such a veto would be an obstacle to the main goals of an international competition regime: fast and simple decisions by a one-stop-shop regime to avoid international conflicts and long-term debates. It is to be expected that a right of veto would be misused in practice by some countries. Because of this, the European Union did not allow its member countries to veto against the merger control decisions of the European Commission. According to Article 9 II ECMR[724], the member countries only have the right to notify the Commission of a significant harm for competition on a distinct domestic market in case of allowing a planned merger: '... a Member State ... may inform the Commission ... that: (a) a concentration threatens to affect significantly competition in a market within that Member State, which presents all the characteristics of a distinct market, or (b) a concentration affects competition in a market within that Member State, which presents all the characteristics of a distinct market and which does not constitute a substantial part of the common market'. The European Commission has to decide whether – 'having regard to the market for the products or services in question and the geographical reference market' – such a distinct market or

[723] Cf. Vaubel (1992) p. 34.
[724] European Council (2004).

threat exists so that either '(a) it shall itself deal with the case in accordance with this Regulation; or (b) it shall refer the whole or part of the case to the competent authorities of the Member State concerned with a view to the application of that State's national competition law'. Only in cases where the distinct market within the territory of a Member State does not form a substantial part of the common market, the European Commission 'shall refer the whole or part of the case relating to the distinct market concerned' (Article 9 III ECMR).

5 Concluding Remarks

5.1 Summary

This investigation has examined the role of *national* competition policy as a factor or dimension of a national economic policy to strengthen the international competitiveness of the nation. It has been assumed the existence of a modern and comprehensive national competition law, enforced by an independent, non-interventionist national antitrust authority that refrains from protectionist and discriminatory antitrust decisions. The advantages of such a *national* competition policy regime have been highlighted in distinction to *international* competition rules. Accordingly, the investigation is closely related to two current economic debates: the demands for an international harmonization of competition policy and the debate about a macroeconomic competitiveness of nations.

The analysis in Chap. 2 has demonstrated that the status quo of international antitrust does not represent a perfect competition policy regime, especially as regards the fight against international cartels. Though, the claims for far-reaching top-down harmonization measures in cross-border antitrust affairs and the alleged benefits resulting from such a harmonization are out of all proportion to the actual necessity for international competition rules and the negative effects which would result from such an international harmonization. Even moderate claims like an international top-down harmonization with regard to minimum standards and a decentralized enforcement of international antitrust rules are questionable. The call for an international harmonization or centralization of competition policy raises several problems.

Firstly, international competition is not severely threatened by an alleged lack of antitrust enforcement. In general, despite the existing deficiencies, the status quo of national and international antitrust enforcement generally works well. Most problems of international competition, especially negative spillovers, result from other political fields like, for instance, protectionist trade measures and diverse forms of industrial policies. Secondly, a part of the existing deficiencies in international antitrust enforcement could be healed by strengthening the existing forms of cooperation, especially by more intensive bilateral antitrust agreements – for example by including the exchange of confidential information – and further advances in international antitrust fora like the ICN. Market foreclosing business practices – in case that these practices are tolerated by the national antitrust authority and used as a substitute for protectionist trade policies – could be tackled by an additional WTO agreement. Thirdly, it is doubtful whether international competition rules and/or a global centralization of antitrust enforcement would result in a fairer and more intensive international competition. The alleged possibility and necessity of an international 'level playing field' is not convincing. It has become a habit of politicians and economists to call for an international harmonization when globalization and regulatory competition produce new challenges, especially supposedly unfair international practices that distort trade. But it is an illusion to create a level playing field. To the contrary, international competition rules could result in negative effects, which could overcompensate its benefits. This aspect refers to the second fundamental debate.

Even working on the assumption that there would be a strong need for *international* competition rules in order to protect international competition, negative effects of an international harmonization could be a justification for keeping up *national* competition rules. The analysis in Chap. 3 has demonstrated that, despite opposing positions, there are sound reasons to hold the *macro*economic concept of an international competitiveness of nations. In times of economic globalization, national economic policy undergoes an international test so that governments have to improve conditions for attracting foreign production factors and to strengthen the international competitiveness of domestic enterprises. *National* competition policy can be considered as an important, though often neglected factor of international macroeconomic competitiveness so that international antitrust rules could impede a nation's efforts to strengthen its competitiveness. Chap. 4 has described two different aspects why especially *national* competition policy – as opposed to *international* competition rules – can be beneficial for the international competitiveness of nations.

On the one hand, from a *general* point of view, the international regulatory competition – which is likely to generate efficient antitrust politics and which is far from resulting in a race to the bottom – should be maintained because a top-down harmonization of antitrust rules would cause several general effects which could reduce both international competition and international competitiveness: inefficient case allocation, distortions through selective harmonization, globalized lobbyism, false international compromises, weakened standards at the lowest common denominator, missing innovativeness, versatility and diversity, time-consuming international negotiations, and political horse-trading which also would involve other political areas.

Furthermore, from a *national* point of view, the international regulatory competition should be kept because an international top-down-harmonization of competition rules or a centralization of antitrust enforcement would make it difficult for a country to use *national* competition policy to practice a flexible and innovative antitrust policy which also can take into account national interests and special characteristics of the domestic economy. The international regulatory competition forces nations to develop national excellence in antitrust enforcement so that, in the long run, all countries can benefit although some countries are more successful than others so that they can strengthen their international competitiveness. Chapter 4.3.2 has pointed to several specific aspects which could be characteristic for a nation and which would necessitate a special consideration in antitrust enforcement in order to protect or strengthen the international competitiveness of the nation. Such a special and careful treatment of national specifics and interests could hardly be provided by an international antitrust regime. Besides the specific needs of small open market economies and developing countries, which would benefit from a sovereign and flexible national competition policy, competition policy often is closely related to other fields of national economic policy which affect the international competitiveness of the nation. Consequently, instead of harmonizing national antitrust rules on the international level, there is a need for a *national* harmonization of competition policy with other national policy sectors, i.e. governments should coordinate and balance *national* policy processes. In several cases, national competition policy 'plays an important role in complementing diverse policies'[725] that have the objective of fostering an efficient, dynamic, and internationally competitive economy. Therefore, every country should be able to use its national competition policy in favour of its international competitiveness and to create its own competitive advantages as long as this does not lead to discriminatory and protectionist practices against foreign countries. As a consequence, the domestic enterprises could become more competitive and this could even have a positive effect on the global competition.

The importance of a sovereign and flexible national competition policy for the international competitiveness has been stated more precisely by the specific advantages and disadvantages of a rather permissive and strict competition policy. The competitive advantage of a nation that is allowed to decide autonomously about the required dose of competition policy from case to case has been illustrated by several applications. A common

[725] Anderson and Khosla (1995) p. ii.

feature of many of these examples is that both private business practices and public antitrust measures often have controversial, ambiguous and ambivalent effects on competition and competitiveness. In contrast to trade policy, there are no easy answers in many cases of antitrust. These cases are characterized by the necessity to carefully weigh the advantages against the disadvantages of certain measures and to take into account national or regional specifics. This problem has been illustrated, for instance, by the following paradox. Both a national market concentration policy and a strategy to increase the number of domestic enterprises can support the export sales and the international competitiveness of a nation. Both strategies can help to intensify international competition. This contradictoriness of strategies results from the complexity of national and global competitive processes. It highlights the necessity for detailed single case studies and a subtle and careful handling of the decision-making. It is likely that a *national* competition authority would show more eagerness and more sense of responsibility to use these legal scopes in favour of the international competitiveness of the own economy. An international competition authority would not be able and willing to consider all these aspects and national interests.

As regards possible fears of a one-sided development to a generally permissive national antitrust policy, several aspects finally can be summarized. Firstly, an alarming spreading of permissive or even protectionist and discriminatory antitrust policies (negative spillovers) is unlikely. The existing forms of international cooperation, the application of the effects doctrine, and further national incentives to practice a strict competition policy prevent such a development, and a race to the bottom is even more unlikely. Empirical evidence underlines this. Secondly, the current core paradigm of national antitrust – especially in industrialized countries – is to practice a strict competition policy and to implement further political liberalization and privatization measures in order to strengthen the competitive forces of domestic enterprises. Consequently, the status quo is characterized by a primacy of strict competition policy, combined with a restrictive use of permissive competition policy in special cases. This is also the most likely scenario for the future because this scenario could be seen as the dominant and most effective way to reach several goals simultaneously: the protection and intensification of national and international competition, the effectiveness of the international regulatory competition, and an increase of a nation's international competitiveness. In contrast to this, international competition rules could even become an obstacle to practice a strict competition policy (cf. Chap. 4.3.3.3.3).

5.2 Recommendations for Economic Policy

To sum up the results of this analysis for a recommendation for economic policy, it has to be highlighted that politicians should exercise restraint with respect to the current claims for international competition rules. The present need for international antitrust rules is rather marginal and limited to specific problems that could be solved without far-reaching measures of international antitrust harmonization and centralization. Comprehensive negotiations on international antitrust rules are in danger to take the proverbial sledgehammer to crack a nut and to produce all the negative effects that have been described in this investigation. In contrast to this, bilateral agreements and other non-binding institutions like the ICN should be supported to generate both confidence between independent national antitrust authorities and to produce international best practices.

Furthermore, governments should become aware of the international locational and regulatory competition and their legal possibilities to improve locational conditions and to strengthen the international competitiveness of domestic enterprises by an effective national economic policy. International regulatory competition is a challenge that has to be taken up if one does not want to lose competitiveness and welfare. In case that a government finds it difficult to adjust its economic policy to the new challenges resulting from globalization and international regulatory competition, it should neither attempt to practice discriminatory and protectionist measures nor should it attempt to reduce the international competitive pressure by searching for international coordination and harmonization as a last resort. The political aim to weaken the international regulatory competition by means of international harmonization is an illusion because (a) it is impossible to generate a level playing field in antitrust, and (b) the international regulatory and locational competition would go on even in case of a total international harmonization of competition laws; the international regulatory and locational competition probably would even get more intense in other political fields. In times of economic globalization, governments cannot evade the international test by mobile production factors.

5.3 Recommendations for Further Research

In order to substantiate the recommendation for economic policy, further research with regard to the advantages of *national* competition policy compared to *international* competition rules would be desirable. This analysis has focused on the international competitiveness of nations, has given an overview of central aspects and has provided a framework for further theoretical and also empirical research on this issue. This investigation could be supplemented

1. by further, more detailed research on single aspects which concern the international competitiveness of nations, for instance as regards the selective effects of international harmonization in antitrust or the limits to practice a strict competition policy after an international harmonization and/or centralization of antitrust;
2. by a more detailed analysis of certain models or concepts of international competition policy – for example a decentralized application of international antitrust rules – with regard to their effect on the international competitiveness of nations;
3. by a country-specific analysis in order to clarify to what extent certain countries include competitiveness considerations into their antitrust policies and how far they would have to give up or change their present competition policy if they participated in an international antitrust regime;
4. by further research on the advantages of *national* competition policy – compared to an international antitrust regime – which do not necessarily refer to the international competitiveness of the nation. National competition policy affects several other economic policies like industrial policy and intellectual property so that these linkages could be eliminated in the course of an international harmonization and/or centralization of antitrust.

References

Acemoglu D, Aghion P, Zilibotti F (2006) Distance to Frontier, Selection, and Economic Growth. Journal of the European Economic Association 4:37-74.

Adaman F, Devine P (1996) The Economic Calculation Debate: Lessons for Socialists. Cambridge Journal of Economics 20:523-537.

Adhikari R, Knight-John M (2004) What Type of Competition Policy and Law Should a Developing Country Have? South Asia Economic Journal 5:1-25.

Adlung R, Langhammer RJ, Klemmer P (1997) Umwelt- und Sozialdumping: Argumente gegen freien Welthandel? Zeitschrift für Wirtschaftspolitik 46:167-192.

Anchordoguy M (2000) Japan's Software Industry: A Failure of Institutions? Research Policy, 29:391-408.

Anderson RD, Khosla SD (1995) Competition Policy as a Dimension of Economic Policy: A Comparative Perspective. Industry Canada Occasional Paper 7.

Angelini P, Cetorelli N (2000) Bank Competition and Regulatory Reform: The Case of the Italian Banking Industry. Banca D'Italia Working Paper 380.

Apolte T (2000) Internationale Koordinierung der Wirtschaftspolitik: Beschränkung des politischen Wettbewerbs oder notwendige Konsequenz der Globalisierung. Jahrbuch für Neue Politische Ökonomie 19:89-120.

Areeda P (1992) Antitrust Law as Industrial Policy: Should Judges and Juries Make It. In: Jorde TM, Teece DJ (eds) Antitrust, Innovation and Competitiveness. New York, pp 29-46.

Bär-Bouyssière B (2002) Wege zu einer einheitlichen Fusionskontrolle. In: Schwarze J (ed) Europäisches Wettbewerbsrecht im Zeichen der Globalisierung. Baden-Baden, pp 97-106.

Baker DI, Miller WT (1997) Antitrust Enforcement and Nonenforcement as a Barrier to Imports – with Illustrations from the Japanese Film Dispute. Empirica 24:83-108.

Balassa B (1962) Recent Developments in the Competitiveness of American Industry and Prospects for the Future. In: Joint Economic Committee (ed) Factors Affecting the United States Balance of Payments. Washington, DC, pp 27-54.

Baron M (2005) Politische Perspektiven einer internationalen Wettbewerbsordnung unter besonderer Berücksichtigung der Empagran-Entscheidung des US Supreme Court. In: Oberender P (ed) Internationale Wettbewerbspolitik. Berlin, pp 111-128.

Barros PP, Cabral L (1994) Merger Policy in Open Economies. European Economic Review 38:1041-1055.

Basedow J (1998) Weltkartellrecht: Ausgangslage und Ziele, Methoden und Grenzen der internationalen Vereinheitlichung des Rechts der Wettbewerbsbeschränkungen. Tübingen.

Baumol WJ, Ordover JA (1992) Antitrust: Source of Dynamic and Static Inefficiencies. In: Jorde TM, Teece DJ (eds) Antitrust, Innovation and Competitiveness. New York, pp 82-97.

Beaulieu E, Gaisford J (2002) Labour and Environmental Standards: The 'Lemons Problem' in International Trade Policy. The World Economy 25:59-78.

Becher KF (2002) Globalisierung und Fusionskontrolle in der Unternehmenspraxis. In: Schwarze J (ed) Europäisches Wettbewerbsrecht im Zeichen der Globalisierung. Baden-Baden, pp 77-87.

Becker WH (1999) Postwar US Antitrust Policy, Corporate Strategy, and International Competitiveness. In: Miyajima H, Kikkawa T, Hikino T (eds) Policies for Competitiveness – Comparing Business-Government Relationships in the 'Golden Age of Capitalism'. Oxford, pp 163-185.

Beninca J (2005) Räumliche Marktabgrenzung in der deutschen Fusionskontrolle. Wirtschaft und Wettbewerb 55:43-48.

Berg H (1983) Internationale Wettbewerbsfähigkeit, staatliche Konzentrationsförderung und nationale Zusammenschlusskontrolle – Erfahrungen und Perspektiven der Europäischen Gemeinschaft. Dortmunder Diskussionsbeiträge zur Wirtschaftspolitik 3, University of Dortmund.

Berg H (1985) Internationale Wettbewerbsfähigkeit und nationale Zusammenschlusskontrolle. Munich.

Berry WD (1984) An Alternative to the Capture Theory of Regulation: The Case of State Public Utility Commissions. American Journal of Political Science 28:524-558.

Berthold N, Hilpert J (1999) Sozialstandards unter globalem Druck: Erhalten, senken, erhöhen. In: Berg H (ed) Globalisierung der Wirtschaft. Berlin, pp 127-156.

Bhagwati J (1958) Immiserizing Growth: A Geometrical Note. Review of Economic Studies 25:201-205.

Bhagwati J (1995) Trade Liberalisation and 'Fair Trade' Demands: Addressing the Environmental and Labour Standards Issues. The World Economy 18:745-759.

Bhagwati J, Hudec RE (1996) (eds) Fair Trade and Harmonization: Prerequisites for Free Trade? Vol 1: Economic Analysis, Vol 2: Legal Analysis. Cambridge, MA.

Blackhurst R (1994) Competition Policies: National versus Multilateral Jurisdiction. Aussenwirtschaft 49:223-229.

Bliss C (1996) Trade and Competition Control. In: Bhagwati J, Hudec RE (eds) Fair Trade and Harmonization: Prerequisites for Free Trade? Vol 1: Economic Analysis. Cambridge, MA, pp 313-328.

Bloch H (2001) Market Power and Foreign Trade: Implications for Competition Policy. In: Bloch H, Kenyon P (eds) Creating an Internationally Competitive Economy. London, pp 105-121.

Bloch H, Kenyon P (2001) Introduction. In: Bloch H, Kenyon P (eds) Creating an Internationally Competitive Economy. London, pp 3-15.

Bloch H, Kenyon P (2001a) The Meaning and Measurement of International Competitiveness: In: Bloch H, Kenyon P (eds) Creating an Internationally Competitive Economy. London, pp 16-35.

Bofinger P (1995) Die internationale Wettbewerbsfähigkeit ganzer Volkswirtschaften: Ein Phänomen auf der Suche nach einer Theorie. Kredit und Kapital 28:467-497.

Boltho A (1996) The Assessment: International Competitiveness. Oxford Review of Economic Policy 12(3):1-16.

Born KE (1989) Jean-Baptiste Colbert (1619-1683). In: Starbatty J (ed) Klassiker des ökonomischen Denkens – Vol 1: Von Platon bis John Stuart Mill. Munich, pp 96-113.

Brown V (1994) Adam Smith´s Discourse: Canonicity, Commerce and Conscience. London.

Brusick P, Alvarez AM, Cernat L, Holmes P (2004) Competition, Competitiveness and Development: Lessons from Developing Countries. United Nations UNCTAD/DITC/CLP/2004/1. New York, Geneva.

Budzinski O (2002) Perspektiven einer internationalen Politik gegen Wettbewerbsbeschränkungen. List Forum 28:234-253.

Budzinski O (2002a) Internationale Wettbewerbspolitik zwischen Zentralität und Dezentralität. In: Schüller A, Thieme HJ (eds) Ordnungsprobleme der Weltwirtschaft. Stuttgart, pp 469-493.

Budzinski O (2003) Pluralism of Competition Policy Paradigms and the Call for Regulatory Diversity. Volkswirtschaftliche Beiträge 14/2003, University of Marburg.

Budzinski O, Christiansen A (2004), Looking Inside the Blackbox: Competence Allocation in EU Competition Policy from an Actor-Centred Perspective. Paper prepared for the international conference on Economic Policies in the New Millennium in Coimbra/Portugal (April 16-17, 2004).

Budzinski O, Kerber W (2003) Megafusionen, Wettbewerb und Globalisierung. Stuttgart.

Budzinski O, Kerber W (2005) International Wettbewerbspolitik aus ökonomischer Perspektive. In: Oberender P (ed) Internationale Wettbewerbspolitik. Berlin, pp 11-40.

Bundeskartellamt (2003) Ausnahmebereiche des Kartellrechts – Stand und Perspektiven der 7. GWB-Novelle. Diskussionspapier für die Sitzung des Arbeitskreises Kartellrecht, September 29.

Busche J (2001) Patente in der Wettbewerbsordnung – Kartellrechtlicher Verwertungszwang versus Innovationsschutz? In: Jahrbuch der Heinrich-Heine-Universität Düsseldorf 2001, pp 345-358.

Bush N (2005) Chinese Competition Policy – It Takes More Than a Law. The China Business Review 32:30-34.

Busse M (2002) Do Labour Standards affect Comparative Advantage in Developing Countries? World Development 30:1921-1932.

Cadot O, Grether JM, de Melo J (2000) Trade and Competition Policy: Where Do We Stand? Journal of World Trade 34:1-20.

Calkins S (1998) Reflections on Vertical Restraints of Trade and National Competition Laws in an Integrated World Economy. In: Hope E, Maeleng P (eds) Competition and Trade Policies: Coherence or Conflict? London, pp 201-219.

Campbell AN (1997) Interjurisdictional Conflict in Merger Review. In: Waverman L, Comanor WS, Goto A (eds) Competition Policy in the Global Economy: Modalities for Cooperation. London, pp 89-126.

Campbell AN, Trebilcock MJ (1992) A Comparative Analysis of Merger Law: Canada, the United States, and the European Community. World Competition 15:5-37.

Cassel D (1996) (ed) Entstehung und Wettbewerb von Systemen. Berlin.

Cernat L (2004) The Role of Competition in the Promotion of Competitiveness and Development: Experiences from a Sample of Developing and Least Developed Countries. UNCTAD Competition and Consumer Policies Branch, Paper prepared for the 3rd International CRC Conference, Cape Town, September 7-9.

Cetorelli N (2001) Competition among Banks: Good or Bad? Economic Perspectives (Federal Reserve Bank of Chicago) 25:38-48.

Cetorelli N, Gambera M (2001) Bank Market Structure, Financial Dependence and Growth: International Evidence from Industry Data. Journal of Finance 56:617-648.

Chamberlin EH (1933) The Theory of Monopolistic Competition: A Reorientation of the Theory of Value. Cambridge.

Cho DS, Moon HC, Cho TS (2000) From Adam Smith to Michael Porter: Evolution of Competitiveness Theory. Asia-Pacific Business Series Vol 2. Singapore.

Christl C (2001) Wettbewerb und internationaler Handel: Eine Analyse ihrer Interdependenzen und institutionellen Voraussetzungen im Rahmen einer internationalen Wettbewerbsordnung. Untersuchungen zur Ordnungstheorie und Ordnungspolitik Vol 42. Tübingen.

Clougherty JA (2003) Industry Trade-Balance and Domestic Merger Policy: Some Empirical Evidence from the US. Discussion Paper SP II 2003 – 19, Social Science Research Center Berlin.

Crandall RW (2006) Has US Antitrust Policy Protected Consumers from the Abuse of Market Dominance? The Research Institute of Industrial Economics. Stockholm.

Daniel, C (2000) The Question of International Competitiveness. International Advances in Economic Research 6:417-426.

Demsetz H (1968) Why Regulate Utilities. Journal of Law and Economics 11:55-66.

Demsetz H (1976) Economics as a Guide to Antitrust Regulation. The Journal of Law and Economics 19:371-388.

Denison EF (1967) Why Growth Rates Differ: Postwar Experience in Nine Western Countries. Washington, DC.

Díaz FEG (2004) The Reform of European Merger Control: Quid Novi Sub Sole? World Competition 27:177-199.

Dornbusch R, Fischer S, Samuelson PA (1977) Comparative Advantage, Trade, and Payments in a Ricardian Model with a Continuum of Goods. The American Economic Review 67:823-839.

Downs A (1957) An Economic Theory of Democracy. New York.

Downs A (1957a) An Economic Theory of Political Action in a Democracy. The Journal of Political Economy 65:135-150.

Drexl J (1998) Perspektiven eines Weltkartellrechts. Center for European Economic Law, Lectures and Reports No 97, University of Bonn.

Dutz M, Hayri A (1999) Does More Intense Competition Lead to Higher Growth? World Bank Working Paper No 2320. Washington, DC.

Easterbrook FH (1992) Ignorance on Antitrust. In: Jorde TM, Teece DJ (eds) Antitrust, Innovation and Competitiveness. New York, pp 119-136.

Easterbrook FH (2004) Antitrust and the Economics of Federalism. In: Epstein RA, Greve MS (eds) Competition Laws in Conflict: Antitrust Jurisdiction in the Global Economy. Washington, DC, pp 189-222.

Eggert, R (2004) Entwicklungen in der Kreditwirtschaft und Mittelstandsfinanzierung: Wohin geht der Weg. Deutsche Bundesbank, Speech at the Wirtschaftsforum Hamburg e.V. Hamburg.

Eguchi K (2003) Cultural Implications in the Framework of Basic Issues of Competition Policy. In: Drexl J (ed) The Future of Transnational Antitrust – From Comparative to Common Competition Law. The Hague, pp 3-8.

Eichengreen B (1999) Toward a New International Financial Architecture. Washington, DC.

Ellis W (1989) David Ricardo (1772-1823). In: Starbatty J (ed) Klassiker des ökonomischen Denkens – Vol 1: Von Platon bis John Stuart Mill. Munich, pp 188-207.

Emmerich V (2001) Kartellrecht. 9th ed. Munich.

Epstein RA, Greve MS (2004) Postscript: In Defense of Small Steps. In: Epstein RA, Greve MS (eds) Competition Laws in Conflict: Antitrust Jurisdiction in the Global Economy. Washington, DC, pp 333-352.

Erlandsson M, Markowski A (2006) The Effective Exchange Rate Index KIX – Theory and Practice. Working Paper No 95, The National Institute of Economic Research. Stockholm.

European Commission (1995) Competition Policy in the New Trade Order: Strengthening International Cooperation and Rules. Report of the Group of Experts, COM(95) 359 final. Brussels, July 12.

European Commission (1997) Decision 97/816/EC of 30 July1997 (Case No. IV/M 877 Boeing/ McDonnell Douglas). Official Journal of the European Union, L 336/16, December 8, pp 16-47.

European Commission (1998) Agreement Between The Government of the United States of America and the European Communities on the Application of Positive Comity Principles in the Enforcement of their Competition Laws. Official Journal of the European Union, L 173, June 18. Brussels.

European Commission (2000) Regulation (EC) No. 2659/2000 of 29 November 2000 on the Application of Article 81 (3) of the Treaty to Categories of Research and Development Agreements. Official Journal of the European Communities, L 304, December 5. Brussels.
European Commission (2002) Benchmarking of Business Incubators. Final Report, Centre for Strategy & Evaluation Services. Brussels.
European Commission (2002a) Regulation (EC) No. 1400/2002 of 31 July 2002 on the Application of Article 81 (3) of the Treaty to Categories of Vertical Agreements and Concerted Practices in the Motor Vehicle Sector. Official Journal of the European Communities, L 203, August 1. Brussels.
European Commission (2004) Commission Notice on Cooperation within the Network of Competition Authorities. Official Journal of the European Union, 2004/C 101/03, April 27.
European Commission (2004a) A Pro-Active Competition Policy for a Competitive Europe. COM (2004) 293 final. Brussels, April 20.
European Commission (2004b) Guidelines on the Assessment of Horizontal Mergers under the Council Regulation on the Control of Concentration between Undertakings. Official Journal of the European Union, 2004/C 31/03.
European Commission (2004c) Commission Regulation (EC) No 772/2004 of 27 April 2004 on the Application of Article 81(3) of the Treaty to Categories of Technology Transfer Agreements. Official Journal of the European Communities, L 123, April 27. Brussels.
European Commission (2004d) European Competitiveness Report. Luxembourg.
European Commission (2006) Time to Move up a Gear: The New Partnership for Growth and Jobs. Luxembourg.
European Commission (2006a) Mergers: Commission Approves Acquisition by E.ON of Endesa. Press Release IP/06/528, April 25. Brussels.
European Commission (2006b) Mergers: Commission Decides that Spanish Measures in Proposed E.ON/Endesa Takeover Violate EC Law. Press Release IP/06/1853, December 20. Brussels.
European Council (2002) Council Regulation (EC) No. 1/2003 of 16 December 2002 on the Implementation of the Rules on Competition Laid down in Articles 81 and 82 of the Treaty. Official Journal of the European Communities, L 1, January 4. Brussels.
European Council (2004) Council Regulation (EC) No. 139/2004 of 20 January 2004 on the Control of Concentration Between Undertakings (the EC Merger Regulation). Official Journal of the European Communities, L 24, January 29. Brussels.
Evans DS (2002) The Antitrust Economics of Two-Sided Markets. AEI – Brookings Joint Center For Regulatory Studies, Related Publication 02-13.
Evenett SJ (2003) Can Developing Countries Benefit from WTO Negotiations on Binding Disciplines for Hard Core Cartels? UNCTAD/DITC/CLP/2003/3, United Nations. New York and Geneva.
Evenett SJ, Levenstein MC, Suslow VY (2001) International Cartel Enforcement: Lessons from the 1990s. The World Economy 24:1221-1245.
Fagerberg J (1988) International Competitiveness. Economic Journal 98:355-374.

Fagerberg J (1996) Technology and Competitiveness. Oxford Review of Economic Policy 12(3):39-51.
Feld LP (1996) Sozialstandards und die Welthandelsordnung. Aussenwirtschaft 51:51-73.
Feldstein M, Horioka C (1980) Domestic Saving and International Capital Flows. The Economic Journal 90:314-329.
Fendel R, Frenkel M (2005) Wozu Studien zur Wettbewerbsfähigkeit von Volkswirtschaften. Wirtschaftsdienst – Zeitschrift für Wirtschaftspolitik 85:26-32.
Fikentscher W, Immenga U (1995) (eds) Draft International Antitrust Code: Kommentierter Entwurf eines internationalen Wettbewerbsrechts mit ergänzenden Beiträgen. Baden-Baden.
Fikentscher W (1994) Competition Rules for Private Agents in the GATT/WTO-System. Aussenwirtschaft 49:281-325.
Fikentscher W (2003) Cultural Implications in the Framework of Basis Issues of Competition Law: Comments on Kiminori Eguchi. In: Drexl J (ed) The Future of Transnational Antitrust – From Comparative to Common Competition Law. The Hague, pp 9-19.
Finsinger J (1991) Wettbewerb und Regulierung. Munich.
First H (2003) Evolving Toward What? The Development of International Antitrust. In: Drexl J (ed) The Future of Transnational Antitrust – From Comparative to Common Competition Law. The Hague, pp 23-51.
Fischer KH, Pfeil C (2003) Regulation and Competition in German Banking: An Assessment. Center for Financial Studies Working Paper No 2003/19, University of Frankfurt a.M..
Fischer HG (2005) Europarecht – Grundkurs des Rechts der Europäischen Union. Munich.
Flanagan RJ, Gould WB (2003) International Labor Standards: Globalization, Trade, and Public Policy. Stanford.
Fontenot RJ, Wilhelm PG (2005) Predicting Core Innovation and Wealth from Technological Innovation and Domestic Competitiveness: The Crucial Role of Anti-Trust Policy Effectiveness. Journal of Nonprofit & Public Sector Marketing 13:233-253.
Fox EM, Pitofsky R (1997) United States. In: Graham EM, Richardson JD (eds) Global Competition Policy. Institute for International Economics. Washington, DC, pp 235-269.
Frankfurter Allgemeine Zeitung (2006) Der Veto-Mann. No 11, January 13, p. 17.
Frankfurter Allgemeine Zeitung (2006a) Die Schweiz ist das wettbewerbsfähigste Land der Welt. No 225, September 27, p 14.
Frenkel M, Menkhoff L (2000) Stabile Weltfinanzen – Die Debatte um eine neue internationale Finanzarchitektur. Berlin.
Fritsch M, Wein T, Ewers HJ (2005) Marktversagen und Wirtschaftspolitik: Mikroökonomische Grundlagen staatlichen Handelns. 6th edn. Munich.
Fuchs A (2000) Ziele, Formen und Grenzen einer internationalen Vereinheitlichung des Kartellrechts. Jahrbuch für Neue Politische Ökonomie 19:356-372.
Fuchs A (2005) Kontrollierte Dezentralisierung der europäischen Wettbewerbsaufsicht. In: Schneider JP, Schwarze J, Müller-Graff PC (eds) Vollzug des Eu-

ropäischen Wirtschaftsrechts zwischen Zentralisierung und Dezentralisierung. Baden-Baden, pp 77-118.

Fullerton L, Mazard CC (2001) International Antitrust Co-operation Agreements. World Competition 24:405-423.

Fung KC (1992) Economic Integration as Competitive Discipline. International Economic Review 33:837-847.

Gal MS (2003) Competition Policy for Small Market Economies. London.

Gal MS (2003a) Competition Policy in Small Economies. OECD Global Forum on Competition, CCNM/GF/COMP/WD(2003)42, February 07. Paris.

Galloway J (2005) Moving Towards a Template for Bilateral Antitrust Agreements. World Competition 28:589-614.

Gapinski JH (2001) Developing ICOM: An Index of International Competitiveness. In: Bloch H, Kenyon P (eds) Creating an Internationally Competitive Economy. London, pp 36-48.

Gelauff GMM, Lejour AM (2006) The New Lisbon Strategy: An Estimation of the Economic Impact of Reaching the Five Lisbon Targets. CPB Netherlands Bureau for Economic Policy Analysis, Report Prepared for the Enterprise and Industry Directorate-General of the European Commission. Brussels.

Gerber DJ (2000) Afterword: Antitrust and American Business Abroad Revisited. Northwestern Journal of International Law and Business 20:307-312.

Gerhardt W (2001) Die WTO als Kernstück einer internationalen Wettbewerbsordnung. In: Gerken L, Graf Lambsdorff O (2001) (eds) Ordnungpolitik in der Weltwirtschaft. Baden-Baden, pp 49-54.

Gilbert RJ, Shapiro C (1998) Unilateral Refuses to License Intellectual Property and International Competition Policy. In: Hope E, Maeleng P (eds) Competition and Trade Policies: Coherence or Conflict? London, pp 65-78.

Gill DG (1994) Hartford Fire Insurance Co. v. California. American Journal of International Law 88:109-114.

Globerman S (1990) Trade Liberalization and Competitive Behavior: A Note Assessing the Evidence and the Public Policy Implications. Journal of Policy Analysis and Management 9:80-88.

Gottwald W (1992) Die EG-Gruppenfreistellungsverordnung für Patentlizenzvereinbarungen (EWG Nr. 2349/84) als Instrument zur Förderung der Wettbewerbsfähigkeit der europäischen Industrie. Munich.

Graham EM (2003) 'Internationalizing' Competition Policy: An Assessment of the Two Main Alternatives. The Antitrust Bulletin 48:947-972.

Gray CB (2001) Computer Complaints in Anti-trust Enforcement: Of Microsoft and Mergers. Economic Affairs 21:38-43.

Greif S (2002) Internationaler Patent- und Lizenzverkehr: Formen – Fakten – Regeln. In: Schüller A, Thieme HJ (eds) Ordnungsprobleme der Weltwirtschaft. Stuttgart, pp 179-200.

Grimes WS (2003) The Microsoft Litigation and Federalism in U.S. Antitrust Enforcement: Implications for International Competition Law. In: Drexl J (ed) The Future of Transnational Antitrust – From Comparative to Common Competition Law. The Hague, pp 237-258.

Großmann H, Busse M, Fuchs D, Koopmann G (2002) Sozialstandards in der Welthandelsordnung. Baden-Baden.

Guzman A (2004) The Case for International Antitrust. Berkeley Journal of International Law 22:355-374.

Härtel HH (2006) The Threat of Economic Patriotism. Intereconomics 41:58-59.

Haucap J, Marcus JS (2005) Why Regulate? Lessons From New Zealand. IEEE Communications Magazine 43(11):14-16.

Haucap J, Müller F, Wey C (2004) How to Reduce Conflicts over International Antitrust? DIW Research Notes 2. Berlin.

Haufler A, Nielsen SB (2005) Merger Policy to Promote 'Global Players'? A Simple Model. CESIFO Working Paper No 1523.

Hauser H, Schoene R (1994) Is There a Need for International Competition Rules? Aussenwirtschaft 49:205-222.

Hawk BE (1996) Antitrust Policy and Market Access. The OECD Observer, Special Edition on International Trade and Investment, Paris, December, pp. 9-10.

Hayek von FA (1968) Der Wettbewerb als Entdeckungsverfahren. Kieler Vorträge im Institut für Weltwirtschaft an der Universität Kiel, edited by Erich Schneider, Neue Folge No 56. Kiel.

Hayek von FA (1952) «Freie Wirtschaft» und Wettbewerbsordnung. In: Hayek von FA (ed) Individualismus und wirtschaftliche Ordnung. Erlenbach-Zürich, pp 141-155.

Head K, Ries J (1997) International Mergers and Welfare under Decentralized Competition Policy. Canadian Journal of Economics 30:1104-1123.

Heckenberger W (2002) Probleme der globalisierten Fusionskontrolle aus der Sicht eines Unternehmensjuristen. In: Schwarze J (ed) Europäisches Wettbewerbsrecht im Zeichen der Globalisierung. Baden-Baden, pp 89-96.

Heckscher EF (1919) The Effect of Foreign Trade on the Distribution of Income. Reprinted in: Ellis HS, Metzler LA (eds) Readings in the Theory of International Trade. Blackiston Series of Republished Articles on Economics Vol. IV. London, 1949, pp 272-300.

Helm D (2001) The Assessment: European Networks – Competition, Interconnection, and Regulation. Oxford Review of Economic Policy 17:297-312.

Hewitt G (2000) Bank Mergers – Background Note. OECD Journal of Competition Law and Policy 2:13-66.

Ho LS (2000) Towards a New International Monetary Order: The World Currency Unit and the Global Indexed Bond. The World Economy 23:939-950.

Hobe S, Kimminich O (2004) Einführung in das Völkerrecht. 8th edn. Tübingen.

Hollis A, Yuan L (2004) Competition Policy in Open Economies. International Economic Journal 18:179-194.

Holmes P, Müller H, Papdopoulos A, Sydorak A (2005) A Taxonomy of International Competition Cooperation Provisions. Paper for the International Research and Policy Symposium on 'Competition Policy for International Development, Growth and Trade' organized by the Centre for Economic Policy Research, Brussels, December 9-10.

Hotelling H (1929) Stability in Competition. Economic Journal 39:41-57.

Hovenkamp H (2005) Federal Antitrust Policy: The Law of Competition and its Practice. 3rd edn. St. Paul.

Huang S (1992) Bankenregulierung und Wettbewerbsfähigkeit - Eine komparative Analyse der Schweiz und der EG. Bern.

Huovari J, Kangasharju A, Alanen A (2001) Constructing an Index for Regional Competitiveness. Pellervo Economic Research Institute, Working Paper No 44. Helsinki.

Hutter M (2006) Staatliche Regulierung in der Medienwirtschaft. WISU – Das Wirtschaftsstudium 35:112-118.

Immenga U (2000) Eine internationale Wettbewerbsordnung? Neue Töne aus Washington. Wirtschaft und Wettbewerb 50:1059.

Immenga U (2004) Internationales Wettbewerbsrecht: Unilateralismus, Bilateralismus, Multilateralismus. Martin-Luther-University Halle Wittenberg, Beiträge zum Transnationalem Wirtschaftsrecht: Issue 31.

Immenga U (2007) Missbrauch eines Grundgesetzes. Frankfurter Allgemeine Zeitung No. 15, January 18, p. 10.

Isele K (2003) Fusionskontrolle im Standortwettbewerb. Potsdam.

Jacquemin A (1993) The International Dimension of European Competition Policy. Journal of Common Market Studies 31:91-101.

Jennings JP (2006) Comparing the US and EU Microsoft Antitrust Prosecutions: How Level is the Playing Field? Erasmus Law and Economics Review 2:71-85.

Jens U (2002) Überlegungen zur Einführung einer Welt-Wettbewerbsordnung. ifo-Schnelldienst 21/2002, pp 13-17.

Jochimsen R (2000) Anforderungen an eine Weltfinanzordnung. Grenzen nationaler Alleingänge und Effizienz internationaler Instrumente. In: Nuscheler F (ed) Entwicklung und Frieden im Zeichen der Globalisierung. Bonn, pp 159-175.

Jorde TM, Teece DJ (1990) Innovation and Cooperation: Implications for Competition and Antitrust. Journal of Economic Perspectives 4:75-96.

Jorde TM, Teece DJ (1992) (eds) Antitrust, Innovation and Competitiveness. New York.

Jorde TM, Teece DJ (1997) Innovation, Market Structure and Antitrust: Harmonizing Competition Policy in Regimes of Rapid Technological Change. In: Waverman L, Comanor WS, Goto A (eds) Competition Policy in the Global Economy: Modalities for Cooperation. London, pp 289-303.

Kantzenbach E (1967) Das Konzept der optimalen Wettbewerbsintensität – Eine Erwiderung auf den gleichnamigen Besprechungsaufsatz von Erich Hoppmann. Jahrbücher für Nationalökonomie und Statistik 181:193-241.

Kantzenbach E, Kinne K (1997) Nationale Zusammenschlusskontrolle und internationale Wettbewerbsfähigkeit von Unternehmen. In: Kruse J, Stockmann K, Vollmer L (eds) Wettbewerbspolitik im Spannungsfeld nationaler und internationaler Kartellrechtsordnungen. Baden-Baden, pp 67-84.

Karceski J, Ongena S, Smith DC (2005) The Impact of Bank Consolidation on Commercial Borrower Welfare. The Journal of Finance 60:2043-2082.

Kelly T (2003) The WTO, the Environment and Health and Safety Standards. The World Economy 26:131-152.

Kennedy KC (2001) Competition Law and the World Trade Organisation: The Limits of Multilateralism. London.

Kerber W (1998) Zum Problem einer Wettbewerbsordnung für den Systemwettbewerb. Jahrbuch für Neue Politische Ökonomie 17:199-230.

Kerber W (2001) Standortwettbewerb und Ordnungspolitik. In: Gerken L, Graf Lambsdorff O (eds) Ordnungpolitik in der Weltwirtschaft. Baden-Baden, p 86-97.

Kerber W (2003) An International Multi-Level System of Competition Laws: Federalism in Antitrust'. In: Drexl J (ed) The Future of Transnational Antitrust: From Comparative to Common Competition Law. Bern, pp 269-300.

Kerber W, Budzinski O (2003) Towards a Differentiated Analysis of Competition of Competition Laws. Zeitschrift für Wettbewerbsrecht – Journal of Competition Law 1:411-448.

Kerber W, Budzinski O (2004) Competition of Competition Laws: Mission Impossible? In: Greve MS, Epstein RA (eds) Competition Laws in Conflict: Antitrust Jurisdiction in the Global Economy. Washington, DC, pp 31-65.

Khemani RS (1998) A Brief Note on the Role of Competition Policy in Economic Development. In: Hope E, Maeleng P (ed) Competition and Trade Policies: Coherence or Conflict? London, pp 143-151.

Kinne K (1997) Internationale Wettbewerbsfähigkeit von Unternehmen in der deutschen und europäischen Zusammenschlusskontrolle. HWWA-Report No 168. Hamburg.

Kinsella NS (2001) Against Intellectual Property. Journal of Libertarian Studies 15:1-53.

Klees AM (2006) Breaking the Habits: The German Competition Law after the 7th Amendment to the Act against Restraints of Competition (GWB). German Law Journal 7:399-420.

Klein J (1997) Anticipating the Millennium: International Antitrust Enforcement at the End of the Twentieth Century. US Department of Justice, Speech Presented at Fordham Corporate Law Institute, 24th Annual Conference on International Law and Policy. New York, October 16.

Klein J (2002) Expanding Our Web of Bilateral Agreements. In: Jones CA, Matsushita M (eds) Competition Policy in the Global Trading System: Perspectives From the EU, Japan & the USA. The Hague, pp 335-340.

Kleinert J, Klodt H (2002) Die fünfte Fusionswelle: Ausmaße und Hintergründe. In: Oberender P (ed) Megafusionen: Motive, Erfahrungen und wettbewerbspolitische Probleme. Berlin, pp 9-19.

Klodt H (2001) Conflict and Conflict Resolution in International Anti-Trust: Do We Need International Competition Rules? The World Economy 24:877-888.

Klump R (2006) Wirtschaftspolitik: Instrumente, Ziele und Institutionen. Munich.

Knieps G (2001) Regulatory Reform of European Telecommunications: Past Experience and Forward-Looking Perspectives. Albert-Ludwigs-Universität Freiburg, May.

Knieps G (2004) Limits to the (De-)Regulation of Transport Services. Institut für Verkehrswissenschaft und Regionalpolitik der Universität Freiburg, Discussion Paper No 99. Freiburg.

Knieps G (2005) Wettbewerbsökonomie: Regulierungstheorie, Industrieökonomie, Wettbewerbspolitik. 2nd edn. Berlin.

Kösters W (2004) Stabilitätsvergessen: Kritische Anmerkungen zum Verfassungsentwurf des Europäischen Konvents. WiSt – Wirtschaftswissenschaftliches Studium 33:1+19.

Kojima T (2001) International Conflicts over the Extraterritorial Application of Competition Law in a Borderless Economy. Weatherhead Center for International Affairs at Harvard University.

Kolb G (1997) Geschichte der Volkswirtschaftslehre: Dogmenhistorische Positionen des ökonomischen Denkens. Munich.

Koopmann G (2000) Internationalisierung der Wettbewerbspolitik: Korrelat zur internationalen Handelspolitik? HWWA Discussion Paper No 108.

Krakowski M (2002) Der Markt für Strom. Wirtschaftsdienst – Zeitschrift für Wirtschaftspolitik 82:296-300.

Kroes N (2006) Competition Policy's Contribution to Growth and Jobs. Speech before EP Economic and Monetary Affairs Committee. Brussels, January 31.

Krugman PR (1994) Competitiveness: A Dangerous Obsession. In: Council on Foreign Relations (ed) A Foreign Affairs Reader. New York (originally published in: Foreign Affairs 73 (1994) No 2, pp 28-44).

Krugman PR (1995) Development, Geography and Economic Theory. Cambridge, MA.

Krugman PR (1996) Making Sense of the Competitiveness Debate. Oxford Review of Economic Policy 12(3):17-25.

Krugman PR (1997) Pop Internationalism. Cambridge, MA.

Kumkar L (2002) The European Electricity Market: Centralization of Regulation or Competition between Regulatory Approaches. Kiel Discussion Papers No 387, University of Kiel.

Kurita M (1995) Recent Developments of Competition Policy in Japan and Their Implications for International Harmonization of Competition Laws. In: Cheng CJ, Liu LS, Wang CK (eds) International Harmonization of Competition Laws. London, pp 361-379.

Kurz HD (1990) Adam Smith, die Regel der freien Güter und die vent-for-surplus-Begründung des Außenhandels. In: Kurz HD (ed) Adam Smith (1723-1790): Ein Werk und seine Wirkungsgeschichte. Marburg, pp 237-260.

Lachmann W (1994) Entwicklungspolitik. Vol 3: Außenwirtschaftliche Aspekte der Entwicklung. Munich.

Lachmann W (1997) Entwicklungspolitik. Vol 2: Binnenwirtschaftliche Aspekte der Entwicklung. Munich.

Lachmann W (1998) Ordnungspolitische Aspekte der Globalisierung. In: Lachmann W, Farmer K, Haupt R (eds) Globalisierung: Arbeitsteilung oder Wohlstandsteilung? Münster, pp 97-119.

Lachmann W (1999) The Development Dimension of Competition Law and Policy. UNCTAD-Series on Issues in Competition Law and Policy. Geneva.

Lachmann W (2001) Improving the International Competitiveness of Nations – What is it and (how) should it be done? WEP-Working Paper No. 6, Friedrich-Alexander-University of Erlangen-Nuremberg, Chair of Economic Policy and Development Policy. Nuremberg.

Lachmann W (2004) Volkswirtschaftslehre 2 – Anwendungen. 2nd edn. Berlin.

Lachmann W (2006) Volkswirtschaftslehre 1 – Grundlagen. 5th edn. Berlin.

Lachmann W (2005) Brauchen wir eine Welt-Ordnungpolitik? In: Lachmann W, Haupt R, Farmer K (eds) Globalisierung der Wirtschaft: Segen oder Fluch? Münster, pp 109-143.

Lachmann W, Mitschke A (2006) Wettbewerbspolitik und die internationale Wettbewerbsfähigkeit von Volkswirtschaften. WISU – Das Wirtschaftsstudium 35:560-566.

Lässig P (1997) Dezentrale Anwendung des europäischen Kartellrechts. Cologne.

Lenel HO (1999) Die Gefahren von Großfusionen werden unterschätzt. Orientierungen 81:7-8.

Lenel HO (2000) Zu den Megafusionen in den letzten Jahren. ORDO 51:1-32.

Leontief WW (1953) Domestic Production and Foreign Trade: The American Capital Position Re-examined. Proceedings of the American Philosophical Society 97:331-349 (Reprinted in Bhagwati J (ed) International Trade – Selected Readings. Harmondsworth, 1969).

Levenstein M, Suslow V, Oswald L (2003) International Price Fixing Cartels and Developing Countries: A Discussion of Effects and Policy Remedies. Political Economy Research Institute PERI, University of Massachusetts Amherst, Working Paper Series No 53.

Levy N, O'Donoghue R (2004) The EU Leniency Programme Comes of Age. World Competition 27:75-99.

Liang G (2004) New Competition: Foreign Direct Investment and Industrial Development in China. Erasmus University Rotterdam, Erasmus Research Institute of Management (ERIM), Ph.D. Series Research in Management 47. Rotterdam.

Lieberman MB, Montgomery DB (1987) First-Mover Advantages. Stanford Business School, Research Paper No 969.

Lin P (2002) Competition Policy in East Asia: The Cases of Japan, People's Republic of China, and Hong Kong. Working Paper Series - Centre for Asian Pacific Studies No 133 (17/02) CAPS, Lingnan University Hong Kong.

Lloyd PJ (1998) Multilateral Rules for International Competition Law? The World Economy 21:1129-1149.

Lloyd PJ, Vautier KM (1999) Promoting Competition in Global Markets: A Multi-National Approach. Cheltenham.

Lopez-Claros A, Porter ME, Sala-i-Martin X, Schwab K (2006) (eds) The Global Competitiveness Report 2006-2007. World Economic Forum. New York.

Maahs C (2005) Wettbewerbsschutz und Verbraucherinteressen im Lichte neuerer ökonomischer Methoden – Tagungsbericht des Bundeskartellamtes. Wirtschaft und Wettbewerb 55:49-55.

Machlup F, Penrose E (1950) The Patent Controversy in the Nineteenth Century. The Journal of Economic History 10:1-29.

Maennig W (1992) Internationale Transmission und Koordinierung der Wirtschaftspolitik. Berlin.

Mantzavinos C (1994) Wettbewerbstheorie – Eine kritische Auseinandersetzung. Berlin.

Mantzavinos C (2004) The Institutional-Evolutionary Antitrust Model. Reprints of the Max Planck Institute for Research on Collective Goods. Bonn.

Margolis SE (1985) The Excess Capacity Controversy: A Critique of Recent Criticism. Economic Inquiry 23:265-275.

Martin S (2004) Globalization and the Natural Limits of Competition. In: Neumann M, Weigand J (eds) International Handbook of Competition. Cheltenham, pp 16-64.

McGinnis JO (2004) The Political Economy of International Antitrust Harmonization. In: Epstein RA, Greve MS (eds) Competition Laws in Conflict: Antitrust Jurisdiction in the Global Economy. Washington, DC, pp 126-151.

McFetridge DG (1993) Mergers, Competition and Innovation. In: Kantzenbach E, Scharrer HE, Waverman L (eds) Competition Policy in an Interdependent World Economy. Baden-Baden, pp 201-220.

Meessen KM (1989) Competition of Competition Laws. Northwestern Journal of International Law & Business 10:17-30.

Meessen KM (2000) Das Für und Wider eines Weltkartellrechts. Wirtschaft und Wettbewerb 50:5-16 (also published in: Jahrbuch für Neue Politische Ökonomie (2000) Vol 19: Globalisierung und Weltwirtschaft. Tübingen, pp. 336-355).

Meiklejohn R (1999) An International Competition Policy: Do We Need It? Is It Feasible? The World Economy 22:1233-1249.

Melamed AD (1998) An Important First Step: A US/Japan Bilateral Antitrust Cooperation Agreement. US Department of Justice, Speech before Japan Fair Trade Institute. Tokyo, November 12.

Melamed AD (1999) International Cooperation in Competition Law and Policy: What Can Be Achieved at the Bilateral, Regional, and Multilateral Levels? Journal of International Economic Law 2:423-433.

Merges RP, Nelson RR (1992) Market Structure and Technical Advance: The Role of Patent Scope Decisions. In: Jorde TM, Teece DJ (eds) Antitrust, Innovation and Competitiveness. New York, pp 185-232.

Mische H (2002) Nicht-wettbewerbliche Faktoren in der europäischen Fusionskontrolle: Wettbewerbspolitik zwischen Schutzpolitik und Gestaltung. Baden-Baden.

Mitchell AD (2001) Broadening the Vision of Trade Liberalisation: International Competition Law and the WTO. World Competition 24:343-365.

Mitschke A (2005) Ethik der Globalisierung: Wie berechtigt ist die Globalisierungskritik? In: Lachmann W, Haupt R, Farmer K (eds) Globalisierung der Wirtschaft – Segen oder Fluch? Münster, pp 1-59.

Mitschke A (2006) The International Competitiveness of Nations: The Role of National Competition Policy. In: Farmer K, Harbrecht W (eds) Theorie der Wirtschaftspolitik, Entwicklungspolitik und Wirtschaftsethik. Münster, pp 21-40.

Moeschel W (2005) Perspektiven einer internationalen Wettbewerbsordnung. Wirtschaft und Wettbewerb 55:479.

Moeschel W (2005a) Wettbewerb der Wettbewerbsordnungen. Wirtschaft und Wettbewerb 55:599-605.

Monopolkommission (1996) Wettbewerbspolitik in Zeiten des Umbruchs. Hauptgutachten XI - 1994/1995. Baden-Baden.

Monopolkommission (2004) Das allgemeine Wettbewerbsrecht in der Siebten GWB-Novelle. Sondergutachten 41 der Monopolkommission gemäß § 44 Abs. 1 Satz 4 GWB. Baden-Baden.

Monopolkommission (2005) Wettbewerbspolitik im Schatten 'Nationaler Champions'. Hauptgutachten XV - 2002/2003. Baden-Baden.

Monti M (2003) Contribution of Competition Policy to Competitiveness of European Economy. Speech/03/264 at the Institute of European Affairs. Dublin, May 26.

Monti M (2004) International Antitrust – A Personal Perspective. Speech at the Fordham Corporate Law Institute. New York, October 7.

Motta M, PoloM (2003) Leniency Programs and Cartel Prosecution. International Journal of Industrial Organization 21:347-379.

Müller M (2000) Systemwettbewerb, Harmonisierung und Wettbewerbsverzerrung: Europa zwischen einem Wettbewerb der Gesetzgeber und vollständiger Harmonisierung. Baden-Baden.

Müller S, Kornmeier M (2000) Internationale Wettbewerbsfähigkeit: Irrungen und Wirrungen der Standortdiskussion. Munich.

Muris TJ (2001) Merger Enforcement in a World of Multiple Arbiters. Prepared Remarks Before the Brookings Institution Roundtable in Trade and Investment, Washington, DC, December 21.

Nagy A (2002) Die Entwicklung einer internationalen Wettbewerbsordnung: Möglichkeiten und Grenzen aus organisationstheoretischer und politökonomischer Sicht. Frankfurt a.M..

Neary JP (2003) Competitive versus Comparative Advantage. The World Economy 24:457-470.

Nehls H, Schmidt T (2004) Credit Crunch in Germany? Kredit und Kapital 37:479-499.

Neugebauer A (2004) Internationale Wettbewerbspolitik: Eine Problemanalyse anhand der Theorie des institutionellen Wandels mit dem Schwerpunkt EU-USA. Aachen.

Neuhaus JE (1981) Power to Reverse Foreign Judgements: The British Clawback Statute under International Law. Columbia Law Review 81:1097-1133.

Neumann M (2001) Competition Policy: History, Theory and Practice. Cheltenham.

Neumann M (2002) Neoklassik. In: Issing O (ed) Geschichte der Nationalökonomie, 4th edn. Munich, pp 271-288.

Neven D, Seabright P (1997) Trade Liberalization and the Cooperation of Competition Policy. In: Waverman L, Comanor WS, Goto A (eds) Competition Policy in the Global Economy: Modalities for Cooperation. London, pp 381-406.

Niederleithinger E (1990) Wettbewerbsfragen der Europäischen Gemeinschaft. In: Gröner H (ed) Wettbewerbsfragen der Europäischen Gemeinschaft. Berlin, pp 103-113.

Norman VD (1998) A Small Open Economy Perspective on International Competition Policy. In: Hope E, Maeleng P (eds) Competition and Trade Policies: Coherence or Conflict? London, pp 57-64.

Norton JJ (1979) Extraterritorial Jurisdiction of US Antitrust and Securities Law. International and Comparative Law Quarterly 28:576-597.

Nunnenkamp P (2000) Globalisierung und internationales Finanzsystem. Aus Politik und Zeitgeschichte - Beilage zur Wochenzeitung 'Das Parlament', September 8, pp 3-11.

OECD (1967) Recommendation on Cooperation between Member Countries in Restrictive Business Practices Affecting International Trade. C(67)53/Final. Paris, October 5.

OECD (1992) Technology and the Economy: The Key Relationships. Paris.

OECD (1995) Revised Recommendation of the Council Concerning Cooperation between Member Countries on Anticompetitive Practices Affecting International Trade. C(95)130/Final. Paris, July 28.

OECD (1998) Recommendation of the Council Concerning Effective Action Against Hard Core Cartels. C(98)35/Final. Paris, May 13.

OECD (2005) Building Competitive Regions: Strategies and Governance. Paris.

OECD (2005a) Recommendation of the Council on Merger Review. C(2005)34. Paris, March 23.

OECD (2006) International Investment Perspectives. Paris.

OECD Secretariat (2001) Competition Policy and Intellectual Property Rights. OECD Journal of Competition Law and Policy 3:123-193.

OECD Secretariat (2003) Capacity Building for Effective Competition Policy in Developing and Transitioning Economies. OECD Journal of Competition Law and Policy 4:7-23.

Ohlin BG (1933) Interregional and International Trade. Harvard Economic Studies Vol 39 (1957). Cambridge, MA.

Ordover JA, Willig RD (1985) Antitrust for High-Technology Industries: Assessing Research Joint Ventures and Mergers. Journal of Law & Economics 28:311-333.

Parisi JJ (1999) Enforcement Cooperation Among Antitrust Authorities. US Federal Trade Commission, Speech before the IBC UK Conferences - Sixth Annual London Conference on EC Competition Law. London, May 19.

Pelkmans J (2001) Making EU Network Markets Competitive. Oxford Review of Economic Policy 17:432-456.

Petersen MA, Rajan RG (1995) The Effect of Credit Market Competition on Lending Relationships. The Quarterly Journal of Economics 110:407-443.

Pieper B (2007) Das Drei-Säulen-System: Erfolgsbremse der deutschen Banken? Wirtschaftsdienst – Zeitschrift für Wirtschaftspolitik 86:452-461.

Phillips BJ (1994) Comments on the Draft International Antitrust Code. Aussenwirtschaft 49:327-348.

Plumpe W (1999) The State and Enterprise in the German Economy after the Second World War. In: Miyajima H, Kikkawa T, Hikino T (eds) Policies for Competitiveness – Comparing Business-Government Relationships in the 'Golden Age of Capitalism'. Oxford, pp 251-290.

Poeche J (1982) Mittelstandspolitik und Wettbewerbsordnung: Nachteilsausgleich für Klein- und Mittelunternehmen. In: Andreae CA, Benisch W (eds) Wettbewerbsordnung und Wettbewerbsrealität. Cologne.

Porter, ME (1990) The Competitive Advantage of Nations. London.

Porter ME (2004) Competitive Advantage – Creating and Sustaining Superior Performance. New York.

Posner RA (1974) Theories of Economic Regulation. NBER Working Paper Series, Working Paper No 1. New York.

Posner RA (1999) Natural Monopoly and Its Regulation. Cato Institute. Washington, DC.

Prestowitz CV (2000) Response 1: Playing to Win. In: Cho DS, Moon HC, Cho TS (eds) From Adam Smith to Michael Porter: Evolution of Competitiveness Theory. Asia-Pacific Business Series Vol 2. Singapore, pp 38-41.

Preusse HG (2001) Konzeptionelle Überlegungen zur internationalen Wettbewerbsfähigkeit: Unternehmen oder Länder? WEP Working Paper No 5, edited by Lachmann W, University of Erlangen-Nuremberg, Chair for Economics and Development Policy.

Pribram K (1998) Geschichte des ökonomischen Denkens. Vol 1, translated by Horst Brühmann. Frankfurt a.M.

Recktenwald HC (1989) Adam Smith (1723-1790). In: Starbatty J (ed) Klassiker des ökonomischen Denkens – Vol 1: Von Platon bis John Stuart Mill. Munich, pp 134-155.

Reichel R (2002) Ökonomische Theorie der internationalen Wettbewerbsfähigkeit von Volkswirtschaften. Wiesbaden.

Renda A (2004) Catch Me if You Can! The Microsoft Saga and the Sorrows of Old Antitrust. Erasmus Law and Economics Review 1:1-22.

Ricardo D (1817) On the Principles of Political Economy and Taxation. Klassiker der Nationalökonomie Vol VIII. Düsseldorf, 1988.

Richter R, Furubotn EG (2003) Neue Institutionenökonomik: Eine Einführung und kritische Würdigung. 3rd edn. Tübingen.

Risch CF (1998) Evolution, Legitimation und Organisation intergouvernementaler Wirtschaftskooperationen: Das Beispiel der EU und der Visegrád-Staaten. Internationale Beziehungen Vol 4. Frankfurt am Main.

Rittaler JB (1989) Industrial Concentration and the Chicago School of Antitrust Analysis. Frankfurt a.M.

Robertson A, Demetriou M (1994) 'But That Was in Another Country ...': The Extraterritorial Application of US Antitrust Laws in the US Supreme Court. International and Comparative Law Quarterly 43:417-425.

Rodemer H, Dicke H (2000) Globalisierung, Europäische Integration und internationaler Standortwettbewerb. Baden-Baden.

Rodrik D (1996) Labor Standards and International Trade: Do They Matter and What Do We Do About Them? In: Lawrence RZ, Rodrick D, Whalley J (eds)

Emerging Agenda For Global Trade – High Stakes for Developing Countries. Overseas Development Council, Essay No 20. Washington, DC, pp 35-79.
Röder E (2000) Kommentar zu Karl M. Meessen – Das Für und Wider eines Weltkartellrechts. Jahrbuch für Neue Politische Ökonomie 19:373-382.
Rosenthal DE, Nicolaides P (1997) Harmonizing Antitrust: The Less Effective Way to Promote International Competition. In: Graham EM, Richardson JD (eds) Global Competition Policy. Washington, DC, Institute for International Economics, pp 355-383.
Ross TW (1988) Movements Towards Free Trade and Domestic Market Performance With Imperfect Competition. Canadian Journal of Economics 21:507-524.
Ryngaert C (2004) The Application of US Law to Foreign-Flag Vessels: The Clear Statement Rule After Spector v. Norwegian Cruise Line (US Supreme Court, 2005). K.U. Leuven, Faculty of Law – Institute for International Law, Working Paper No 84.
Schefold B, Carstensen K (2002) Die klassische Politische Ökonomie. In: Issing O (ed) Geschichte der Nationalökonomie. 4th edn. Munich, pp 67-91.
Scherer FM (1998) International Trade and Competition Policy. In: Hope E, Maeleng P (eds) Competition and Trade Policies: Coherence or Conflict? London, pp 13-30.
Schmalensee R (1992) Agreements between Competitors. In: Jorde TM, Teece DJ (eds) Antitrust, Innovation and Competitiveness. New York, pp 98-118.
Schmidt I (2001) Wettbewerbspolitik und Kartellrecht. 7th edn. Stuttgart.
Schmidt I, Rittaler JB (1986) Die Chicago School of Antitrust Analysis – Wettbewerbstheoretische und –politische Analyse eines Credos. Baden-Baden.
Schmidt KH (2002) Merkantilismus, Kameralismus, Physiokratie. In: Issing O (ed) Geschichte der Nationalökonomie. 4th edn. Munich, pp 37-66.
Scholz CM, Staehler F (1999) Unilateral Environmental Policy and International Competitiveness. Tübingen.
Schumpeter JA (1975) Der Prozeß der schöpferischen Zerstörung. In: Herdzina K (ed) Wettbewerbstheorie. Cologne, pp 118-121.
Scott S (2004) Cartel Enforcement: International and Canadian Developments. Commissioner of Competition Bureau Canada, Speech given at Fordham Corporate Law Institute – Conference in International Antitrust Law & Policy. New York, October 7.
Sedemund J (2002) Zur Notwendigkeit einer einheitlichen Aufsichtsbehörde für globale Fusionen. In: Schwarze J (ed) Europäisches Wettbewerbsrecht im Zeichen der Globalisierung. Baden-Baden, pp 107-115.
Seong S (1989) Strategic Antitrust Policy Promoting Mergers to Enhance Domestic Competitiveness. Ph.D. thesis, Yale University.
Shelton JR (1999) Competition Policy: What Chance for International Rules. OECD Journal of Competition Law and Policy 1:59-71.
Siebert H (2000) The Paradigm of Locational Competition. Kiel Discussion Papers No 367.
Siebert H (2005) Locational Competition – A Neglected Paradigm in the International Division of Labour. Kiel Working Paper No 1258.

Sinn HW (1997) The Selection Principle and Market Failure in Systems Competition. Journal of Public Economics 66:247-274.

Sinn HW (1999) Competition Between Competition Rules. NBER Working Paper 7273. Cambridge, MA.

Sinn HW (2003) The New Systems Competition. Yrjö Jahnsson Lectures. Oxford.

Smith A (1776) An Inquiry into the Nature and Causes of the Wealth of Nations. In: Eliot CW (ed) The Harvard Classics. New York, 1937.

Stapelfeldt G (2001) Der Merkantilismus: Die Genese der Weltgesellschaft vom 16. bis zum 18. Jahrhundert. Freiburg.

Stearns-Bläsing B (2004) Die Funktionsfähigkeit wettbewerbspolitischen Systemwettbewerbs: Eine Analyse der zwischenstaatlichen Konkurrenz bei der Gestaltung von Institutionen zum Schutz vor privaten Wettbewerbsbeschränkungen. Lohmar-Cologne.

Steckelbach L (2002) Wirkungen wettbewerbspolitischer Regulierungen auf oligopolistischen Märkten. Hamburg.

Stennek J, Verboven F (2001) Merger Control and Enterprise Competitiveness – Empirical Analysis and Policy Recommendations. The Research Institute of Industrial Economics, Working Paper No 556. Stockholm.

Stephan PB (1999) Regulatory Cooperation and Competition: The Search for Virtue. University of Virginia School of Law, Legal Studies Working Papers Series, Working Paper No 99-12. Charlottesville.

Stephan PB (2004) Against International Cooperation. In: Epstein RA, Greve MS (eds) Competition Laws in Conflict: Antitrust Jurisdiction in the Global Economy. Washington, DC, pp 66-98.

Stigler GJ (1971) The Theory of Economic Regulation. Bell Journal of Economics and Management Science 2:3-21.

Stierle MH (2002) Volkswirtschaften in der Globalisierung – Konzeptionelle Analyse der zentralen Indikatoren der internationalen Wettbewerbsfähigkeit von Volkswirtschaften. Speyerer Forschungsbericht No 182.

Straubhaar T (1994) Internationale Wettbewerbsfähigkeit von Volkswirtschaften – was ist das? Wirtschaftsdienst 74:534-540.

Streit M (1998) Competition among Systems, Harmonisation and Integration. Journal des Economistes et des Etudes Humaines 8:239-254.

Streit M, Wohlgemuth M (1999) (eds) Systemwettbewerb als Herausforderung an Theorie und Politik. Baden-Baden.

Suranovic S (2002) International Labour and Environmental Standards Agreements: Is this Fair Trade? The World Economy 25:231-245.

Swindle O (2001) Between Competition and Cooperation – Changing Business-to-Business Relations. United States Federal Trade Commission, Outline of Remarks Before the 8th World Business Dialogue, University of Cologne, April 4.

Swinnerton KA (1997) An Essay on Economic Efficiency and Core Labour Standards. The World Economy 20:73-86.

Tarullo DK (1999) Competition Policy for Global Markets. Journal of International Economic Law 2:445-455.

Tiebout CM (1956) A Pure Theory of Local Expenditures. Journal of Political Economy 64:416-424.

Todino M (2003) International Competition Network: The State of Play after Naples. World Competition 26:283-302.

Torrens R (1815) An Essay on the External Corn Trade. London.

Tritell RW (2006) International Antitrust Issues. Statement at Antitrust Modernization Commission Hearing on International Antitrust Issues. Washington, DC, February 15.

Tritell RW, Kraus EF (2006) The Federal Trade Commission's International Antitrust Program. FTC International Antitrust Division. Washington, DC.

Ullrich H (2003) Competitor Cooperation and the Evolution of Competition Law: Issues for Research in a Perspective of Globalization. In: Drexl J (ed) The Future of Transnational Antitrust – From Comparative to Common Competition Law. The Hague, pp 159-223.

UNCTAD (1980) Set of Multilaterally Agreed Equitable Principles and Rules for the Control of Restrictive Business Practices. UN Document A/Res./35/63, Geneva.

UNCTAD (1997) World Investment Report 1997: Transnational Corporations, Market Structure and Competition Policy. New York and Geneva.

UNCTAD (1998) Empirical Evidence of the Benefits From Applying Competition Law and Policy Principles to Economic Development in Order to Attain Greater Efficiency in International Trade and Development. Trade and Development Board, Intergovernmental Group of Experts on Competition Law and Policy, Revised Report by the UNCTAD Secretariat, TD/B/COM.2/EM/10/Rev.1. Geneva, 25 May.

UNCTAD (2001) The Role of Consumer and Competition Policies in Enhancing Competitiveness and Development. Outcome of the Expert Meeting, TD/B/COM.1/ EM.17/L.1. Geneva, 25 October.

UNCTAD (2002) The Relationship between Competition, Competitiveness and Development. Issues note prepared by the UNCTAD Secretariat, TD/B/COM.2/CLP/ 30. Geneva, 23 May.

UNCTAD (2004) The Role of Competition in the Promotion of Competitiveness and Development: Experiences from Latin America and the Caribbean and Other Regions. Preparatory Seminar for UNCTAD XI, Eleventh Session, Sao Paulo 13-18 June 2004, Background Note TD(XI)/BP/7. Geneva, 5 May.

Vaubel R (1992) Die politische Ökonomie der wirtschaftspolitischen Zentralisierung in der Europäischen Gemeinschaft. Jahrbuch für Neue Politische Ökonomie 11:30-65.

Venables AJ (1996) Localization of Industry and Trade Performance. Oxford Review of Economic Policy 12(3):52-60.

Vernon R (1966) International Investments and International Trade in the Product Cycle. Quarterly Journal of Economics (May), pp 190-207.

Vernon R (1979) The Product Cycle Hypothesis in a New International Environment. Oxford Bulletin of Economics & Statistics 41:255-267.

Vickers J (1995) Concepts of Competition. Oxford Economic Papers 47:1-23.

Vietor RHK (1999) Regulation American Style 1933-1989. In: Miyajima H, Kikkawa T, Hikino T (eds) Policies for Competitiveness – Comparing Business-Government Relationships in the 'Golden Age of Capitalism'. Oxford, pp 212-247.

Voß DP (2000) Ansätze zur Behandlung internationaler kartellrechtlich relevanter Sachverhalte: Insbesondere der Draft International Antitrust Code. Europäische Hochschulschriften, Series II: Rechtswissenschaft, Vol 2921. Frankfurt a. M..

Wagner H (2003) Einführung in die Weltwirtschaftspolitik: Internationale Wirtschaftsbeziehungen – Internationale Organisationen – Internationale Politikkoordinierung, 5th edn. Munich.

Weimann J (2006) Wirtschaftspolitik: Allokation und kollektive Entscheidung. 4th edn. Berlin.

Williamson OE (1968) Economies as an Antitrust Defense: The Welfare Tradeoffs. American Economic Review 58:18-36.

Wils WPJ (2003) Self-Incrimination in EC Antitrust Enforcement: A Legal and Economic Analysis. World Competition 26:567-588.

Wils WPJ (2004) The Combination of the Investigative and Prosecutorial Function and the Adjudicative Function in EC Antitrust Enforcement: A Legal and Economic Analysis. World Competition 27:201-224.

Wins H (2000) Eine internationale Wettbewerbsordnung als Ergänzung zum GATT. Baden-Baden.

Winslow T (2001) OECD Competition Law Recommendations, Developing Countries, and Possible WTO Competition Rules. OECD Journal of Competition Law and Policy 3:116-137.

Wißmann T (2000) Decentralised Enforcement of EC Competition Law and the New Policy on Cartels – The Commission White Paper of 28th of April 1999. World Competition 23:123-154.

Wohlgemuth M (1995) Economic and Political Competition in Neoclassical and Evolutionary Perspective. Constitutional Political Economy 6:71-96.

Wolfram C (2004) Competitive Bidding for the Early US Airmail Routes. UC Berkeley.

Worm H (2004) Grundlagen eines dezentralen Systems internationaler Wettbewerbspolitik. Hamburg.

WTO (1997) Annual Report 1997. Geneva.

WTO (1998) Communications from the United States to the Working Group in the Interaction between Trade and Competition Policy. WT/WGTCP/W/66, March 26.

WTO (1998a) Japan – Measures Affecting Consumer Photographic Film and Paper. Report of the Panel, WT/DS44/R (98-0886). Geneva, March 31.

WTO (2003) Report (2003) of the Working Group in the Interaction Between Trade and Competition Policy in the General Council. WT/WGTCP/7. Geneva, July 17.

Zanettin B (2002) Cooperation Between Antitrust Agencies at the International Level. Portland.

Printed in the United States
116318LV00002B/217-246/P